St. Louis

Documentary History of American Cities
Tamara K. Hareven and Stephan Thernstrom, Series Editors

Detroit
Edited by Melvin G. Holli

Pittsburgh
Edited by Roy Lubove

St. Louis
Edited by Selwyn K. Troen and Glen E. Holt

ST. LOUIS

**Edited by Selwyn K. Troen
and Glen E. Holt**

New Viewpoints
A Division of Franklin Watts
New York | London | 1977

Library of Congress Cataloging in Publication Data

Main entry under title:

St. Louis.

(Documentary history of American cities)
Includes index.
1. St. Louis—Social conditions. 2. St. Louis
—Economic conditions. 3. St. Louis—History.
4. Cities and towns—Growth. I. Troen, Selwyn K.,
1940–   II. Holt, Glen E.
HN80.S2S24   309.1'778'66   77–5907
ISBN 0–531–05393–8
ISBN 0–531–05603–1 pbk.

New Viewpoints
A Division of Franklin Watts
730 Fifth Avenue
New York, New York 10019

Acknowledgments

PART I

"Fragment from Chouteau's Narrative Concerning the Founding of St. Louis," Missouri Historical Society Collections, III (1911), pp. 335–66. Reprinted by permission of the Missouri Historical Society, St. Louis.

"Population Tables, 1764–1800." From Glen E. Holt, "The Shaping of St. Louis, 1763–1800" (Unpublished Ph.D. Thesis, Department of History, The University of Chicago, 1975), Appendix A, Tables 1 and 2. Reprinted by permission of the author.

"Local Ordinances . . . Published by Lieutenant-Governor Don Francisco Cruzat . . ." From Document #12, "Papers from Spain," Missouri Historical Society Archives, St. Louis. Reprinted by permission of the Missouri Historical Society.

"St. Louis as a Focus of Imperialist Aspirations and Intrigues." From the Spanish Archives, Rare Book Department, Washington University Library, St. Louis. Reprinted by permission of Washington University Library.

"Early History of the St. Louis Police Force." From History of the Metropolitan Police Department of St. Louis, 1810–1910 (St. Louis: Board of Police Commissioners, 1910), pp. 108–10. Reprinted by permission of the St. Louis Board of Police Commissioners.

"The St. Louis Hospital . . ." From Edward Stiff, "Nine Days in St. Louis Hospital" (St. Louis: Published by the Author, 1843), pp. 2–3. From St. Louis Imprint Collection, Rare Book Department, Washington University Library, St. Louis. Reprinted by permission of Washington University Library.

PART II

"Gottfried Duden's 'Report.'" From William G. Bek, trans., "Gottfried Duden's Report, 1824–1827," *Missouri Historical Review,* XIII (January, 1919), pp. 174–80. Reprinted by permission of the State Historical Society of Missouri, Columbia, Missouri.

"Lutheran Parochial Schools." From Thomas Graebner, *The Lutheran Church Guide of St. Louis Missouri* (St. Louis: Concordia Seminary, 1916), pp. 166–67. Reprinted by permission of Concordia Seminary, St. Louis.

"Education of Immigrant Children, 1880." Table reprinted from Selwyn K. Troen, *The Public and the Schools: Shaping the St. Louis System, 1838–1920.* Copyright 1975 by the Curators of the University of Missouri. Reprinted by permission of the University of Missouri Press.

"Private Places in St. Louis." From John Noyes, "The 'Places' of St. Louis," *The American City,* XII (March, 1915), pp. 206–208. Reprinted by permission of *American City & County.*

"Meet Me in St. Louis, Louis," by Andrew B. Sterling & Kerry Mills. Copyright 1904 by F. A. Mills. Reprinted by permission of Jerry Vogel Music Co., New York.

PART III

"The Geography of the St. Louis Trade Territory, 1924." From Lewis Thomas, *The Geography of the Saint Louis Trade Territory* (St. Louis: St. Louis Globe-Democrat, 1924), pp. 5–7, 21–22. Reprinted by permission of the *St. Louis Globe-Democrat.*

"The Geographic Landscape . . . , 1927." From Lewis F. Thomas, "The Localization of Business Activities in Metropolitan St. Louis," *Washington University Studies,* I (October 1927), pp. 2–10. Reprinted by permission from Washington University, St. Louis.

"Education of the Labor Force." From the *Fifty-fifth Annual Report of the Board of Education of the City of St. Louis, Missouri, for the Year Ending June 30, 1909,* pp. 43–45; *Sixty-sixth Annual Report of the Board of Education of the City of St. Louis, Missouri, for the Year Ending June 30, 1920,* p. 114. Reprinted by permission of the Board of Education of the City of St. Louis.

"East St. Louis Race Riot of 1917." From the *St. Louis Post-Dispatch,* July 3, 1917. Reprinted by permission of the *St. Louis Post-Dispatch.*

"Post-World War I Suburban Expansion." Pages 280–86 from Stuart A. Queen and Lewis F. Thomas, *The City: A Study of Urbanism in the*

United States. Copyright 1939 by McGraw-Hill, Inc. Reprinted with the permission of McGraw-Hill Book Company.

"The Consolidation Plan of 1959." Pages 38–42 from Henry J. Schmandt, Paul G. Steinbicker, and George D. Wendel, *Metropolitan Reform in St. Louis: A Case Study.* Copyright 1961 by Holt, Rinehart and Winston. Reprinted by permission of Holt, Rinehart and Winston.

"Zoning for St. Louis . . ." From Harlan Bartholomew, *Zoning for St. Louis: A Fundamental Part of the City Plan* (St. Louis: The City Plan Commission, 1918), pp. 10–17. Reprinted by permission of the Department of Planning, Community Development Agency, City of St. Louis.

"The Planned City, 1916–1944." From Harlan Bartholomew, "The Saint Louis Plan in Action," *American Planning and Civic Annual* (American Planning and Civic Association, 1944), pp. 112–15. Reprinted by special permission of the National Urban Coalition.

"The Comprehensive City Plan of 1947 . . ." From *Comprehensive City Plan, Saint Louis, Missouri* (City Plan Commission, 1947), pp. 27-33. Reprinted by permission of the Department of Planning, Community Development Agency, City of St. Louis.

"Decline in Municipal Services . . ." From Gary A. Tobin, *The St. Louis School Crisis: Population Shifts and Voting Patterns* (St. Louis: Washington University, 1970), Table 6. Reprinted by permission of the author.

"Population Decline: The Nature of the Loss." From Peter A. Morrison, "Urban Growth and Decline: San Jose and St. Louis in the 1960's," *Science* (August 20, 1974), pp. 758–62. Copyright 1974 by the American Association for the Advancement of Science. Reprinted by permission of the American Association for the Advancement of Science, and Peter A. Morrison.

"The Gateway Arch . . ." From "Topping-Out Day," *St. Louis Post-Dispatch,* October 28, 1965; John McGuire, "Gateway Arch Now Spanning 10 Years," *St. Louis Post-Dispatch,* October 27, 1975. Reprinted by permission of the *St. Louis Post-Dispatch.*

For our children:

Aron, Deborah, Gordon, Joshua,
Judah, Karen, Kris and Lisa

Contents

INTRODUCTION   XV

PART ONE
From Colonial Outpost to Frontier Town, 1763–1830

1 | Fragment from Chouteau's Narrative Concerning the
     Founding of St. Louis   3
2 | The Tenor of Life in the French Frontier Settlement   5
3 | Population Tables, 1764–1800. Compiled by Glen E. Holt   7
4 | Indenture as a Form of Labor in the St. Louis Economy   15
5 | Local Ordinances for St. Louis and General Ordinances
     Published by Lieutenant-Governor Don Francisco Cruzat
     from October 7, 1780, to November 24, 1787   16
6 | St. Louis as a Focus of Imperialist Aspirations and Intrigues   21
7 | The Progress of the Town, 1804–1818   25
8 | Sources of Immigration to St. Louis, 1804–1816   26
9 | The Town and Its Surroundings, 1810   26
10 | Disciplining Slaves, 1808   31
11 | Early History of the St. Louis Police Force   33
12 | Organization of Fire Companies, 1810   35
13 | The St. Louis Hospital, an Early Charity Institution   37

14 | Religious Conditions in St. Louis, 1818   40
15 | St. Louis Present and Future, 1829   45
16 | The Seal of St. Louis   49

PART TWO
From Town to City, 1830–1910

1 | Situation and Prospect for the
    Midwestern River Economy, 1847   53
2 | The First Locomotive West of the Mississippi, 1852   55
3 | The Shift from Water Transport to Rails   57
4 | The St. Louis–Illinois (Eads) Bridge: Symbol for an
    Industrializing City and Transportation Center, 1874   60
5 | "The Central Continental Metropolis," 1897   62
6 | Gottfried Duden's "Report"   66
7 | Lutheran Parochial Schools   68
8 | German Cultural and Intellectual Life in St. Louis:
    An 1874 Report   70
9 | An Irish Celebration, 1869   74
10 | The Burning of the Mulatto McIntosh:
    Racial Disorder in the Nineteenth-Century Urban Society 76
11 | Colored Teachers for Colored Schools:
    A Petition for Blacks to Instruct Blacks   80
12 | The St. Louis Residential Segregation Referendum, 1916 82
13 | The Teaching of Urban Discipline and Industrial Skills 85
14 | The Social Benefits of Kindergarten   89
15 | Education of Immigrant Children, 1880   91
16 | The Street Arabs of St. Louis, 1878   93
17 | The "Social Evil" Experiment   95
18 | The Suppression of the "Social Evil"   97
19 | The Proper Functions of the Police Force, 1868   100
20 | The Organization of the Western Sanitary Commission in
    St. Louis, 1861   103
21 | Organizing Charity in the City:
    The St. Louis Provident Association, 1863 and 1902   106
22 | Causes of Disease: A Report on Public Health, 1885   110
23 | Trying to Clean Up Smoky St. Louis, 1895   113
24 | St. Louisans Try to Beat the Tenement, 1908   117
25 | An Invitation to Move to the Suburbs, 1866   121

26 | Private Places in St. Louis   124
27 | Forest Park, 1875   127
28 | The Association between Reform and the
        Coming of a World's Fair   129
29 | "Meet Me in St. Louis"   133

PART THREE
From City to Region: Growth and Dispersal, 1910–1975

 1 | The Geography of the St. Louis Trade Territory, 1924   137
 2 | The Geographic Landscape of Metropolitan St. Louis, 1927   141
 3 | The Labor Market, 1930   144
 4 | The Education of the Labor Force   147
 5 | East St. Louis Race Riot of 1917   150
 6 | The Satellite Cities of St. Louis, 1912   155
 7 | Post–World War I Suburban Expansion   160
 8 | Suburban Subdivisions: Lake Forest, 1929   164
 9 | Country Club Swingers: Suburban Society, 1929   166
10 | The Separation of the City from the County   168
11 | The Consolidation Plan of 1959   171
12 | The City Beautiful in St. Louis:
        Improvement of Kingshighway, 1903   175
13 | The Model Street:
        A Contribution of the World's Fair of 1904   176
14 | The Civic League's Plan for St. Louis, 1907   178
15 | The Introduction of Zoning, 1918   181
16 | The Planned City, 1916–1944   185
17 | Problem Areas of St. Louis, 1937   189
18 | Housing the Poor: Pruitt-Igoe   191
19 | The Comprehensive City Plan of 1947:
        Post–World War II Housing Problems   195
20 | Decline in Municipal Services: The School Bond Issue   199
21 | Population Decline: The Nature of the Loss   202
22 | The Gateway Arch: Symbol for the St. Louis Metropolis   206

APPENDIX

Table 8: Selected Characteristics of Population Growth   211

INDEX
213

Introduction

St. Louis is an important midwestern metropolis that deserves
more attention than it has received. It is hoped that this volume
will demonstrate that the absence of scholarship is not because the
city's past is unimportant or uninteresting. Indeed, St. Louis was
one of the great boomtowns of American history. Its distant past is
connected with the settlement and conquest of the western frontier, and its more recent past and present are illustrative of the
development and problems of modern, urban society. However,
this lack of a written history has influenced the organization of
this book. Our purpose is not only to establish the chronological
outline of St. Louis' development, but also to suggest by our documentary choice a large number of important topics that could be
pursued by those interested in exploring and enlarging the history
of the city.

As is consistent with the general purpose of New Viewpoints'
Documentary History of American Cities series, this volume examines and relates both the similarities and the differences between St. Louis and other cities. Readers totally unfamiliar with
St. Louis, for example, may be surprised to learn that St. Louis
during its colonial period was Spanish and French, a distinction

only a few other major midwestern cities can claim. Moreover, through the nineteenth century, St. Louis was in the forefront of reform, pioneering in the organization of modern charity through the Western Sanitary Commission, passing the first laws to decriminalize and regulate prostitution, and establishing an outstanding school system which other cities looked to as a model for dealing with industrialization. In the twentieth century, civic leaders engaged in vigorous and innovative planning to stem decay, channel growth, mitigate social problems, and ameliorate life in a complex metropolis. St. Louis often has followed national trends, but nearly as often, its unique features have made its development somewhat different from that of other American cities. The separate introductions to the various documents attempt to cover both of these aspects in the city's development.

In compiling a documentary history, the greatest problem always is determining what to omit. Early in the project, we decided that this history would deal principally with social, economic, and cultural themes with minimal coverage of politics. Readers, therefore, will find few documents dealing with the various fights over annexation until 1876, the reform efforts to drive corrupt boodlers out of office, or the numerous attempts to build effective political liaisons throughout the metropolis in the twentieth century. Other readers undoubtedly will find that their particular interest has been slighted or omitted. Nevertheless, we hope that scholars, students, and casual readers will enjoy and profit from this volume, even as the authors have while collecting the documents and writing the various introductions.

In reviewing St. Louis history, we have identified three natural and distinct periods. The first section, which covers the history of the city from its founding in 1763 to about 1830, is organized to reflect the imperialistic setting of the first years, as well as the relative simplicity of life in what was first a colonial outpost and a fur-trading village and then another kind of outpost—a way station for American expansion into the Midwest and the Far West. The second section, which carries the history from the 1830s to the Louisiana Purchase Exposition in 1904, relates the transition from a commercial to an industrial-based economy. This middle timespan also was the major period for domestic and foreign immigration into the city, and adjustments were necessary to deal with the consequent social tensions and problems. The main theme of the third section, the city since the turn of the century, is the expansion of St. Louis into a metropolis. In this enlarged setting, the old central city faced difficult social and economic problems, even though the metropolis generally appeared to be making a satisfactory adjustment to the changing population and economic challenges of the twentieth century.

From Colonial Outpost to Frontier Town, 1763–1830

St. Louis was founded in 1763, a product of competition between European nations over control of the Mississippi Valley. When Pierre Laclède obtained his monopolistic grant from the French governor at New Orleans, led his party up the Mississippi, and laid out the site for St. Louis, both the royal government and Laclède understood that the patent was bestowed for purposes of solidifying French hegemony over this vast region. That aim was subverted by a new diplomacy. By the time the Laclède party began to erect the first buildings in the St. Louis settlement, in March 1764, France had given England the territory on the east side of the Mississippi, what is now the state of Illinois. Soon after construction of the settlement began, the inhabitants discovered that their king, Louis XV, had traded the west bank, including the area where they resided, to Spain, in return for a throne over a small duchy.

Despite the transfer to Spain, the Frenchmen continued to build their settlement. With the wilderness as the crucible for their efforts, the French colonists were joined by other French Catholics, who migrated across from the Illinois territory to avoid English Protestant rule and to protect their slaves, whom they feared the English would set free. When the French-Spanish treaty concerning the territory surrounding St. Louis was finally implemented in 1770, the French character of the place already was firmly established. The Spanish numbers were so small that they were engulfed by the French populace. Thus, although under Spanish rule, St. Louis grew up French.

Technically, Spain ruled St. Louis for three and a half decades. In reality, that fact made little difference in the way local life was conducted. The Spanish applied their power with kid gloves, and most questions of local importance were settled by informal meetings of leading village residents. Early decisions concerning land use, for example, were made by Laclède. He determined the location of the three original downtown streets paralleling the river, designated cross streets, and located the original common fields and the village commons. The importance of these decisions was that they determined the original city lot lines. When St. Louis spread out in the nineteenth century, it was superimposed over these original lots and grants later made by the Spanish. Many of St. Louis' streets still follow those old land-use patterns.

In establishing the social as well as the physical form of the village, the controlling group was an elite aristocracy composed of a few Creole trading families like the Chouteaus, Labbadies, and Papins. This group ran the civil government and the village economy. They were the chief recipients of the wealth gained through trading and hunting expeditions, and they lived in luxury compared with other members of St. Louis society.

A second group consisted of numerous unattached rivermen and boatmen, mostly French, but it also included free mulattos and free Negroes. As befitting a society with feudal traditions, there were also indentured servants. This group worked for the big traders, but they had little wealth. They were unable to accumulate savings because of irregular employment.

The third and lowest layer of St. Louis society was composed of Negro, mulatto, and a few Indian slaves. Although small in number, they performed valuable service as traders, farmers, and houseworkers. In the pioneer economy, the work of slaves could not be differentiated easily from that of lower-class free persons. They "toted," paddled, and cooked just as members of the free population did. The Indians, meanwhile, generally were held at a distance. Although they traded with the St. Louisans, their presence was not welcomed by the villagers, especially if they arrived or congregated in large numbers.

By 1800, this community numbered a little more than a thousand inhabitants. Although equivalent in size to many New England towns of the period, St. Louis was far wealthier, more cosmopolitan, and possessed greater pretensions. Such characteristics naturally created tensions. Both Indians and slaves were problems: the former required defensive measures, the latter needed discipline. Controlling a group that was common to all frontier communities, the abnormally large number of single males—military men and laborers—also was difficult. In addition to managing these elements, the more general need to secure the safety, health, and order of the village brought numerous decrees from the Spanish governors.

The most serious issue confronting the Spanish rulers, however, was the relatively slow pace of development. Indeed, during some years in the 1790s, St. Louis lost population and the economy stagnated. As a result, the Spanish governor sought to stimulate agriculture and encourage the exploitation of the region's considerable resources by inducing American immigrants from Illinois through dispensation of land grants. This lure was effective, and even before the United States purchase of Louisiana in 1803, St. Louis began its transformation from an outpost of European nations into an American frontier town.

The process of change was slow, however; the French predominated until 1810 in economic as well as social affairs. Between 1800 and 1810, the population increased by only 361, since few pioneers, either urban and rural, reached as far west as the Mississippi. During the next decade, the town grew dramatically from 1,400 to 4,598. The foundation of the economy continued to be the fur trade. This was supplemented through the 1820s by an expansion of the Santa Fe trade, by lead exports, and by the provisioning of growing federal army installations in the West. The War of 1812 had a powerful effect, stimulating both the economy and new immigration. Moreover, the first steamboat arrived in 1817, although this event was more a symbol of the future role of the city as a great commercial entrepôt than a decisive turning point. Not until after 1825 did the steamboat substantially affect the St. Louis economy.

As a territorial town, St. Louis had a very weak government. Nearly every action required that the local citizens petition the territorial legislature or the federal government for enabling legislation. The result was that most decisions shaping the city were made by private individuals. The most important example was the town's inability to control land use. In 1816 and in 1819, subdivisions were added north and west of the town, and new buildings were erected within them. As in most American cities and towns, the subdividers decided the direction and width of the streets, the length and depth of the lots, whether or not there would be alleys, and the size of the blocks. In sum, patterns of growth were set by private entrepreneurs, not by public decision-makers. In this respect the unregulated growth that characterized American cities of the period was enhanced by the loose frontier quality of the town.

The population increase that St. Louis experienced between 1800 and 1820 reflected the emerging national significance of the city. The largest portion of the new residents came from Virginia and other southern coastal states. Significant percentages migrated from the Middle Atlantic and New England states as well. An important consequence of this immigration was the increasingly Protestant component in what previously had been a largely Catholic community. Many of the newcomers, however, held to no religion. Protestant as well as Catholic missionaries were attracted to the town to deal with this element. If many missionaries were dismayed by irreligion and the diversity of sects, there were others who welcomed the richness and variety of cultures in what was an open and changing society.

Missouri had sufficient numbers by 1821 to claim statehood. St. Louis was granted its first town charter in 1823, but the local government's powers were nearly as limited as they had been in the territorial period. Most importantly, the new charter allowed the city to raise its tax rate only slightly. Because of this limit, the town government was not able to levy sufficient taxes to provide the urban services that residents were demanding by the late 1820s. Out of economic necessity, town government assumed only those public expenditures for which no private entrepreneurs could be induced to accept responsibility. From its inception, then, St. Louis' government was characterized by minimal services. It did no more than necessary, and then usually only after some crisis inspired public involvement.

By the 1820s, after more than half a century of relatively slow growth under three different nations, St. Louis had made the transition from an isolated colonial outpost to the most important trading center in the western portion of an aggressively expanding nation. When the dynamic economy and incessant movement of a restless people reached the Mississippi in the second quarter of the nineteenth century, St. Louis would become a ready and natural focus for growth. The foundations had been laid for the emergence of an important American city.

From Town to City, 1830–1910

After 1830, St. Louis became a boomtown. Rapid expansion began when the tide of westward migration reached mid-continent. For uncounted thousands from the East, the South, and from Europe, St. Louis became the "gateway" to the American West. For others, it was the place to settle down and build a future. Population figures demonstrate the pace of growth: from 16,649 in 1840, St. Louis increased to 310,864 by 1870 and 787,029 by 1910. During the forty years between the two latter dates, it was the fourth-largest city in the United States. Even by 1870, St. Louis not only was one of America's five largest cities, but internationally it would have ranked as the third largest in France, the second largest in Prussia and the Netherlands, and greater than any in Belgium or Sweden.

In assembling this population, St. Louis lost its former French and native-born character. In 1860, its population was nearly 60 percent foreign-born, a proportion larger than that of any other major American city. Among the immigrants, the Germans constituted the largest group, followed by the Irish. However, this predominance of foreign-born declined steadily in St. Louis after the Civil War, although it did not decrease in most large industrial cities.

By 1900, the Mound City's population growth was attributable less to the arrival of successive waves of foreigners than to natural increase and domestic migrations. Between 1890 and 1930, the proportion of foreign-born dropped from 25 percent to 10 percent. Boston's percentages for the same dates were 35 and 30, Chicago's 40 and 26, and New York's 42 and 34. Moreover, a majority of St. Louis foreign-born continued to be drawn out of the "old immigrant" countries—from Germany and Ireland—rather than from eastern or southern Europe. This migration pattern was unusual for a midwestern industrial city, and it gave a peculiar cast to St. Louis' social and political history.

The shape of these movements also meant that the period of greatest ethnic and religious tensions occurred during the mid-nineteenth century. A consequence of such tensions was the building of institutions and the framing of legislation that encouraged a sense of community or enforced universal standards of behavior on those who held different values than did the city's civic leaders. Since the schools were regarded as a key instrument to instill conformity and discipline, the politics of public education were particularly abrasive. Temperance reform, gambling, and prostitution, however, similarly involved conflict, as some groups attempted to prescribe models of public and private behavior for others unlike themselves. The drive for uniformity is not unusual in any society. In nineteenth-century St. Louis, however, the movement was reinforced by the absence of common traditions: the city was essentially a community of strangers, many of whom maintained their loyalties to inherited cultures.

St. Louis also attracted blacks. Those bound for destinations farther north used the city as a way station. Others settled permanently to take advantage of opportunities not found in the South. There were only 2,000 slaves and free blacks in 1840, but together they accounted for more than 12 percent of the total population. While their number rose to 3,300 by 1860, they comprised just slightly over 2 percent of the total. The greatest numerical growth occurred over the next twenty years, as the black population multiplied fivefold, reaching 22,256. In 1880, St. Louis had the third-largest black community in the nation. Only Baltimore and Philadelphia attracted more. In the antebellum period, blacks in the Mound City suffered from the same restrictions and hostilities that existed in the South. The Civil War and the reconstructed Missouri constitution of 1865 legislated new freedoms, but prejudice and discrimination did not dissolve in the postwar period. Blacks were forced to reside mostly in enclaves, were so limited in economic opportunities that the great majority worked only as unskilled laborers, and were allocated separate and substandard public facilities. Despite adversity, blacks established an independent social and cultural life generally preferable to what they had in the rural South. Something of the spirit of the black experience in St. Louis was captured in the popular expression that referred to one of the landmarks of a black ghetto: "I'd rather be a lamppost on Targee Street than be mayor of all Dixie."

All immigrants to nineteenth-century St. Louis came for the

same basic reasons: opportunities for work and wealth. The city's commercial prosperity was based on its relationship to the river. Travelers and cargo had to make one of two changes in transport: from land to water, or between larger vessels which navigated the deeper Lower Mississippi waters below the city and smaller vessels with a lighter draught which traveled the Upper Mississippi, Missouri, and Illinois rivers. St. Louis, therefore, was a natural point where one size boat was exchanged for another, new pilots who were acquainted with different waters boarded, goods were unloaded and redistributed to and from the land, and the manifold transactions accompanying these activities were arranged and concluded.

Such services became more significant as the agricultural frontiers pushed westward. Between 1840 and 1870, for example, the populations of Missouri and Illinois more than tripled. Wisconsin and Iowa, which contained only scattered settlements in 1840, attracted nearly a million and a half people during these decades. Hundreds of thousands more moved to Kansas and Minnesota. As the Midwest filled up and flourished, St. Louis' position as a major regional, commercial entrepôt was assured.

The river trade increased steadily until the 1880s, then declined and stabilized. Eventually, it became a small though significant factor in the city's commerce during the twentieth century. Not until the 1850s did St. Louisans begin investing heavily in railroads, which supplanted riverboats as the major form of inland freight and passenger transportation. Their efforts, while extensive, were not supported by eastern and foreign capitalists, who chose to emphasize routes elsewhere. Between 1864 and 1875, the city transferred its trade allegiance to the rails, but failed to make St. Louis either the commercial capital of the Midwest or the political capital of the United States. Population movements, decisions made by foreign and eastern financiers, and, to some degree, conservatism on the part of St. Louis capitalists, worked together by 1880 to raise Chicago into preeminence as the nation's largest rail center and biggest midwestern city. St. Louis was relegated to second position in both categories.

With good transportation and a hinterland rich in agricultural and mineral resources, however, St. Louis developed into an industrial center. The process was well under way in the latter part of the century, as St. Louis beer, shoes, meats, textiles, stoves, chemicals, streetcars, and a host of other finished products were distributed both regionally and nationally. This transformation marked off St. Louis, as it did Cincinnati, Chicago, and other successful major cities, from the host of stagnant and underdeveloped communities that remained relatively dormant as midwestern frontiers were rolled back and the region prospered.

The emergence of the city as a commercial-industrial center brought not only a broader distribution of wealth but a greater awareness of poverty. While no adequate social statistics exist to delineate the gradations in St. Louis society, inequalities were apparent to those who lived in or visited the city. By the end of the nineteenth century, the city's industry was located in three corridors: north and south along the river and westward along the southern edge of the old downtown. Close to the factories and rail lines which serviced the manufactories in these corridors, there developed two- and three-story slums housing industrial workers and the poor. In large areas both north and south of the westerly Mill Creek Valley corridor, there were brick detached dwellings and row houses for artisans and the middle class. Farther west, beginning in the 1850s, the wealthy built handsome suburbs and discrete residential areas called "places." In 1876, St. Louis had a major annexation. After that its boundaries became permanently frozen. As one of the first major cities to stop spatial expansion, it was increasingly hemmed in by communities of the well-to-do, who drew their wealth from the city but who lived in suburbs that had a separate political and social identity.

This spatial and social segregation has become a serious problem in the contemporary period. Through the turn of the century, however, there was an important and vigorous tradition of involvement by the wealthy, who promoted public amenities for the citizenry as a whole: a succession of civic-minded reformers agitated for improvements such as parks, boulevards, playgrounds, and smoke abatement.

This agitation coalesced during the 1890s in the movement to bring a world's fair to the city. While the campaign resulted in the Louisiana Purchase Exposition of 1904, the broader movement to obtain it was accompanied by campaigns for political as well as physical reform. Although rooting out political corruption met with short-term success during the first decade of the new century, the movement for planning a more humane and orderly environment had greater continuity and more impressive results. Thus, the Louisiana Purchase Exposition not only celebrated the city's past but also was an important catalyst in establishing traditions of municipal planning for the future. A more immediate consequence of the fair was that it attracted nearly twenty million visitors, who joined in celebrating the progress of urban industrial society, of which St. Louis was so outstanding a product and which it typified.

From City to Region:
Growth and Dispersal, 1910–1975

At the beginning of the twentieth century, St. Louis was the nation's fourth city and confident of its future growth. Seventy years later, it ranks eighteenth, and its prospects are the subject of much controversy. Just as earlier prophecies of unbridled expansion were not realized, so present forecasts of doom are premature. In order to understand the apparent change in the city's fortunes, it is important not to conclude too much from a decline in its comparative ranking. The story is more complicated: it requires placing St. Louis into its metropolitan and regional framework.

The same factors that stimulated the Mound City's growth through three-quarters of the nineteenth century continued to sustain it in the twentieth. First, St. Louis retained its crossroads position within the national transportation network. What the city lost relatively in rail and river commerce, it gained in trucking and air transport. Second, industry, which had begun to supplant commerce in the 1850s as the city's primary economic focus, became the dominant activity. By 1910, St. Louis claimed the nation's largest brewery, shoe manufacturing establishment, and tobacco products plant. More stoves, chemicals, streetcars, and clay products were made in the St. Louis area than in any other. Through World War I and the 1920s, this industrial base expanded. Thousands of new jobs were created, with automobile assembly, electrical components, chemicals, and communications in the lead but hardly alone. In 1929, the year of the Great Crash, 80 new firms were established and 135 more expanded. During the de-

pression decade that followed, the St. Louis economy was sufficiently diversified to weather the lean years better than other cities
that were dependent on narrow or single-industry employment
bases.

Since the late 1930s, federal defense spending has contributed
to the maintenance and growth of area manufacturing. By June
1940, St. Louis plants had obtained $440 million in military
contracts. Not only did existing industries expand, but new ones
were created. In terms of employment, the most important was
McDonnell Aircraft Corporation, which opened in 1939. This
company, rechartered as McDonnell-Douglas in 1967, now is the
area's largest employer, with 29,000 workers. While it is the biggest, the aerospace firm is not anomalous. In 1968, of the fifteen
corporations in the region with at least 4,000 employees, only
three—the Famour-Barr department store chain and the electric
and telephone utilities—were not engaged in production or proc-
essing. A final indication of the dominance of manufacturing is
that in 1971 nearly 44 percent of the total area labor force worked
in factories.

While factories continue to be the most important source of income for St. Louisans, other areas of the economy expanded as
well. The public, parochial, and other private elementary and
secondary schools in the region together employ more people than
McDonnell-Douglas—a total of 32,000 persons. Higher education
also has been a major growth industry since World War II. In
1950, Harris Teachers College, with 500 students, was the region's single publicly supported postsecondary institution. By
1975, there were eleven, instructing 60,000 full-time students. In
the same period, the twenty-four private universities, colleges,
and seminaries increased their enrollment by 16,000 students.
Another "non-polluting industry" that generates income is hospitals. In the last quarter decade, St. Louis has become a national
health center. In 1973, for example, one-third of all patients
treated at the Washington University Medical Center came from
outside the region. Tourism, a newer name for the old American
phenomenon of travel, also has become big business. The city that
hosted four national political conventions before World War I now
performs the same function for more than 212,000 persons who
attend 300 different conventions annually. Thus, even as St. Louis

produces and processes goods, and as it continues to occupy a primary place in a commercial and financial market that embraces portions of Missouri, Illinois, Kentucky, Tennessee, and Arkansas, its "service sector" prospers as well. Metropolitan population figures mirror the economy. In 1970, the St. Louis SMSA (Standard Metropolitan Statistical Area) ranked tenth in the nation, and even the most pessimistic recent calculations mark it among the top dozen.

The overall trend of the St. Louis regional economy during the past seventy-five years, then, has been one of at least substantial, and sometimes even spectacular, growth. It is within this perspective that the twentieth-century history of the Mound City should be considered. While this technique is necessary in analyzing the recent history of all older cities, especially those in the northeastern industrial corridor of which St. Louis is a part, it is particularly important for this one. As it turned out, the annexation of 1876 marked the last time that St. Louis City was allowed to add territory to its political jurisdiction. For the past sixty years, various attempts to widen the bounds have been defeated. St. Louis in 1975 has 61.3 square miles inside its corporate limits, the same amount it contained a century ago. Had consolidation continued into the twentieth century as it did in many other places, the old River City's relative decline would not have been so dramatic. For just as the central thrust in the regional economy has been growth, the main theme of the St. Louis region's internal movement has been dispersal—of industry, population, business, and services.

Even before 1900, large industries began moving to the American Bottoms, the extensive floodplain on the Illinois side of the river which began to be secured by dikes and levees after the Civil War. The large industries were attracted to the east side by cheap land, good water and rail connections, and lower freight rates on shipments to and from the East than were granted on the same items in and out of St. Louis. In 1873, Owens-Illinois Glass Company built a plant in Madison County. Two years later, the 656-acre National Stockyards opened in East St. Louis, and a number of large packing firms soon clustered around the regional facility. During the 1890s, Granite City Steel made a company town out of the previously chartered Granite City. The modern consequence of this movement is apparent in the 1970s. In the Illinois counties of Madison and St. Clair, the area directly across the Mississippi from St. Louis, about two out of every five factory workers are employed by just six corporations—Granite City Steel, Laclède Steel, Olin-Mathieson, Owens-Illinois Glass, Swift and Company, and Shell Oil.

Light manufacturing also has tended to disperse, although its movement was more to the counties on the Missouri side of the river than to Illinois. Before 1930, most light industry, which often is labor-intensive, was located within the city. The Washington Avenue shoe and garment district, for example, became world famous. It grew so large before the depression that a cluster of hotels, restaurants, and entertainment places were located especially to serve those who came to buy. After World War II, however, trucks, automobiles, and railroads contributed to decentralization, and industrial parks, catering to clean manufacturing and wholesalers, were developed mainly beyond the municipal limits. The effects of this movement were revealed in a 1958 survey, which found 2,135 manufacturing establishments with 100,412 wage earners in the city and 3,150 plants with 179,971 workers in the five counties surrounding it. The trend continues, as new plants entering the region have mostly chosen outlying locations.

Population movement coincided with this dispersal of employment opportunities. In 1900, the city had 570,000 inhabitants, and its boosters confidently predicted that a population of one million soon would be achieved. The prognostication was not realized. The city reached 822,000 in 1930, declined by 6,000 during the depression decade, then rose to its apex of 857,000 in 1950. Over the next quarter century, it dropped to 625,000. The regional population, meanwhile, continued to increase. The largest portion of the rise took place in St. Louis County. Numbering only 50,000 in 1900, it more than doubled by 1920. It doubled again by 1930, as large numbers of automobile suburbs were established. After only a modest increase during the depression, the county trend arched upward again. Between 1950 and 1970, its population rose from 406,000 to 950,000.

While the region increased in wealth and numbers, St. Louis City faced many difficult and some intractable problems. Along with the loss of jobs, St. Louis encountered policy issues of a different texture and scale from those of previous decades. There was, for example, deteriorating housing. St. Louisans had battled slums before, but never on the scale required in the mid-twentieth century. As more houses decayed, more people moved away. By the 1940s, a massive urban renewal effort, including demolition and the building of new public housing, was under way. The results of these efforts were dramatic. By 1973, the St. Louis Land Reutilization Authority owned more land parcels than any other property holder.

Complicating the housing problem was a massive population shift. As middle- and upper-income whites departed, they were replaced largely by those who were black and poor. In 1940, only 13 percent of St. Louis City's population was black, but the postwar influx increased that figure to 41 percent by 1970. In the years since then, their proportion has declined. Like whites before them, blacks are moving to the county, since large-scale demolition and continued deterioration of existing residences leave them with insufficient city housing. The composition of the population also changed, because it was mostly the middle- and upper-income whites who left. The remaining white population is older and lacks the resources necessary to rehabilitate the housing stock. Unable to make up the revenues lost through a diminishing tax base, the city has not been able to provide all the services for which its various groups of citizens have asked. Inadequate tax revenues and the limited funds granted by the state and federal governments are not sufficient to finance major rebuilding of residential areas.

It is ironic that St. Louis should face such difficulties, for it has one of the longest and best-articulated traditions of city planning in America. The preparations for the Louisiana Purchase Exposition of 1904 marked the beginning of the tradition; numerous citizens were involved in laying out an impressive array of public improvements. The city plan of 1907 was one of the most comprehensive and visionary of the period. And after the St. Louis City Plan Commission was created in 1916, that agency produced a constant flow of creative and innovative ideas that dealt not only with current conditions but also with future needs. Much of this work was accomplished under the direction of Harlan Bartholomew, the commission's chief engineer and one of the leading city planners of the twentieth century. In reviewing the history of St. Louis planning over the past seventy years, it appears that the greatest successes occurred before the 1940s, when the city had more resources and the problems were seemingly soluble by mortar and brick. During the last several decades, as the focus of planners has widened to encompass social concerns, the resources have been wanting and the issues have been less amenable to social engineering.

While St. Louis City's public agencies have been no more successful than other American cities in dealing with what are national as well as local trends, many area residents have effected their own solutions. Beginning early in the nineteenth century, the affluent moved west into new subdivisions. By the time of the 1904 exposition, the grounds of which bordered on the western edge of the city, developers had begun building up the contiguous areas in the county. This westward movement remained steady for the next twenty years, but it was limited to a few corridors where adequate transportation connected with the central city until widespread ownership of automobiles in the 1920s provided the necessary release from limited space. Automobile suburbs—those residential areas in which access to a car was an absolute necessity for both economic and social existence—made their appearance in large numbers in that decade. In the mid-1930s, federal housing policies began to reinforce the trend of building new dwellings on open land outside the central city. Finally, the guidelines under which the Federal Housing Administration and the Veterans Administration guaranteed loans during the massive post-World War II building boom discriminated against remodeling older housing and favored construction of lower-density suburban subdivisions.

Along with low densities, suburbs generally shared another characteristic: they were removed from the central business district, which had limited and expensive parking. Since suburbs were away from downtown, developers installed competing commercial and civic centers in them. Although planned shopping centers dependent on the motor truck for supply and the automobile for customers appeared initially in the second decade of the twentieth century, they were built on a massive scale after World War II. Northwest Plaza, Crestwood Plaza, and Westport Plaza—to name only three of the largest—drew trade not only from the suburbs that surrounded them but to some extent from the wider region. The time when the downtown retail center offered the best selection of goods for the upper and middle classes was gone. Moreover, the St. Louis central business district had difficulty retaining its traditional administrative functions. Clayton, which began as the county seat of St. Louis County in the 1870s, began in the early 1960s to compete with downtown St. Louis for the regional administrative headquarters of financial institutions and large corporations.

Despite these developments, a rigorous distinction cannot be made between affluent, white suburbs and an impoverished, black city. Both the central political unit and the counties that surround it contain many different class, ethnic, and racial groups. The Germans still predominate on the city's South Side, but they are located throughout the region. "The Hill" in South St. Louis has remained an Italian section throughout the twentieth century. Enclaves of Irish and Slavs still exist as well, with the latter group concentrated mainly on the East Side. Moreover, just as the poverty of St. Louis City's black slum is obvious to even the most casual observer, so too is the wealth of its Westmoreland, Portland, and Cabanne places. The county contains similar gradations. Poor blacks are found in Wellston and Meacham Park; the white middle class occupies old Webster Groves and newer Lake St. Louis. The wealthy may be found on their ample estates in West County or in Clayton condominiums.

In recent years, residents of numerous localities within both the city and the region have endeavored to find the means to express their distinctiveness. This tendency has been encouraged by local and federal planners who continue to endorse the idea that neighborhoods are the basic building blocks of sound communities. During the 1960s, the residents of Soulard, Carondelet, and Lafayette Park neighborhoods joined together in active local associations. "Hill Day" has come to symbolize the integrity and vitality of a predominantly Italian Catholic neighborhood. For a few days each summer, the area in front of City Hall is reserved for the Strassenfest, a celebration of the continuing German culture in the region. On the predominantly black north side of St. Louis, the residents of the Yeatman and Murphy-Blair areas also utilize associations for celebrating group identity and meeting group needs. Beyond the city's edge, in the old, inner-ring suburb of University City, Jewish, Greek Orthodox, Catholic, and Protestant groups sponsor an annual fair which demonstrates the racial and ethnic mix in the community. Farther south and west in the county, the former railroad suburbs of Kirkwood and Webster Groves hold annual celebrations attesting to their civic consciousness and unique identities. While all this activity is tinged with boosterism and political opportunism—in addition to being good business—it is rooted in vital and authentic diversity.

This staunch localism, however, has often been maintained at a high cost. In the city, social divisions have inhibited cooperation on important issues and have contributed to the decline in essential services like public education. In the county, rampant balkanization has stymied efforts for all but the most minimal cooperation between political units. In 1900, St. Louis County had 8 incorporated towns. There were 22 by 1935 and 92 in 1950. The proliferation of incorporated areas has slowed in the past quarter century as the county government has encouraged de-incorporation and attempted to improve basic services to all those who are not part of some smaller, incorporated unit. Despite these efforts, the county at present contains about 100 discrete political entities, along with numerous overlapping service districts.

Recognizing the essential interdependence of peoples, institutions, and businesses within the region, some politicians, civic leaders, and academics have argued for various forms of metropolitan integration. A few have been forthcoming. The Regional Commerce and Growth Association, founded in 1964 as the Regional Industrial Development Council, is a nongovernmental group chartered to further economic growth in the St. Louis area. It performs functions previously carried out by the Metropolitan Chamber of Commerce. An interstate compact is the legal basis for the Bi-State Development Agency, founded in 1949 with the Port of New York Authority as its model. On paper this agency has enormous powers, especially in the transportation area, but its successes have been something less than anticipated. The East-West Gateway Coordinating Council was established in 1966, when the governors of Illinois and Missouri empowered it to serve as the regional review agency and clearinghouse for nineteen different federal funding programs. By mid-1971, it was mandated to review ninety different program areas.

Inherent in the development of more power by these or other agencies is a fundamental tension. The great mass of St. Louis area citizens desire privacy, independence, and the intimacy of neighborhoods or relatively small local government units that contain people who are much like themselves. Governments, including the newest agencies for the articulation of regional cooperation, meanwhile, seek to increase their authority for rational planning and the execution of programs. The quality of life and the prospects of modern, metropolitan St. Louis depend on how and to what extent this tension is resolved.

PART ONE

From Colonial Outpost to Frontier Town, 1763-1830

1 | Fragment from Chouteau's Narrative Concerning the Founding of St. Louis

"Rootless" modern urban Americans find some comfort in investing their city and town beginnings with an epic aura. While St. Louisans have no mythological heroes to compare with Rome's Romulus and Remus, they have cast their city's founder into the heroic mold. Auguste Chouteau, who at thirteen was a member of the original party of thirty that established St. Louis, wrote a history of the trip upriver and the first years of the settlement. Although much of this work has been lost, fourteen manuscript pages of the document were located in 1855 and were first translated and published in 1858. This excerpt is from a translation printed in the Missouri Historical Society Collections, *III (1911), pp. 335–66.*

In the year 1762, M. D'Abbadie, at that time Director General and Commandant of Louisiana, granted to a company the exclusive trade with the savages of the Missouri and all the nations residing west of the Mississippi, for the term of eight years. This company was formed under the name of Pre Laclède Ligueste,

Antoine Maxan and Company. . . . At the head (of the expedition) . . . was placed M. P. Laclède Ligueste, known as a man of great merit. . . . He left New Orleans the 3rd of August, 1763, and arrived in Illinois the 3rd of November following.

Observe, that all the establishments which the French had on the left bank of the Mississippi, were ceded to the English by the treaty of 1762, and that upon the right bank, remained to the French, there was only the small village of Ste. Geneviève, in which M. de Laclède could not find a house capable of containing one-fourth of his merchandise. M. de Neyon, Commandant of Fort de Chartres, learning the embarrassment of M. de Laclède, sent an officer to him, to tell him that he could offer him a place for his goods. . . . Necessity made him accept this generous offer of M. de Neyon. He left Ste. Geneviève, and arrived at Fort Chartres on the 3rd of November, 1763, where he disembarked all his goods, and prepared immediately all the supplies for the different nations. After all the business of the trade was done, he occupied himself with the means of forming an establishment suitable for his commerce, Ste. Geneviève not suiting him, because of its distance from the Missouri, and its insalubrious situation. These reasons decided him to seek a more advantageous site. In consequence, he set out from the Fort de Chartres in the month of December, . . . and examined all the ground from the Fort de Chartres to the Missouri. He was delighted to see the situation (where St. Louis at present stands); he did not hesitate a moment to form there the establishment that he proposed. Besides the beauty of the site, he found there all the advantages that one could desire to found a settlement which might become very considerable hereafter. After having examined all thoroughly, he fixed upon the place where he wished to form his settlement, marked with his own hand some trees, and said: "Chouteau, you will come here as soon as navigation opens, and will cause this place to be cleared, in order to form our settlement after the plan that I shall give you." We set out immediately afterwards, to return to Fort de Chartres, where he said, with enthusiasm, to Monsieur de Neyon, and to his officers that he had found a situation where he was going to form a settlement, which might become, thereafter, one of the finest cities of America—so many advantages were embraced in this site, by its locality and its central position, for forming settlements. . . . I arrived at the place designated on the 14th of February, and, on the morning of the next day, I put the men to work. They commenced the shed, which was built in a short time, and the little cabins for the men were built in the vicinity. In the early part of April, Laclède arrived among us. He occupied himself with his settlement, fixed the place where he wished to build his house, laid a plan of the village which he wished to found (and he named it Saint Louis, in honor of Louis XV, whose subject he expected to remain, for a long time;— he never imagined he was a subject of the King of Spain).

2 | The Tenor of Life in the French Frontier Settlement

Frederic L. Billon was seventeen when his family moved to St. Louis from Philadelphia in August 1818. Ten years later he was elected a city alderman and later was appointed twice as city comptroller. Throughout his adult life he was involved in numerous "booster" activities and served as an official of the Missouri Pacific Railway Company. After 1863, Billon retired from business to write about the early history of St. Louis. Like most nineteenth-century urban historians, Billon's work tends to be encyclopedic and narrative. Because of his early arrival in the city, however, his history contains information that is not readily accessible except in original documents, some of which are no longer extant. In one of his books on early St. Louis, Billon outlined numerous aspects of economic and social life in the period when Spain ruled while the French prevailed in St. Louis. Frederic L. Billon, comp., Annals of St. Louis in Its Early Days under the French and Spanish Dominations *(St. Louis: G. I. Jones and Company, 1886), pp. 74–77, 81–88.*

[*The Settlement*]

. . . St. Louis contained in the year 1770, at the conclusion of her first and French administration, one hundred and fifteen houses—one hundred of wood and fifteen of stone—of which number seventy-five, about two-thirds of the whole, had been put up in her two first years—1765 and 1766—with a population of about 500 souls. And at the transfer of the country to the United States in 1804 they had increased to one hundred and thirty of wood and fifty-one of stone—one hundred and eighty-one in all; an increase in the thirty-four years under Spanish rule of sixty-six buildings; an average of barely two per annum, and this included stores, warehouses, kitchens and other buildings, etc., some twenty or so. The dwellings being about one hundred and sixty, and the population 925 souls—an average of less than six to a house. . . .

During the thirty-four years of Spanish authority succeeding the first six years of French rule, the place continued to be French in every essential but the partial use of Spanish in a few official documents; the intercourse of the people with each other, and their governors, their commerce, trade, habits, customs, manners, amusements, marriages, funerals, services in church, parish registers, everything was French; . . . Outside of the Spanish officials and soldiers not more than a dozen Spaniards came to the place during the domination of Spain. . . . The country was only Spanish by possession, but practically French in all else.

Early Houses

Until some years after the transfer in 1804, the houses were of but two materials, stone and timber. The stone was quarried with a crow-bar and sledge-hammer, from along the river bluffs in front of the village, and much of the timber for the first houses was cut on the ground and in the near vicinity. . . .

About four-fifths of the houses were of posts set in the ground, the best of them hewed about nine inches square, the others of round posts set about three feet deep; a few of the best of these houses were of hewed posts set on a stone wall from four to five feet high above ground. The largest portion of these houses were from twenty to thirty feet in size, divided usually into two and some of them three rooms; some smaller, of fifteen to twenty feet square, a single room, which had to serve as parlor; bed and dining-room and kitchen; a few had a shed attached to the house for the latter purpose. A few of the larger houses were divided into three rooms, with a stone chimney in the center and a fire-place in each room; they were mostly floored with hewed puncheons, the ceilings from eight to ten feet high.

Agriculture

The agricultural operations in the early development of the

settlement were on a very limited scale, confined at first mainly to corn for their bread; potatoes and turnips, pumpkins and melons in their common fields, and no more of these than were necessary for their own consumption, as there would have been no market for any surplus, and each one his little garden patch contiguous to his residence, where he raised his little supply of kitchen truck.

In a few years, after the erection of Laclède's water mill [in 1767], they added wheat to their bread stuffs. . . . They needed no meadows, the wild prairie grass abounding all over the country affording an abundance of nutritious hay for their animals. . . . Their gardens furnished them peas, beans, cabbages, beets, carrots, etc., the woods and prairies plenty of wild game, the streams plenty of fish, and with their beef, poultry, eggs, milk and butter there was an abundance in the land, because the consumers were but few.

Amusements

For the men, the amusements were billiards, cards and pony races, for amusement only—rarely anything staked. For the females, fiddling and dancing and the usual amount of gossiping and small-talk. In 1767, the village hardly two years old, there were two billiard establishments, and a year or two later, a third. Their horses for many years being exclusively a small breed of Indian ponies peculiar to the country, mostly natural pacers, their races were seldom more than a few hundred yards in length, or at most, a quarter of a mile to the extent, usually in the prairie back of the village, there being then no race track. . . .

Their dancing parties were sometimes on a Saturday evening, after the labors of the week were ended, and were always kept up until daylight the next morning. But more frequently on Sundays, afternoons and evenings, the Sabbath being considered over by most of the people at the conclusion of the High Mass at twelve o'clock noon,—the afternoons were devoted to amusement, a few only of the most devout, largely females, would attend the evening vespers.

3 | Population Tables, 1764–1800

*The introductory essay suggests that the main factors in St. Louis'
early growth were the desires of immigrants to continue practicing*

the Catholic religion, retain ownership of slaves, and obtain free land. Table 1 provides a basis for asserting these relationships. The figures are for the St. Louis District, a geographical area roughly equivalent to present-day St. Louis County. They were compiled from Spanish censuses and other sources. The first growth period, lasting from 1764 to 1770, was associated with the fear of the French residents who lived on the Illinois side of the Mississippi that the English would be oppressive rulers, especially in the area of religious practice. For nearly a full decade the growth remained relatively slow. Immigration to the St. Louis District increased only a little more rapidly as the effects of the American War of Independence were felt in Illinois. While the Spanish experienced less frontier disorder than did the English, it was not until 1787 that a new incentive occurred. When the Northwest Ordinance was passed by the Congress in that year, slaveholders on the Illinois side feared that their chattel slaves would be freed. A second brief growth spurt was associated with this law, lasting until 1791. St. Louis actually lost population in the next five years. The third population increase was associated with the great land giveaway which the Spanish started in 1795. This surge abated when all the land in the district was claimed, which occurred by 1800. Table 2 provides a breakdown of the composition of St. Louis' population between 1772 and 1800. Some observations follow. Glen E. Holt, "The Shaping of St. Louis, 1763–1860" (Unpublished Ph.D. thesis, Department of History, University of Chicago, 1975), Appendix A, Tables 1 and 2.

TABLE 1

Population, Actual and Estimated, of the St. Louis District Settlements,
1764–1804 *

Year	Population	Rate of Increase for Previous Five-Year Period	Year	Population	Rate of Increase for Previous Five-Year Period
1764	40				
1765	(193)				
1766	(215)		1786	(962)	
1767	(311)		1787	1,028	
1768	(316)		1788	1,197	
1769	(320)		1789	(1,257)	
1770	500	159.1%	1790	(1,318)	41.8%
1771	(548)		1791	1,378	
1772	597		1792	1,362	
1773	637		1793	1,348	
1774	(644)		1794	1,331	
1775	(651)	31.2%	1795	1,316	−.2%
1776	(658)		1796	1,522	
1777	(665)		1797	(1,674)	
1778	(672)		1798	(1,827)	
1779	(680)		1799	1,979	
1780	687	4.7%	1800	2,447	78.2%
1781	(729)		1801	(2,530)	
1782	(771)		1802	(2,613)	
1783	(813)		1803	(2,670)	
1784	(855)		1804	2,780	13.6%
1785	897	30.6%	1805		

* Numbers in parentheses are estimates.

TABLE 2

Composition of the Population of the District of St. Louis (1772–1787) and the Village of St. Louis (1791–1800)

Year	1772	%	1773	%	1787	%	1791	%	1794 –95	%	1796	%	1799	%	1800	%
Whites																
Males—																
to 14	72	12.1	74	11.6	63	5.3	134	13.0	120	12.3	114	11.7			110	10.6
14 to 50	169	28.3	188	29.5	494	41.8	217	21.1	209	21.4	241	24.7			270	26.0
over 50	7	1.2	23	3.6	30	2.5	62	6.0	39	4.0	35	3.6			21	2.0
Males—																
total	248	41.5 *	285	44.7	587	49.7 *	413	40.2	368	37.7	390	40.0			401	38.6
Females—																
to 14	77	12.9	78	12.2	123	10.4			119	12.2	113	11.6			117	11.3
14 to 50	64	10.7	71	11.1	170	14.4			126	12.9	130	13.3			140	13.5
over 50	10	1.7	10	1.6	16	1.3			23	2.3	18	1.8			44	4.2
Females—																
total	151	25.3	159	25.0 *	309	26.1	270	26.3	268	27.4	261	26.8 *			301	29.0
Total Whites	399	66.8	444	69.7	896	75.8	683	66.4	636	65.1	651	66.7 *	601	65.0	702	67.6
Free Mulattos																
Males—																
to 14					6	.5			12	1.2	10	1.0			14	1.3
14 to 50					7	.6			8	.8	6	.6			17	1.6
over 50															1	.1
Males—																
total					13	1.1	10	1.0	20	2.0	16	1.6			32	3.1

TABLE 2 (cont'd)

Composition of the Population of the District of St. Louis (1772–1787) and the Village of St. Louis (1791–1800)

Year	1772	%	1773	%	1787	%	1791	%	1794 -95	%	1796	%	1799	%	1800	%
Females—																
to 14					6	.5			11	1.1	6	.6			13	1.2
14 to 50					2	.2			6	.6	10	1.0			12	1.1
over 50																
Females—																
total	—		—		8	.7	13	1.2	17	1.7	18	1.8			26	2.5*
Total Free Mulattos					21	1.8	23	2.2*	37	3.8*	34	3.5*	50	5.4	58	5.6
Free Negroes																
Males—																
to 14					2	.2									1	.1
14 to 50					3	.2			1		1	.1			1	.1
over 50					1	.1										
Males—																
total	—		—		6	.5	8	.8	1	.1	1	.1			2	.2
Females—																
to 14					1	.1			1	.1					1	.1
14 to 50					4	.3			4	.4	5	.5			6	.6
over 50					1	.1					2	.2				
Females—																
total					6	.5	6	.6	5	.5	7	.7			7	.7

TABLE 2 (cont'd)

Composition of the Population of the District of St. Louis (1772–1787) and the Village of St. Louis (1791–1800)

Year	1772	%	1773	%	1787	%	1791	%	1794 –95	%	1796	%	1799	%	1800	%
Total Free Negroes					12	1.0	14	1.4	6	.6	8	.8	6	.6	9	.9
Total Free Mul/Blacks					33	2.8	37	3.6	43	4.4	42	4.3	56	6.0	67	6.4 *
Mulatto Slaves																
Males—																
to 14					16	1.3			25	2.6	19	1.9			29	2.8
14 to 50					24	2.0			26	2.7	18	1.8			9	.9
over 50															6	.6
Males— total					40	3.4	38	3.7	51	5.2 *	37	3.8 *			45	4.3
Females—																
to 14					14	1.2			23	2.3	24	2.5			31	3.0
14 to 50					20	1.7			19	1.9	22	2.2			27	2.6
over 50					2	.2			4	.4	2	.2			2	.2
Females— total					36	3.0 *	36	3.5	46	4.7 *	48	4.9			60	5.8
Total Mulatto Slaves					76	6.4	75	7.2	97	9.9	85	8.7			104	10.0 *

TABLE 2 (cont'd)

Composition of the Population of the District of St. Louis (1772–1787) and the Village of St. Louis (1791–1800)

Year	1772	%	1773	%	1787	%	1791	%	1794 –95	%	1796	%	1799	%	1800	%
Negro Slaves																
Males—																
to 14	40 a	6.7	25 a	3.9	11	.9			31	3.2	23	2.3			24	2.3
14 to 50	76	12.7	80	12.5	68	5.5			55	5.6	58	5.9			36	3.5
over 50					2	.2			24	2.4	19	1.9			15	1.4
Males— total	116	19.4	105	16.4	81	6.8 *	126	12.2	110	11.3 *	100	10.1 *			75	7.2
Females—																
to 14	22	3.7	20	3.1	32	2.7			17	1.7	21	2.1			18	1.7
14 to 50	60	10.0	68	10.7	61	5.2			60	6.1	68	7.0			62	6.0
over 50					3	.2			13	1.3	8	.8			10	1.0
Females— total	82	13.7	88	13.8	96	8.1	108	10.5	90	9.2 *	97	9.9			90	8.7
Total Negro Slaves					177	15.0 *	234	22.8 *	200	20.5	197	20.2 *			165	15.9
Total Mul/Black Slaves	198	33.2 *	193	30.3 *	253	21.4	308	30.0	297	30.4	282	28.9	268	29.0	269	25.9
Total Population	597	100.0	637	100.0	1182	100.0	1168	100.0	976	99.9 *	975	99.9 *	925	100.0	1039	99.9 *

* Indicates that sum is not equal to total of previous figures because of rounding.

a Slaves not classified as Negro or mulatto; only two age categories were used for slaves: capable of work and too young to work.

Observations on Table 2

Whites

1 | Between 1772 and 1787, the proportion of whites in the area population rose significantly from 66.8% to 75.8%. From 1791 to 1800 the percentage of whites in the village remained relatively stable, fluctuating from a low of 65% in 1799 to a high of 67.6% in 1800, only a year later.

2 | The most volatile group in the population were white males between the ages of 14 and 50. In the early 1770s, this group accounted for between 28.3% and 29.5% of the population. They form a less sizable proportion in 1791 (21.1%) and in 1795 (21.4%), when the St. Louis District was in the doldrums. After 1795, their proportion rose to a high of 26% by 1800.

3 | In spite of the periods of expansion and contraction in the three growth cycles between 1772 and 1800, the percentage of white adult women rose steadily in the population. Those of child-bearing ages, between 14 and 50, increased from 10.7% in 1772 to 13.5% in 1800. Women over 50 more than doubled in the same period, going from 1.6% of the total population in 1773 to 4.2% of the population in 1800.

4 | The number of children under 14 dropped steadily in proportion to the number of women of childbearing age. For each white woman in 1772, there were 2.3 children under 14; in 1773, 2.1 children; in 1795, 1.9 children; in 1796, 1.7 children; in 1800, 1.6 children. Several interpretations are possible: Unmarried females of childbearing age were not marrying so quickly between 1772 and 1800, each woman was bearing fewer children in the later years, or infant mortality was very high.

Free Blacks and Mulattos

1 | Within the village the proportion of free mulattos and Negroes rose steadily from 1787 until 1800. Mulattos made up almost all of this increase. They constituted 5.6% of the total population of the village in 1800.

2 | Remarkably, there are no free Negro children in any of the three village censuses that contain such a category between 1795 and 1800. This lack of children may well indicate the freeing of former single slaves, with these ex-slaves remaining unmarried.

3 | The birth rate for free mulattos and Negroes was remarkably low. In 1795, for every free black or mulatto woman there were only 1.6 children under 14; in 1796, only .6 children; and in 1800 only 1 child. Free blacks and mulattos thus appear to have borne less children than did whites.

Slaves

1 | The proportion of slaves in the total population declined steadily between 1772 and 1787, from 33.2% to 21.4%. With the passage of the Northwest Ordinance in 1787, the proportion of slaves increased to 30% in 1791 and, within the village, to 30.4% in 1795. Thereafter it declined substantially, to 25.9% in 1800.

2 | In the 1770s, the number of male slaves of workable age tended to be greater than the number of females. This result might be anticipated since the populations of 1772 and 1773 included agricultural areas, where field hands were used for labor. In the censuses of the village after 1795, the reverse is true. Increasingly female slaves, both mulatto and Negro, outnumber males in the total population.

3 | There is a noticeable decline in the number of Negro slaves and a rise in the proportion of mulatto slaves within the village between 1796 and 1800.

4 | The number of children in the population was lower in relation to slave women of childbearing age than it was for white women. In 1795, there were 1.2 children for every woman between the ages of 14 and 50; in 1796, 1 child; and in 1800, 1.1 children.

4 | Indenture as a Form of Labor in the St. Louis Economy

Along with slavery, another form of labor existed in colonial St. Louis. While it is impossible to determine their numbers, indentured servants—persons who contracted their labor for their keep and often to learn a trade as well—played a part in building the city. The indenture contract presented here included a substantial economic incentive for the apprentice to complete his indenture successfully. From Billon, Annals of Early Days, *pp. 73–74.*

Personally present Francis Baribault, a free boy, living in the post of St. Louis, aged about 19 years, who by these presents voluntarily binds himself for two years and a half to James Denis, joiner, also of this place, as an apprentice to learn the trade and mystery of a joiner—commencing with this day, and to end, without discontinuance, at the close of the two and half years; said Denis binds himself to feed, clothe and maintain said apprentice, with proper medical assistance if sick, during the term of his apprenticeship, and to use his best endeavours, as a good citizen and master, to teach said apprentice his said business as a joiner; and in like manner said Baribault binds himself to work with all his ability and strength for the interest of his master in acquiring his trade, and to obey his proper commands in all things connected with the said business. Denis to have no claim on said apprentice's services beyond the expiration of his term, unless for loss of time through fault of said apprentice.

In addition said Denis is to put up at his cost and expense, at the close of said apprenticeship, a small house of posts in the ground of 12 by 15 feet, with an earthern chimney and covered with shingles, on such lot of ground as Baribault may then have acquired, so that he may have a place to live in when he leaves said Denis.

Done at office in St. Louis, of Illinois, April 4, 1770, in presence of the undersigned witnesses and parties, who have signed the same, after being read, except Baribault, who knows not how to write.

JULIEN LEROY ⎫
BEAU SOLIEL, ⎬ *Witnesses*
HERVIEUX, ⎭

JACQUES DENIS,
LABUSCIERE, *Notary.*

5 | Local Ordinances for St. Louis and General Ordinances Published by Lieutenant-Governor Don Francisco Cruzat from October 7, 1780, to November 24, 1787

The early history of St. Louis is often presented in the quiet pastels of an idyllic society where order and harmony prevailed. Local and general ordinances as decreed by Spanish Governor Francisco Cruzat offer an important corrective. They demonstrate that by the 1780s, establishing both public safety and public order, the underlying tenets of what later came to be called "municipal housekeeping," were of great concern in colonial St. Louis. Governor

Francisco Cruzat's edicts, issued in a seven-year period, were official attempts to promote a more disciplined and safer existence for citizens in the nascent urban environment. Excerpted from Document #12, "Papers from Spain," located in the Missouri Historical Society Archives, St. Louis. Translation by Richard C. Amelung, 1977.

We see with displeasure that many persons, despising the wisdom of the . . . ordinances and public tranquillity, give themselves up to drinking with savages, in the hope of obtaining by their methods their personal ends—without considering the effects of such a proceeding. . . , of which a baneful experience ought to lead us to avoid dangers by foreseeing them. Consequently, we most strictly forbid every person, of whatever occupation, rank, condition, and sex that he may be, from giving any liquor to the savages . . . under any pretext whatever. . . . October 7, 1780.

The deadly experience which we have had from the unavoidable effects which always result from confusion in an unexpected alarm requires of our duty an active zeal to remedy the situation. Consequently, we prescribe the following rules and signals, so that in case of attack there may be exact compliance with them; to wit: when by day the colors are seen hoisted, and two cannon-shots are heard—one fired from the government building, and the other from the Exchange—and the drums beat the general [alarm], the [military] company which is composed of persons who live from the government house as far as the extremity of the village on the north side shall repair, immediately and without any delay, to the entrenchment on the north; and the company composed [of residents] from the government house as far as the end of the lower part of the village shall at the same time repair to the entrenchment on the south. If in the night a cannon-shot is heard, with the general alarm by the drums, everyone shall repair immediately to the entrenchment assigned to him. . . . October 29, 1780.

It has come to our knowledge that various persons, who are wallowing in a shameful condition of sloth and negligence, employ their time and are too free in retailing to the public false tidings and unreliable reports, in the hope of alarming and disturbing that very public, which is sometimes too easily led astray by the marvelous of anti-political affections and of talk that is unbridled, clandestine, and opposed to good sense; that these persons, uneasy, restless, and giddy, thrust themselves in to stir up the people, for the malicious pleasure of disturbing the public tranquillity, and by the vanity of wanting to raise themselves above the common—imposing upon them by a tissue of sophistical reasonings without foundations or likeness to truth, but seductive. Desiring (since it is a part of our duty) to remedy these abuses, so opposed to the general peace and to the respect which ought to be felt for the government in a country that is civilized and under a monarch, we forbid expressly with all our power, right, and full authority, any person, of whatever sex, rank, occupation, and condition he may be, to spread abroad, communicate, or make known to the public, or even to a single individual, any news—whether true or false, favorable to the state, or otherwise—before he has privately announced it to the government, which alone must make public that which concerns the nation, or be known by it. In consequence, any person whosoever who is proved and duly convicted of having opposed or infringed this ordinance, in whole or in part, will be regarded as rebellious against the government, and, as such, will be sent with the case against him to New Orleans, at his own cost and expense, that he may be judged according to the full severity of the laws. . . . February 9, 1781.

Experience demonstrates every day how necessary it is to provide by foresight against the treacherous blows which the savages very often deal to those to whom they had seemed most trustworthy, covering their foul projects by an apparent friendship which has all the external marks of a sincere attachment, the falseness of which is almost never known until after the remedy fails to be efficacious, and one has been the dupe of blind confidence. Consequently, we most strictly order every person, whatever may be his rank, occupation, and condition, not to leave his dwelling by day or night (whether or not there be savages in the village) without being well armed—as one must be in so critical a time of war, in a country where one cannot take too many precautions against the events to which one is daily exposed. . . . February 25, 1781.

We again notify all persons, generally, in order to prevent the soldier from incurring more debts than he can pay, and the public from being wronged, that those who shall give credit to any soldier for a larger sum than that of twenty sols shall lose all the advances that they may have made to him and shall be granted no hearing; nor shall the soldier be compelled to pay what such person has advanced to him or given him on credit. . . . May 24, 1781.

The infraction of the ordinances published at various times by our predecessors that one dares commit when one is out of the view of the government building and which very strictly forbid horse-racing in the streets of the village obliges us to renew those ordinances at this time, in order to prevent the misfortunes which may result from an abuse so diametrically opposed to the public safety. Consequently, we very strictly forbid, with all our power and full authority, every person, of whatever sex, occupation, rank, or condition he may be, to go on horseback, or in a cart, sledge, or carriole, faster than at a foot-pace [*le petit pas*], no matter for what motive, reason, or pretext that it may be, under penalty to the offender—for the first time, fifteen days' imprisonment and a fine of twenty-five livres, to be applied to the treasury; and double [that amount] for the second offense.

We command all those who shall see any act of disobedience to the above command, or who shall have knowledge of it, to come to us and make a faithful report of it; if they do not, they will be punished like the aggressors. . . . June 10, 1781.

The abuses which are daily creeping in through the unruly conduct of the slaves at this post of St. Louis, owing to the criminal tolerance in some masters who are so careless of their authority and of public welfare—in which they ought to feel an interest, as [all are] members of the same body—oblige us, notwithstanding the orders previously published on this subject, again to prohibit the slaves, under the penalty of fifty lashes of the whip, to hold any assembly at night, in the cabins or elsewhere; and they will incur a more severe punishment according to the result of their said assemblies.

We most strictly forbid all the slaves to leave their cabins at night or otherwise, after the beat of tattoo [*retraite*], unless it be for some errand of their masters, and with the consent (either written or verbal) of the latter—under the penalty of fifty lashes of the whip for the first time (if they are found in the streets), received in a public square and double the penalty if they repeat the offense.

The slaves are likewise forbidden, under the same [penalty], to receive in their cabins other slaves, except those who belong to their own masters; and they are commanded to detain slaves who are strangers, and notify the masters of these—who shall be obliged to put them in prison, and themselves to be responsible for the tranquillity and good conduct of their slaves; if they do not, they shall be punished with imprisonment of one week, and shall pay a fine of fifty livres, to be applied to the public works of this post. The slaves shall not be allowed to dance, either by day or night, in the village or elsewhere, without an express permission from their masters and the consent of the government; and those who shall be arrested for failure to observe this order shall each receive in public fifty lashes of the whip. . . . August 12, 1781.

As it has come to the knowledge of the government that the savages, both free and slaves, and the negroes on this post often dress themselves in barbarous fashion, adorning themselves with vermilion and many feathers which render them unrecognizable, especially in the woods: in order to avoid the misfortunes which may follow from the surprises which these men, thus metamorphosed, could occasion to those who might see them in an unexpected moment, and who, taking them for enemies, would shoot at them, we most strictly forbid all savages, whether free or slave, and negroes of this said post to clothe themselves in any other manner than according to our usage and custom, either in the village or in order to go into the woods or fields—under penalty of being punished with severity. . . . August 15, 1781.

The fires, of which there has been no instance until the present time, and which are singularly making their appearance for some days past without our being able to discover their causes, constrains us to take measures for preventing still greater happenings in such cases. Consequently, we ordain that all the inhabitants and other persons who reside on this post repair, as soon as they hear the drums sound the general [alarm], or the alarm bell ring, to the place where the fire shall be seen appearing, each one carrying his gun or other defensive weapon, in order by this precaution to forestall any feint or ambush on the part of the enemy. But, as it is necessary to be able to check the progress of the fire, we enjoin the said inhabitants and residents who shall have slaves to send them to the place where the fire is, without distinction of sex, with axes, spades, and mattocks. . . . October 1, 1785.

Notice is given to all the inhabitants settled in this province that the wise and pious laws of his Majesty most strictly forbid any subject [of his], of whatever rank or condition he may be, to make any Indian a slave, or to hold one as such, under any pretext whatsoever, even though one might be in open war with the nation from which the Indian might come. Consequently, it is most strictly prohibited and forbidden to all the subjects of his Majesty, and even to travelers who chance to be in this province, to acquire, buy, or appropriate any savage slave, from the day of the publication of this edict; it is also ordained that the present owners of the said savage slaves shall not [be] allowed to get rid of those whom they have, in any manner whatsoever, except it be by giving them their freedom. . . . November 24, 1787.

6 | St. Louis as a Focus of Imperialist Aspirations and Intrigues

Between 1770 and 1804 Spanish governors resided in St. Louis. By most accounts their superintendence over domestic affairs was effective even though the Spanish element comprised a small minority of the town's predominantly French population. Control over external affairs was another matter. The governors' main concern was to exploit the riches of the frontier and to protect it from first English, then American competition and expansionism. The following three documents which are drawn from the governors' correspondence illustrate their external concerns and activities. The letters reflect St. Louis' strategic significance in the development of the West.

The first item is a commission from the Spanish authorities in New Orleans to one of the leading citizens of St. Louis, Pierre or Pedro Chouteau. It instructs him to build forts among the Indians in order to protect the lucrative fur trade upon which early St. Louis fortunes, including that of the Chouteau family, were founded.

The second item, a letter from the Spanish governor in New Orleans to the governor at St. Louis, demonstrates that smuggling furs across the Mississippi was a more difficult problem than controlling the Indians.

The final item amplifies the American threat. Despite the Louisiana Purchase, important Spanish interests remained throughout the West. Moreover, the borders were not well-drawn and, based on their experience with American aggressiveness, Spanish officials feared a continued erosion of their territory and influence. The background of this letter is the suspicion that expeditions such as that led by Lewis and Clark were engaged in gathering military as well as scientific information and that Spain should attempt to plant a double-agent in such a venture as a prelude to waging war against the United States.

The following documents are located in the Spanish Archives, Rare Book Department, Washington University Library, St. Louis.

A Commission to Pierre Chouteau by the Baron of Carondelet, 1794

In consideration of the service rendered by Don Augusto and Don Pedro Chouteau, they have proposed to His Majesty to erect a Fort in the Nation of the great Osages and maintain order and discipline among them as well as in the Nation of the Small Osages, preventing raids and incursion which they have already accomplished; being essential to appoint a Commander of this Fort, one of those brother's influence over said nation is such that I have appointed Don Pedro Chouteau Lieutenant of Militia as its Commander, with Military Powers subject to the Lieutenant Governor of the Illinois, and besides the above circumstance he has valor, courage and the necessary qualifications for the above position. Therefore I order to said Lieutenant Governor, Commanders, citizens and inhabitants of the establishments of Illinois to obey him as such Commander, and give to him the obedience, honors, privileges and exemptions which belong to him as such, and will best serve His Majesty and the tranquility of these Provinces.

Given under my hand and seal in New Orleans and attested by the undersigned Secretary for His Majesty of this Government and Dependence of New Orleans on the 17th of May, 1794.

THE BARON OF CARONDELET

*Spanish Governor at New Orleans
to the Governor of St. Louis, 1802*

To Don Carlos Denault Delassus.

After comparing the present shipment of goods which left this market for those establishments, and the arrival of furs, with these of the previous years of 1781 and 82 and others, the difference resulting is of consideration and against the commerce of this Capital, and therefore also against the Royal interests, because the duties are not paid as before when goods were shipped. I am well aware of the fact that the Indian works do not produce as much as they use to before, but I also know that this is not the only reason of the decline of the mercantile relations between that country and this Capital. The secret importation and exportation that I am informed the Englishmen and Americans are doing contribute largely to the present condition of affairs. Therefore it is my duty to ask you to exercise all your efforts in this direction and prevent such acts that may result against the State in general, you can do this without going into any expense, and advise me what you think would be necessary to do, and if any expenditure would be indispensable, so I will consider the matter and try to do what will be in my power, or to submit same to the decision of His Majesty.

May the Lord keep you for many years, New Orleans, January 21st, 1802.

JUAN VENTURA MORALES

*To the Marqués de Casa Calvox from
His Excellency Don Pedro
Ceballos, New Orleans, July 18, 1805*

Most Excellent Sir:-

In confidential reports numbers 14 and 15 of June 21 and September 24, 1804, I informed your Excellency of the design of the President of the United States to examine and explore the Rivers of San Francisco de Arkansas and the Colorado from their discharge into the Mississippi to their source; I intimated in those reports what I thought ought to be done immediately not only to prevent this undertaking but also to hinder the progress of the Expedition which in the early part of 1804 and with a like object, ascended the River Missouri in command of Captain Lewis Merry Whether [Meriwether Lewis], who has already made several shipments of Plants, Stones, Fossils, Skins and other curiosities of Natural History, which are at this time in the hands of the Governor of this Territory, to be sent shortly to the President, together with a lot of live animals and birds which will arrive within a few days.

I have just lately received through Governor Claiborne, who intimated its purpose, the petition No. 1, he having advised me some days before under the pretext of making me a visit, on behalf of the said President, manifesting ardent desires to preserve the harmony and good understanding which exists between both Nations, and his design to take advantage of the opportunity in order to promote useful knowledge among the same, and to this end he notified the Governor to ask me for a passport for Don William Dumbar, an intelligent and literary person, who was to direct the operations of exploration of said Rivers: adding that in order to remove all suspicion of any hostile intention on the part of the United States, he proposed that our Government should name one or two persons who should witness said operations and take part at the same time in the advantageous and useful knowledge and discoveries which might be attained, all the expenses being paid by the U.S.

I was not a little embarrassed at the beginning of this proposition; but after well reflecting over the matter, and considering how far advanced Captain Merry is upon the Missouri, and having in view the particular utility and advantages which we would derive under the circumstances, I have acceded for my part without compromising myself, leaving the Commandant General and Governors of the internal Provinces to act, not doubting but they will comply with their duties.

I well know that the President, under the pretext of advancing the sciences, and making use of his maxims of an apparent Philosophy and of an astute and democratic policy, is endeavoring to obtain knowledge of the country which we possess and which he has so much ambition to possess; but in the circumstances in which we find ourselves, if it is not possible to oppose with open force, after the considerable progress which has already been made, nothing remains to me but to make war against them with their own arms, by finding out all their plans, views and ideas, which cannot but appear and be penetrated through conversations and operations which necessarily must occur during the exploration and survey of said Rivers. The opportunity is so favorable that there will hardly be presented another of like nature in a great while.

7 | The Progress of the Town, 1804–1818

Even after the transfer to America in 1804, St. Louis continued to grow slowly. The town still was an urban outpost on the far-western frontier, shaped more by traditional factors than by new developments due to accession by the United States. Then, as historian Frederic Billon points out in this brief excerpt, a critical national event stimulated economic activity that brought new population and forced spatial expansion. Frederic L. Billon, Annals of St. Louis in Its Territorial Days. . . *(St. Louis: G. I. Jones, 1888), pp. 22–25.*

For the first few years after the transfer, there was but little, if any, increase in either population or houses, a few of the latter, generally log, were now and then added to the place, as the gradual increase of the population seemed to require.

Then came the war with England, in June, 1812, which continued until the early part of the year 1815. During the three years' continuance of this war, the General Government deemed it necessary to keep up a pretty large force of men here, as a protection to our frontier inhabitants, from inroads on the part of the British and Indians, this post being then the westernmost military post of the United States.

These troops were cantoned at Fort Bellefontaine, on the Missouri, in this county, and the officers had almost daily intercourse with the people of the place. After the close of the war, and the consequent reduction of the army to the peace establishment, many of these troops, both officers and men remained in the west, and became permanent residents of the country, thereby adding materially to the population. Added to this was the revival of business throughout the country, east and west, consequent upon the peace, which gave an impetus to the place, so that . . . at the date of my arrival here in 1818, the population was estimated at three thousands souls.

During this period up to 1816, the Town was confined to the three original streets on the lower plateau, but after the close of the war, the prospective increase in the place induced Col. Chouteau and Judge Lucas, who were the sole owners of the land on the "hill," back of the village, as it was then called, in contradistinction to the old or lower Town, Col. C. owning south and Judge Lucas north of Market street, their dividing line, to lay out an addition to the Town, which was accordingly done in May, 1816, and the lots brought into market. A number of them in the center near to Market street were sold, and a few houses erected thereon of brick and frame.

8 | Sources of Immigration to St. Louis, 1804–1816

Early censuses of St. Louis lack detail. Before 1821, when Missouri became a state, local territorial censuses indicate only that St. Louis grew from 925 to 1,400 between 1799 and 1810, and to 4,900 by 1820. Using the family biographies of those who arrived between 1804 and 1816, in Billon's Annals of St. Louis in Its Territorial Days, *some indication of the sources of St. Louis leadership can be ascertained (Table 3). Immigration to St. Louis was heavily American, and there was a discernible pattern in the originating points of the sixty-four arrivals. Robert L. Kirkpatrick, in "History of St. Louis, 1804–1816" (M.A. thesis, Washington University, 1947), p. 16, first compiled this raw information in a different format. Some of the percentage subtotals do not come out even because of rounding.*

9 | The Town and Its Surroundings, 1810

One of the most graphic descriptions of St. Louis in any period was written by Henry M. Brackenridge. In 1793, his father asked a friend, St. Louis Judge John B. C. Lucas, to take the seven-year-old boy, whose mother had died, and place him with a French family so that he could learn the language. After living more than a year in Spanish-held Louisiana, he was returned to Pittsburgh. In April 1810, Brackenridge returned to Louisiana Territory and practiced law in and around St. Louis until January 1811. His interests, however, were more catholic than legal. His extensive travels over the territory included a long expedition to Fort Man-

TABLE 3

Sources of Immigration to St. Louis, 1804–1816

States, by Census Region	Number of Families	%	States, by Census Region	Number of Families	%
New England			*East North Central*		
New Hampshire	0		Ohio	1	1.6
Vermont	1	1.6	Indian Territory	1	1.6
Massachusetts	3	4.7		2	3.1
Rhode Island	0		*South Atlantic*		
Connecticut	4	6.3	Delaware	0	
	8	12.5	Maryland	5	7.8
Mid Atlantic			Virginia	19	29.7
New York	0		North Carolina	2	3.1
New Jersey	3	4.7	South Carolina	0	
Pennsylvania	10	15.6	Georgia	0	
	13	20.3		26	40.6
East South Central			*Foreign Countries*		
Kentucky	1	1.6	France & Santo Domingo	5	7.8
Tennessee	1	1.6	Italy	1	1.6
	2	3.1	British Isles		
West South Central			Ireland	5	7.8
Louisiana	0		Scotland	1	1.6
			Wales	1	1.6
				13	20.3
			Total	64	99.9

dan on the Upper Missouri River. In 1814, he published his Views of Louisiana, *from which this description of St. Louis and its surroundings is excerpted. Henry M.* Brackenridge, Views of Louisiana, Together with a Journal of a Voyage up the Missouri River in 1811 *(Pittsburgh: Cramer, Spear & Eichbaum, 1814), pp. 120–24.*

This place occupies one of the best situations on the Mississippi, both as to site and geographical position. . . . It is perhaps not saying too much, that it bids fair to be second to New Orleans in importance, on this river.

The ground on which St. Louis stands is not much higher than the ordinary banks, but the floods are repelled by a bold shore of limestone rocks. The town is built between the river and a second bank, three streets running parallel with the river; for the sake of the pleasure of the promenade, as well as for business and health, there should have been no encroachment on the margin of the noble stream. The principal place of business ought to have been on the bank. From the opposite side, nothing is visible of the busy bustle of a populous town; it appears closed up. The site of St. Louis is not unlike that of Cincinnati. How different would have been its appearance, if built in the same elegant manner: its bosom opened to the breezes of the river, the stream gladdened by the enlivening scene of business and pleasure, compact rows of elegant and tasteful dwellings, looking with pride on the broad wave that passes!

From the opposite bank, St. Louis, notwithstanding, appears to great advantage. In a disjoined and scattered manner it extends along the river a mile and an half, and we form the idea of a large and elegant town. Two or three large and costly buildings (though not in the modern taste) contribute in producing this effect. On closer examination, the town seems to be composed of an equal proportion of stone walls, houses, and fruit trees: but the illusion still continues.

On ascending the second bank, which is about forty feet above the level of the plain, we have the town below us, and a view of the Mississippi in each direction, and of the fine country which it passes. When the curtain of wood which conceals the American bottom shall have been withdrawn, or a vista formed by opening farms to the river, there will be a delightful prospect into that rich and elegant tract. The bottom at this place is not less than eight miles wide, and finely diversified with prairie and woodland.

There is a line of works on this second bank, erected for defence against the Indians, consisting of several circular towers, twenty feet in diameter, and fifteen in height, a small stockaded fort, and a stone breast work. These are at present entirely unoccupied and waste, excepting the fort, in one of the buildings of which, the courts are held, while another is used as a prison. Some distance from the termination of this line, up the river, there are a number of Indian mounds, and remains of antiquity; which, while they are ornamental to the town, prove, that in former times, those places had also been chosen as the site, perhaps, of a populous city.

Looking to the west, a most charming country spreads itself before us. It is neither very level nor hilly, but of an agreeable waving surface, and rising for several miles with an ascent almost imperceptible. Except a small belt to the north, there are no trees; the rest is covered with shrubby oak, intermixed with hazels, and a few trifling thickets, of thorn, crab apple, or plum trees. At the first glance we are reminded of the environs of a great city; but there are no country seats, or even plain farm houses: it is a vast waste, yet by no means a barren soil. Such is the appearance, until turning to the left, the eye again catches the Mississippi. A number of fine springs take their rise here, and contribute to the uneven appearance. The greater part fall to the S.W. and aid in forming a beautiful rivulet, which a short distance below the town gives itself to the river. I have been often delighted in my solitary walks, to trace this rivulet to its sources. Three miles from town, but within view, amongst a few tall oaks, it rises in four or five silver fountains, within short distances of each other: presenting a picture to the fancy of the poet, or the pencil of the painter. I have fancied myself for a moment on classic ground, and beheld the Naiads pouring the stream from their urns.

Close to the town, there is a fine mill erected by Mr. Cho[u]teau, on this streamlet; the dam forms a beautiful sheet of water, and affords much amusement in fishing and fowling, to the people of the town.

The common field of St. Louis was formerly enclosed on this bank, consisting of several thousand acres; at present there are not more than two hundred under cultivation; the rest of the ground looks like the worn common, in the neighborhood of a large town; the grass kept down and short, and the loose soil in several places cut open into gaping ravines. . . .

St. Louis contains according to the last census 1,400 inhabitants. One fifth Americans, and about 400 people of color. . . . It remained nearly stationary for two or three years after the cession; but it is now beginning to take a start, and its reputation is growing abroad. Every house is crowded, rents are high, and it is exceedingly difficult to procure a tenement on any terms. Six or seven houses were built in the course of last season, and probably twice the number will be built the next. There is a printing office, and twelve mercantile stores. The value of imports to this place in the course of the year, may be estimated at two hundred and fifty thousand dollars. The outfits for the different trading establishments, on the Mississippi or Missouri, are made here. The lead of the Sac mines is brought to this place; the troops at Belle Fontaine put sixty thousand dollars in circulation annually. The settlers in the vicinity on both sides of the river, repair to this place as the best market for their produce, and to supply themselves with such articles as they may need. . . .

The manners of the inhabitants are not different from those in other villages: we distinctly see the character of the ancient inhabitants, and of the new residents, and a compound of both. St. Louis, however, was always a place of more refinement and fashion, it is the residence of many genteel families, both French and American.

A few American mechanics, who have settled here, within a short time, are great acquisitions to the place; and there is still ample room for workmen of all kinds. There is a French school and an English one.

St. Louis will probably become one of those great reservoirs of the valley between the Rocky mountains and the Alleghany, from whence merchandise will be distributed to an extensive country. It unites the advantages of the three noble rivers, Mississippi, Illinois and Missouri. When their banks shall become the residence of millions, when flourishing towns shall arise, can we suppose that every vender of merchandise, will look to New Orleans for a supply, or to the Atlantic cities? There must be a place of distribution, somewhere between the mouth of the Ohio and the

Missouri. Besides a trade to the northern parts of New Spain will
be opened, and a direct communication to the East Indies, by
way of the Missouri, may be more than dreamt: in this, St. Louis
will become the Memphis of the American Nile.

10 | Disciplining Slaves, 1808

*Before the incorporation of the Town of St. Louis in 1809 by the
Territorial Legislature, local affairs and the preservation of law
and order were supervised by Spanish, French, and United
States military officers. Among the first acts passed by the town's
trustees were ordinances for insuring municipal peace. The concern with public order stemmed from St. Louis' boisterous frontier
character and from the apprehension evoked by the presence of
numerous slaves, who amounted to a quarter of the total population during this period. The code that follows would be characteristic of Southern communities throughout the antebellum
period, and when compared with the regulations enacted by the
Spanish (document 5), its terms suggest that American rule both
continued and improved on colonial precedents. Because St. Louis
was the major city of a slave state, these and similar regulations
remained in force until after the Civil War. Acts of Board of
Trustees for the Town of St. Louis, August 27, 1808, in John
Thomas Scharf,* History of Saint Louis City and County *(2 vols.;
Philadelphia: Louis Everts & Co., 1883), vol. 1, pp. 648–49.*

Be it ordained by the Board of Trustees for the town of St.
Louis, That no person or persons shall sell nor give to any slave
any spirituous or ardent liquor without a written permission from
the master or mistress of such slave, under the penalty of ten dollars for each and every offense.

Sec. 2. No person nor persons shall sell or furnish to any slave
any kind of goods, wares, and merchandise without a written permission from the master or mistress of such slave, under the
penalty of paying for each offense the sum of six dollars.

Sec. 3. Every person who shall find any slave in a state of in-
toxication in the streets or other public place in the said town of
St. Louis is hereby authorized to carry or cause to be carried such
slave to the master or mistress of such slave, who shall immediately

cause the said slave to receive and be whipped on his or her bare back ten lashes; and in case the said master or mistress shall neglect or refuse to cause such slave to be so whipped, such master or such mistress shall for every such neglect or refusal pay and forfeit the sum of five dollars.

Sec. 4. Slaves shall not assemble together for amusement and recreation, unless at the house of their master or mistress, except in the daytime, and having previously obtained a written permission from the chairman of the board of trustees for the town of St. Louis for the time being, or in his absence from some two members of the said board; and if any number of slaves exceeding four shall be so found assembled together for amusement and recreation without such written permission, any person or persons are hereby authorized to carry or cause to be carried such slave to the master or mistress thereof, who shall immediately cause the said slave to receive and to be whipped on his or her bare back ten lashes; and in case the master or mistress shall neglect or refuse to cause the said slave to be so whipped, such master or mistress shall for every such neglect or refusal forfeit and pay the sum of five dollars.

Sec. 5. Every free person of color giving balls, amusements, or public diversion and admitting a slave therein without the written permission of the master or mistress of said slave shall for every such offense forfeit and pay the sum of ten dollars, and the occupier of the house where such balls, amusements, or public diversions are held, and where a slave or slaves are admitted without such written permission, shall for every such ball, amusement, or public diversion as aforesaid forfeit and pay the sum of twenty dollars.

Sec. 6. No slave shall take or ride the horse, mare, or gelding of his master or mistress, or that of any other person without permission first had and obtained from the owner thereof; and any person finding a slave offending herein is hereby authorized to carry or cause to be carried the said slave to his or her master or mistress, and the said master or mistress shall immediately cause the said slave thus found offending to receive and be whipped upon the naked back of such slave twenty stripes; and in case the master or mistress shall neglect or refuse to cause the said slave to be so whipped, such master or mistress shall for every such neglect or refusal forfeit and pay the sum of ten dollars.

11 | Early History of the St. Louis Police Force

The enactment of codes regulating blacks required a means of enforcement, so the Board of Trustees accompanied the foregoing ordinances with the establishment of a small police force. In so doing, St. Louis antedated older cities in the East, which did not create similar municipal offices until the late 1830s. The need for law and order was so great that more than half of the 1818 budget of $1,500 was allocated for maintaining the watch. Nevertheless, the watch could not have succeeded without the participation of private citizens. Indeed, as the comparatively small budget of 1818 indicates, most of the town's limited services could not have been offered without the initiative, cooperation, and largesse of individuals. This spirit of volunteerism, which was common to early nineteenth-century American cities, especially those of the western frontier, would end when professional police and other hired officials supplanted the unpaid citizen. History of the Metropolitan Police Department of St. Louis, 1810–1910 *(St. Louis: Board of Police Commissioners, 1910), pp. 108–10.*

In 1808 . . . the first police force of St. Louis was arranged for. It consisted . . . of four men and the provision for the force was drawn up in the shape of an ordinance and signed by the Board of Trustees of the "Town of St. Louis," composed of Auguste Chouteau, E. Hempstead, B. Pratte, A. McNair and P. Chouteau. The four men were proudly distinguished as the "Constabulary." They were appointed and served without pay. Every male inhabitant of the town was subject to four months' duty each year, provided he were over eighteen years of age. No one was exempt. Service was practically compulsory, a fine of $1 being imposed for each refusal to serve. But it was a good force, albeit a small one, for the labor was one of love, and duty was a pride. It sufficed to manage the police end of the little community for ten years.

January 1, 1818, the city of St. Louis, then of respectable size and giving promise of the greatness that has come to bear, increased her police force, appointed her first Police Captain and paid her first salary to a policeman. This was to Captain Mackey Wherry. He was selected to head the force when the title of "Constabulary" was dropped and another ordinance substituted for the old. The old system of conscription was followed, but the regular watch was augmented by two men and a "Night Watch" of two men was also enrolled. Captain Wherry was paid $400 a year as commander of the first real police force of this city. Gabes Warner, a one-armed man was his "Night Chief," and a constable aided him. The force was small but adequate and competent. It was able to cope with every situation, to run down crime and handle the ordinary run of duties that appeared. Its duties like that of the preceding force had been mainly preservation of the peace. The patrol went armed, furnishing their own weapons. They had the power to: "Command order and silence of all persons after 9 o'clock in the evening on all streets and public highways." It was their duty to apprehend all persons "Disturbing the public tranquility." Negro slaves who perchance were caught on the streets after 9 p.m. were subject to a flogging, ten lashes being prescribed or a fine of $2 to be paid by their masters, providing they were abroad without written permits from their owners. Persons found in "Gardens or lots not their own," were subject to a fine of $5. They were ordinances suited to the times and made necessary by circumstances.

In 1826 the town had spread out and trebled in population. It was too unwielddy [*sic*] for the small, but efficient force which had done valiant duty so long and the subject became one of general discussion. The growth of the city was steady. For almost a year, prior to February 23, 1826, the question of a larger police force had been talked of, pro and con. Daily meetings were held. Plans were submitted. Innovations were offered. Nothing was done till the Board of Trustees took action February 23 of that year. The Board compiled a list, or roster of citizens. It was the groundwork of the police and from it, we are told, "All free white males—clergymen, paupers and invalids excepted—between the ages of eighteen and sixty years" were enrolled to serve as peace officers when summoned.

A Captain of Police and twenty-six Lieutenants were appointed by the Mayor and sanctioned by the Board of Aldermen. The city made provision for the care of its increased force by establishing through ordinance suitable guard room with necessary furniture, fuel and candles. The duties of the police were added to by commanding them to ring the church bells in the evening as a signal for the slaves to retire, the hours being ten o'clock from May to October 1 and 9 o'clock the other six months. This force and its duties sufficed for over a decade.

12 | Organization of Fire Companies, 1810

At the same time that the town's trustees concerned themselves with keeping the peace, they attempted to insure the physical safety of the community by enacting an ordinance "for forming the inhabitants of the town of St. Louis into fire companies and other purposes." As they had with the first police, the trustees, in this 1810 enactment, relied heavily on the cooperation and initiative of citizens. Equipment, for example, was purchased by private subscription until 1841, when the city purchased buckets, hoses, and engines out of public funds. Not until 1850 did St. Louis place an "inspector" on the public payroll to oversee the companies, and not until 1857 was a citywide system established on anything like a professional basis. An important factor in the resistance to professionalization and municipal sponsorship of fire fighting was the reluctance to disband the volunteer companies which were organized along ethnic, religious, and class lines. Despite enactment of the ordinance of 1810, an excerpt of which follows, the first companies were not formed on a regular basis until 1819, when St. Louisans belatedly reacted to several attempts to burn down the town. From Scharf, History of St. Louis, *vol. 1, pp. 788–89.*

All the free male inhabitants within the said town above the age of eighteen years . . . shall be enrolled to form [two fire companies] to be commanded by Pierre Didier, Esq., and . . . by Bernard Pratte, Esq.

Sec. 2. It shall be the duty of the said officers, immediately after the passage of this ordinance and once every six months, to enroll all the free male inhabitants as aforesaid and appoint their under officers, and to exercise their respective companies at least one hour in each and every month, at such time and place as shall by them be thought most fit within the limits of their companies.

Sec. 3. The said officers shall immediately, on notice that a fire has broke out in a dwelling-house or other building, assemble their respective companies and march them to the spot, and arrange them in such a manner as to render the most effectual service.

Sec. 4. Any person thus enrolled who shall neglect or refuse to meet at the time and place appointed for exercise as aforesaid, after being notified thereof, or who shall neglect or refuse to obey any legal orders from his commanding officers, shall be fined a sum not exceeding one dollar for every such neglect or refusal. And if an officer shall refuse or neglect to do his duty as aforesaid, he shall be fined in a sum not exceeding three dollars, to be recovered, with costs, before the chairman of the board of trustees or a justice of the peace of the said town.

Sec. 5. Each and every householder, occupier of a store or shop within the limits of the town of St. Louis shall within two months from the passage hereof furnish himself or herself with two leather or other buckets to be made use of in cases of fire, and in case of neglect or refusal to provide the same within the limited time as aforesaid, then in each and every case the captain is hereby empowered to supply such deficiency; and on complaint of such captain to the chairman of the board, or any justice of the peace of the said town, process shall issue against such delinquent or delinquents for the purchase-money of such bucket or buckets with costs.

Sec. 6. The captain of each company shall, once in each month, make a return of the delinquents in his limits who have neglected to furnish buckets as aforesaid to the chairman of the board, under the penalty of five dollars.

Sec. 7. It shall be the duty of each occupier of a house, store, or other building to cause the chimneys thereof to be swept at least once in each month; and if any chimney shall take fire, the occupier of such house, store, or other building shall forfeit and pay a sum not exceeding ten dollars, to be recovered with costs before the chairman of the said board or a justice of the peace of the said town, unless such person proves to the satisfaction of such chairman or justice that such chimney has been swept within one month.

13 | The St. Louis Hospital, an Early Charity Institution

French and Spanish army surgeons provided the limited "professional" health care available during the first decades of St. Louis' existence. After the American takeover, there arrived in the Mound City a small but steady influx of physicians from such diverse places as France, Germany, England, New England, and the South. While providing medical care, these men also engaged in commerce, real estate speculation, urban promotion, and politics. Their importance as civic leaders was exemplified when a physician, Dr. William Carr Lane, was elected the city's first mayor. Doctors such as Lane, however, usually served only those who could pay. The poor had to seek medical attention in hospitals, which were charitable institutions. St. Louis obtained its first hospital in 1828, when John Mullanphy, a wealthy Irish Catholic, financed its opening through the Sisters of Charity. Other religious groups followed this example, but it was not until 1845 that the city began to develop a public facility. Meanwhile, because hospitals connoted charity, the wealthier members of society preferred to receive medical treatment at home. Not until after 1900, when hospitals had become more professionalized, did people choose to enter them in order to obtain high-quality medical care. The following document, an excerpt from a satirical nativist tract aimed at Catholics and their institutions, captures the neglect and crude medical attention that awaited the indigent if they had to enter this important early St. Louis charity. Edward Stiff, "Nine Days in St. Louis Hospital" (St. Louis: published by the author, 1843), pp. 2–3. Pamphlet from St. Louis Imprint Collection, Rare Book Department, Washington University Library, St. Louis.

It was on Thursday, the 28th of March, when I entered the portals of the Saint Louis Hospital, a homeless, houseless wanderer, without a penny in my pocket, and suffering the most excruciating misery, both in body and in mind. The implements of my trade, as well as my clothes, had one by one gone to procure sustenance for an infant son, and medicine for myself. For a long time I had been unwell, and for near two months the use of my left arm had been entirely lost. The proceeds of the last remnant of property within my reach, had squared accounts at my boardinghouse, and I was then told, "that if my money was gone, I could remain no longer." In this dilemma, a choice of evils presented themselves, which, I trust, may never more be seen or felt by another human being; and it sufficient for my present purpose to say, I chose the one above alluded to, and to furnish the public with a brief detail of its results.

Before applying for admission, I had waited upon the attending physician, Dr. Prather, and put him in possession of the facts of my case. I told him, that during the fore part of the winter, in fitting up my shop and working at my trade, I had been much exposed, had entirely overdone myself, had been cured of the ague, had taken a violent and obstinate cold, which had settled in my left shoulder, and that in every other respect I was restored to perfect health. The Doctor gave me a critical exmination, said I was well, all but rheumatic pains, advised me to come to the Hospital, said he would cure me in a few days, & c., & c. Upon this assurance, I acted promptly, placed my son where I thought he was safe, obtained the certificate of an eminent medical practitioner, that I was a "fit subject,"—an order from the Register for admission, and for the first time in my life became the recipient of the name of charity, either public or private, or any other kind, and even then, but for the "stay law," an unprincipled villain, I could have used my hard earnings, and not have been driven to this pressing extremity.

Although my stomach and bowels were in perfect order, I was forthwith drugged with emetics and calomel, and from my entrance, forty-eight hours had scarcely elapsed, before my whole system was deranged, the functions of nature suspended, and their place usurped by copious doses of mineral poison! My strength was soon gone. The pain, always before confined to the shoulder-joint, spread rapidly over near half my body, and with greatly increased violence. Then came cupping and blistering, without a single opiate to allay the joint effect of internal and external pain, even while going through the inevitable operations of an emetic. For four days and nights, sleep, that "sweet restorer," had forsaken my pillow; I was in an agony of misery, which human nature is incapable of supporting a long time, when the "Sisters," in compassion, I suppose, administered a drug not prescribed, which gave partial relief for about half the night. At this time I viewed them as angels of mercy. In vain had I supplicated the Doctor; he had turned a deaf ear to my repeated requests, and he now left me, in that kind of silence which forced the conviction that he was a cruel and unfeeling despot, if not something infinitely worse. I knew I was sinking rapidly. The effects of the Sisters' kindness had passed away. From unmitigated misery, for want of nourishment, which my disordered stomach would not bear, and the unceasing tortures heaped upon me, death must soon come to my relief, or I must cease to be made the victim of experiments—must decline voluntary submission to the knights of the dissecting knife. Under such circumstances, I resolved on the latter, and the Doctor next found me writhing under the joint effects of my first malady, and the means prescribed, which had made it a thousand times worse! In this situation another emetic was prescribed, and a refusal, as usual, to afford even sufficient relief to enable me to go through the operation, was meted out to me by this tyrant, in whose keeping are confided the lives of so many unfortunate human beings. I told the Doctor that I knew I should die under a vomit, that from my back to my heart was a continuous sore, my strength entirely prostrated, and that every nerve and muscle in one half of my body was in a ceaseless tremor and pain. Upon this, he directed my discharge! !

I then addressed myself to the "Sisters." I told them I had come there without consulting my friends; that, although destitute my-self, and comparatively a stranger in the city, if my case was known, there were a few gentlemen who knew me well, and would loan me money, that I would immediately send for them, and also for a physician, and if they would let me remain until partially recovered, their money should be paid that day. This they positively refused to do, assigning as the only reason, "that it would displease Dr. Prather," and acknowledging that they "knew I was unable to go out." Tortured with bodily pain and mental agony, and goaded to desperation by such unheard-of cruelty, could I at that moment have seen the author of my accumulated misery, the last convulsions of my frame should have sent him, steeped in crime, to the bar of his God. Moralize upon this, ye prating guardians of the public weal! Reflect, ye champions of religion and philanthropy, about which we hear so much!

Learn a lesson from it, ye purse-proud and well-to-do lords of creation; and mark! the person now addressing you has been accustomed to as many of this world's blessings as you are now. Nothing but the excitement of the moment enabled me to emerge from the Hospital. I felt fully prepared to swoon and die in the street, rather than remain an instant longer under this inhospitable roof, and in about two hours I was enabled to reach the office of Dr. Howe, in Locust-street, (a few squares only,) and in perhaps two hours more, for the first time in near two months, I was entirely freed from pain, and have felt but little since.

14 | Religious Conditions in St. Louis, 1818

By 1818, St. Louis was in the midst of a minor growth boom that marked its transition into a more American, but still very diverse, community encompassed within an area of less than one square mile. It was to this newly Americanized St. Louis that John Mason Peck, a Baptist missionary whose observations on the frontier were to influence the thinking of historian Frederick Jackson Turner, came in 1817. In this document, Peck speaks first of the economic conditions in St. Louis upon his arrival, then moves into a longer discussion of the rough, free, and even libertarian nature of life in the frontier town. His interpretation of the character of St. Louis society forms the basis for justifying his missionary, or "civilizing," efforts. Rufus Babcock, ed., Forty Years of Pioneer Life: Memoir of John Mason Peck *(Philadelphia: American Baptist Publication Society, 1864), pp. 84–90.*

At the commencement of 1818, St. Louis was crowded with inhabitants, including families temporarily residing there for the winter. Every house and room that could shelter persons was occupied. There was no regular hotel, nor were there even boarding-houses, that afforded nightly accommodation. Alexandre Bellissame kept a French tavern at the corner of Second and Myrtle streets, where farmers from the country found food and shelter for themselves and horses. The storekeepers, most of whom were without families, in many instances, kept "bachelor's hall" in their counting-rooms, and cooked their own meals. "Shin-plaster" currency abounded. The bills were the droppings of the first generation of banks instituted in the far West without any adequate specie basis. Their leaves were scattered over the frontiers like the leaves of the trees by an autumnal frost, and the price of every article of necessity (for articles of luxury were not thought of) was high in proportion.

This bore heavily on us as missionaries, under sacred obligations to use an economy bordering on parsimony, in all our expenses. . . . The houses, shops, and stores were all small. Many only one story, and limited to two or three small rooms, were thought to be quite commodious. For the single room my family occupied for nine months, we paid twelve dollars per month. Mr. Welch engaged a room in the rear of a store, for school purposes, about fourteen by sixteen feet, for fourteen dollars per month. Eatables were not easily obtained, and only at extravagant prices. Butter was from thirty-seven to fifty cents per pound, sugar from thirty to forty cents, coffee from sixty-two to seventy-five. Flour of an inferior quality cost about twelve dollars per barrel. . . .

Oppressive as were the prices for every article of living in St. Louis at the commencement of 1818, and inconvenient as were our accommodations, the morals and religion of the place were the most likely to awaken our attention and call forth our sympathies.

It is here expedient to draw an accurate picture of St. Louis as it appeared to the writer, during a few months of his early acquaintance, in the beginning of 1818. There was a class of gentlemen of the bar, the medical profession, merchants, and officers in civil and military authority, Indian traders, etc., whose character and behavior, for men of the world, and destitute of any strong religious principles, were not gross, but respectable. They played cards for amusement, and of course bet liberally. They had social "sprees" occasionally, and indulged in habits of conviviality. Yet they exhibited some noble qualities, were generous and liberal, and governed by principles of honor. Some of these men . . . at subsequent periods, made a profession of true religion, joined a Christian church, and lived and died as Christian men should do. Some, with hoary heads and feeling the infirmities of age still live, and are honored, respected, and beloved by all who know them.

We would delight in giving the impressions, as among our most vivid reminiscences, made on our mind from the casual social intercourse, without any attempt at intimacy, with many whose names and peculiar traits of character come within memory's vision. But the field is too large, and propriety and delicacy forbid saying anything. Of the law profession there was the late Judge Carr (Wm. C.), Edward Bates—still among us in the vigor of his profession—David Barton, his brother Joshua, who was killed in a duel by one of the rectors in 1823. This victim was an intelligent man, of a sprightly mind, and possessed many amiable qualities, but fell a sacrifice to the barbarous and unchristian practice of dueling. There had been several duels within a year; and I gave out an appointment to preach on the subject at my next monthly visit to St. Louis. . . . In the interval of time, two more duels had taken place. One had proved mortal to one of the party, from a shot through the abdomen; while his antagonist, who escaped without a wound, took a severe attack of fever, caused, probably, by the preternatural excitement, and died within a week. My text was from Isaiah i. 15, last clause: *"Your hands are full of blood."* The old Baptist church-house, which stood on the corner of Third and Market streets, was the place; and it was crowded by all classes, amongst whom I discovered the Hon. David Barton, then a Senator in Congress, whose lamented brother was one of the victims, and the late Rev. Samuel Mitchell, whose eldest son was another. I had taken the precaution to write out every word of my discourse. I did my utmost to hold up the practice of dueling to the abhorrence of all right-minded men, as a crime of no small magnitude against God, against man, against society.

The discourse made a little "town-talk" in the village, and I received the thanks and approbation of many citizens. I made no personal reflections, but portrayed to the best of my ability the disastrous effects of dueling on the social relations, and the folly of obtaining satisfaction for injuries in such a mode.

There was another class in St. Louis at the period of these reminiscences that merit only that sort of notice which will place in wide and vivid contrast the advances in morals and social order by the American and French population. One-half, at least, of the Anglo-American population were infidels of a low and indecent grade, and utterly worthless for any useful purposes of society. Of the class I allude to, I cannot recollect an individual who was reclaimed, or became a respectable citizen. The reader will keep in mind that at that period there were no foreign emigrants from their native country among us.

This class despised and vilified religion in every form, were vulgarly profane, even to the worst forms of blasphemy, and poured out scoffings and contempt on the few Christians in the village. Their nightly orgies were scenes of drunkenness and profane revelry. Among the frantic rites observed were the mock celebration of the Lord's Supper, and burning the Bible. The last ceremony consisted in raking a place in the hot coals of a wood fire, and burying therein the book of God with shoutings, prayers, and songs.

The boast was often made that the Sabbath never had crossed, and never should cross the Mississippi. The portion of the Anglo-American population who had been trained to religious habits in early life, and manifested some respect for the forms of worship, were kept away from the place of worship by an influence of which perhaps they were not fully conscious. Though the profane ribaldry of the class already noticed did not convince their judgments of the fallacy of all religion, it affected their feelings and pride of character. But there was another class whose influence was far more effective, because it carried with it a degree of courtesy, respectability, and intelligence. I refer to the better-informed French population. These constituted at least one-third of the families. They were nominally Roman Catholics, and their wives, sisters, and daughters adhered to the Catholic faith, attended mass, and went to confession regularly. The men attended church on festival occasions. But every Frenchman, with whom I formed an acquaintance, of any intelligence and influence, was of the school of French liberalists—an infidel to all Bible Christianity. But they would treat Christian people, and even Protestant ministers of the gospel, with courtesy and respect. Romanism was the religion of their fathers, but the casual correspondence held with France, where infidelity was demolishing the thrones of political and religious despotism, and tearing up the foundations of superstition, led them to regard all religion as priestcraft, necessary perhaps for the ignorant, superstitious, and vicious, but wholly unnecessary for a gentleman—a philosopher.

The good-natured jokes and *badinage* of their French acquaintances, and the bitter taunts of the profane and drunken scoffers, made it unpopular and unfashionable to be seen on the way to church on Sunday, except on special occasions.

The Sabbath was a day of hilarity, as in all Catholic countries. Mass was attended in the morning by females and illiterate Frenchmen; and in the afternoon, both French and Americans assembled at each other's houses in parties for social amusement. Dances, billiards, cards, and other sports, made the pastime. Four billiard-rooms were open throughout the week, but on the Sabbath each was crowded with visitors and gamblers. With few exceptions, the stores and groceries were open on that day, and in some of them more trading was done then than on any other day in the week. The carts and wagons from the country came to market, and sold their provisions at retail through the village.

Another source of irreligion may be traced to officers in the United States Army, who, with few exceptions, were irreligious themselves, having vague notions of a future state, with some crude Universalian notions as the basis of their own prospects. . . .

In addition to the obstacles to the propagation of a pure Christianity found in the laxity of morals, want of reverence for the Sabbath, and disinclination to regular attendance on a preached gospel, there is another class which should be noticed. I refer to the colored people, both free and bond. The number of free blacks and mulattoes was small in comparison to the whole population. Of these, two persons, the late J. B. Meachum and his first wife, were Baptists, and truly religious. Of the rest, some were more moral than others; but all alike were without religious instruction. The Sabbath to them was a relief from toil. There was an open space, of a square or more, between Main and Second streets, and not far probably from Green street. Here the negroes were accustomed to assemble in the pleasant afternoons of the Sabbath, dance, drink, and fight, quite to the annoyance of all seriously-disposed persons.

The character of negroes in general is a tolerably correct index to that of the white population among whom they reside. They are characteristic for imitation, and are quick in catching the living manners, and quite successful in cultivating the low vices of their superiors. Such was the condition of the negroes, which prompted us as missionaries to make an effort to reclaim them through religious instruction.

15 | St. Louis Present and Future, 1829

By 1830, St. Louis had ended its transition from a frontier trading post to a regional entrepôt. Its population, which had declined in the 1820s, was on the rise again, and the city was soon to experience a great growth boom. New England Senator Caleb Atwater arrived in St. Louis on June 12, 1829. He was an American expansionist who saw the Mound City as a vibrant testimonial to the greatness of the country and to its bright future. As an urban outpost in the expanding nation, St. Louis was destined to become a great city. While Atwater was not a city resident, his account is representative of the growth mentality of many St. Louis leaders. The city's future, according to Atwater, was predetermined by its geography and resources. The Writings of Caleb Atwater *(Columbus: published by the author, 1833), pp. 212–15, 217–24.*

St. Louis is a town containing, now, I presume, about seven thousand inhabitants, about forty stores, a considerable number of lawyers, who are very respectable in their profession, several physicians, well bred and well educated; and several clergymen.

The government expends large sums of money in St. Louis, and no small portion of all that is expended for the support of the army, is laid out here. The navy department, too, purchases provisions in this place; and the Indian department has expended millions of dollars here. Six military posts come here for every thing almost they need; and the officers of the army are here in greater numbers, than they are at any other one point. It was no uncommon occurrence, for forty officers to sit down at the table to dinner, at Town's, where I lodged; and I saw them in other parts of the city daily, and in considerable numbers.

The trade to New Orleans is a heavy business, as to the amount of its value, and steam vessels of the largest class arrive and depart, not only every day, but several of them in each day.

They were always well freighted, both ways. Steamers ply regularly between this place and Franklin, on [the] Missouri river, and they often ascend the Upper Mississippi. From New Orleans, they bring European goods, molasses, sugar, cotton, alum, salt, coffee, and every article produced in the states of Tennessee, Mississippi and Louisiana, as well as the productions of the West Indies. From Pittsburgh, Cincinnati and Louisville, they bring whisky, beer, porter, ale, pork, flour, beef, iron in castings, bars, bolts, and nails—indeed, all the articles manufactured of either iron or steel—cabinet furniture, hats, tobacco, gun powder, salt-peter, hemp and cordage. These articles are bought to sell again to the upper-country people.

The trade in lead, manufactured, either in Missouri, or in the mineral region of the Upper Mississippi, has been a great business. The manufacture of lead, into the form of shot, has been carried on to a considerable extent, at Herculaneum, below this town. From my imperfect knowledge . . . I should estimate the commerce and trade of St. Louis, at this time, at ten millions of dollars annually. It cannot be less, I think, and may be more, much more.

The town occupies the western side of the river, from its very edge, a distance, from north to south, of about two miles, and it may be about half a mile in width from east to west. The streets are laid out parallel with the river, intersecting each other at right angles, like all our western towns. Main street, running parallel with the river, and nearest to it, is well paved with limestone. In this street are located nearly all the stores, and the buildings in it are, many of them, large and elegant. . . .

Limestone underlays the whole surface of this country at no great depth, of exactly the right thickness and texture for building stone.

This rock lies in strata, about four inches in thickness, and is easily quarried, and cut into fragments of the size of a common brick. . . .

The fuel used in town I should suppose was fossil coal, to a considerable extent, as I saw grates for using it, in nearly every house I entered. This coal . . . is found in the highest ridge of rocks bounding the American bottom . . . and exists in such quantities that it will supply the town with it forever, at twelve and a half cents a bushel. . . . This coal . . . will, at no future day, ever become scarce or dear. . . .

Land, in and about town, is cheap; so much so, that good land, on the Missouri side of the river, can be purchased now, within sight of the town, for three and four dollars an acre; and on the other side, in Illinois, for one dollar and twenty-five cents an acre.

Farmers and horticulturists may here locate themselves as soon as they please, and make fortunes. . . .

All the boards and scantling used in building here . . . came from Pittsburgh, and were brought down the Alleghany river from the pine groves at the heads of that river and its branches. Though these boards were dearer, of course, than the same articles were at Cincinnati and Louisville, they were much cheaper than I should have supposed, considering the great distance they had been transported from their native forests, and the mills where they had been manufactured. . . . Every other species of timber, except the pine, used by the house builder, the joiner and cabinet maker, may be found near St. Louis, on the east side of the river, and floated to it in rafts. . . .

I regret deeply my total want of information, as to the number of schools and churches in St. Louis, though I do know, that the children and youth of both sexes, belonging to the best families, are well bred and well educated, and those I saw in the streets, behaved, at all times and in all places, where my eye saw them, with the greatest propriety. I should hardly suppose though, that schools existed in this city, in which the young ladies of this town had obtained all the education they most certainly had received. I have seen no where, young ladies better educated, and the young gentlemen were very little behind them, in this respect.

The Presbyterian church was well attended on Sunday, and so was a Sunday school also. The state of society is doubtless improving here, as it is every where, west of the mountains.

The westwardly wind, that generally prevails here, does not pass over one drop of stagnant water near the town. The bright sparkling eye, the ruddy cheek, firm, quick and elastic step, indicate good health among the people of the place.

The market is good, and not very dear, though I saw chickens brought to it from the state of Illinois, a distance of one hundred miles. To me it appeared strange and unaccountable, that the whole plain west of the town, wide spread, and not wanting in fertility, nor dear in price, should be suffered to grow up with bushes, instead of being cultivated by the farmer and the gardener.

Why gentlemen of fortune should all prefer, in summer, the sight of a heated pavement, to the green grass, the orchard loaded with delicious fruit, the corn field and garden; and why they should all prefer at the same season, the sound of the guns of the steamers arriving or departing, to the lowing of herds, and flocks of their own raising, I cannot divine. It is one of those freaks of taste, for which there is no accounting, and I almost regret the absence of a law which would punish this, and some other of its strange vagaries.*

The Philadelphians would manage these matters much better, if they lived here, I am sure, and so would the Bostonians. Let us hope that a people so worthy, deserving every pleasure this earth has to bestow on human beings, will soon build villas and country seats near the town, where they can assemble and enjoy, not only all the pleasure they now do, under their delightful groves, but even an additional one, the company of their beautiful and accomplished wives, daughters, sisters, and sweethearts. . . .

Trade and Commerce

Considering the size of the place, these [trade and commerce] must amount to a large sum indeed. The American Fur Company have here a large establishment, and the furs, skins and peltry cannot amount to less than one million of dollars annually, which are brought down the Mississippi and Missouri rivers. . . . The company trade over a vast region, occupying all the country north and west of this place, quite to the Rocky mountains, and to as low a latitude as the Arkansaw river. . . .

This town has the trade of nearly all the State of Illinois, along and near the Mississippi; it supplies the retail merchants of the State of Missouri, with goods of all sorts, and nearly all the produce of the upper country passes through the hands of the merchants of St. Louis.

This trade is increasing and must increase for ages yet to come, as the country fills up with people, over a surface larger than that of all France—a country, for fertility of soil, and healthy and invigorating climate, equal any other country in the world. At some

---

* The reason for the vacancies was that landowners just west of the built-up area were holding their land off the market waiting for prices to rise.

day, not very distant, either, four or five millions of people, will transact nearly all their mercantile business at St. Louis. When the country is fully settled, and properly improved, on all the Mississippi and Missouri waters, thirty millions of people will trade here.

From thirty-seven to forty-eight degrees north; from the Wabash river or near to it, to the Rocky mountains in the west, in all future time, the people of that whole region, will go to St. Louis to trade; because located as it is, no town can ever grow up, nearer to it than Louisville, and that will add to the business of St. Louis, but never will, and never can injure it, in the smallest degree. The same may be said of Cincinnati, the trade of each, adds to each, and not the reverse.

. . . The framers of our constitution intended the whole country to be filled up with civilized people, and then see what this vast country would be. This process is going on as rapidly as the heart of the patriot can wish, and that process will make St. Louis, situated as it is, the future capital of a great nation.

16 | The Seal of St. Louis

Official government seals are invested with symbols and images that reflect economic, political, and social values. When St. Louis was incorporated as a city after Missouri was granted statehood, the seal it chose was eminently simple. The City Council, as its first official act, outlined its design.

Ordinance #1

An ordinance prescribing the emblem and devices of the Common Seal of the City of St. Louis.

Be it ordained by the Mayor and Board of Aldermen of the City of St. Louis:

Sec. 1. That the device for the Common Seal of the City of St. Louis shall be a steamboat carrying the United States flag. And the seal of the said city shall be so engraved as to represent by its impression the aforesaid surrounded by a scroll inscribed with the words: "The Common Seal of the City of St. Louis" in Roman capitals, which seal shall be circular and not more than one and a half inches in diameter.

Sec. 2. Be it further ordained, That the Register procure the said seal at the expense of the city.
Approved April 22, 1823.

That the United States flag was included in the seal was not unusual. The fact that the steamboat occupied such a place of prominence is unusually significant given the city's historical development. The first steamboat, the Pike, *had not arrived in St. Louis until 1819, and steamboat traffic escalated only slowly. Between October 1, 1823, and July 1, 1824, only 50 steam-driven vessels docked at St. Louis wharves. By 1828, the annual number had risen to 250, by 1832, to 596. The use of the steamboat as the preeminent symbol in the City Seal then suggests great expectations for the future rather than a long experience in the past. The symbol also had long-term significance in shaping local economic thinking. Leaders of the city, a child of the Mississippi, continued to believe in the steamboat even when more technologically advanced forms of transport were utilized by other cities to gain trade territory.*

PART TWO

From Town to City, 1830-1910

1 | Situation and Prospect for the Midwestern River Economy, 1847

Throughout the 1850s, St. Louis competed with Cincinnati for preeminence in the inland waterway trade. Demonstrating the instability of building the economy of a city on such a base, the number of arrivals and departures in the decade fluctuated with the floods and low water of the Mississippi. During the peak of the boating season, numerous packet lines offered almost daily passenger and freight service to New Orleans, Louisville, Cincinnati, and Pittsburgh; regular and frequent connections with Peoria on the Illinois, Keokuck on the Upper Mississippi, St. Joseph and Kansas City on the Missouri, and Nashville on the Cumberland; plus numerous ferries each day to Alton and what became East St. Louis on the Illinois shore. Mound City leaders wanted to keep these connections intact and to extend them as well. To do so required a stable navigable channel, an objective not easy to achieve on midwestern rivers, with their episodic, dramatic fluctuations and their uncontrollable shifts in course through the loose alluvial soil of the region. The federal government took a narrow view of its responsibility for protecting inland navigation in the mid-nineteenth century. For the first time, in 1837, St. Louisans got Congress to appropriate a small amount to help stabilize their harbor. After that, the fight for federal funds was constant. This document, a memorial presented to the Rivers and Harbors Convention held at Chicago in 1847, outlines the importance of the river for St. Louisans and, characteristically, uses the opportunity to make a typical booster statement about the city's future. Thomas Allen, The Commerce and Navigation of the Valley of the Mississippi; and Also That Appertaining to the City of St. Louis *(St. Louis, 1847), pp. 3–9.*

The people of the City of St. Louis, hail with satisfaction, the assemblage of a general convention, with reference to the great interests of interior commerce and navigation. From such commerce and navigation St. Louis derives its origin, its increase, and its future hopes of greatness. In such it has lived, flourished and suffered, until experience has given it full knowledge of their nature, and a clear apprehension of their capacities, their deficiencies, and their relations. . . .

This vast area, this fat and fertile valley, comprehended between the sources of the Mississippi on the north, and the Gulf of Mexico on the south, the Rocky Mountains on the west, and the Alleghanies on the east, though but recently a wilderness, already embraces eleven entire states, and parts of two others, and two territories, and is busy with the industry, and burdened with the immediate support and all the earthly interests of half the population of the United States of North America. Comprising within its limits 1,200,000 square miles, . . . its importance can no more be calculated than that of the Union itself. Its influence must be co-extensive with the habitable globe, of which it will be the Garden and the Granary; going beyond the United States, of which it must become the seat of Empire, the source of vitality, the diadem of pride, the base of their pyramid of grandeur. The Creator of the universe has no where on the face of the earth, spread more lavishly the means of human prosperity, or stamped more legibly the lineaments of beautiful and convenient adaptation to the wants and necessities of mankind. Visit it not with the evils of bad government; obstruct not the hand of improvement within it; stay not the tide of population pouring in upon its bosom; and let its broad acres receive that proportion of population which vexes the soil of the kingdom of Great Britain, and the Bountiful Giver of this great and good gift, will smile from Heaven upon a happy family of more than 275 millions of human beings. Indeed, looking forward for 60 years, for an increase of population keeping pace with the ratio of the past 60 years, (that is, doubling every 10 years,) the world would behold in the year 1907, (60 years hence) swarming in this valley, more than 640 millions of inhabitants. This astonishing result, has for its demonstration, the past statistical history of the country, though it would seem scarcely possible that the past ratio of increase can be maintained. At the first census (1790) the population of the valley of the Mississippi, did not exceed 200,000. In 1800, it had increased to about 560,000; . . . and in 1847, . . . it exceeds 10,520,000. In the year 1850, . . . it will exceed 12 millions, and be about equal to the population of all the Atlantic states. . . .

At the period of the introduction of steam upon the Mississippi, 1817, the whole commerce from New Orleans to the upper country, was transported in about twenty barges of an average of 100 tons each, and making but one trip in a year. The number of keel boats on the Ohio was estimated at 160, carrying thirty tons each. The total tonnage was estimated at between 6,000 and 7,000.

In 1834, the number of steamboats on the Mississippi and its tributaries was 230, and their tonnage equal to about 39,000. . . . The tonnage had increased by the last of June, 1845, to 159,713, making the number of boats 789.

A report from the same authority, for 1846, exhibits the steamboat tonnage enrolled and licensed at the several districts in the Mississippi Basin to be a total [of] 249,054.77 tons. [St. Louis has 22,425.92 enrolled tons.]

. . . To such an extent has the commerce of this Valley grown, while yet in its infancy. Who can comprehend its magnitude when the banks of our streams shall be populated to the density of the Old World, and the resources of the country shall be fully developed?

2 | The First Locomotive West of the Mississippi, 1852

The first public discussion by city leaders over the need for rail-

roads into St. Louis occurred in 1830, when a small model line was set up and operated. Through the next twenty years, St. Louis, like other midwestern and southern cities, hosted a series of conventions trying to obtain financial support for railroad connections from the East.⌈The State of Missouri by 1850 had chartered more than two dozen different companies which proposed to build railroad lines within Missouri, most of them connected to St. Louis in one way or another. The State of Missouri, St. Louis County, and St. Louis City all went in debt to purchase railroad bonds in support of these efforts. A number of St. Louis capitalists invested in these ventures, as well as in lines that were coming westward toward the city. Viewed in this context, the running of the first locomotive in 1852 was of more than passing importance.⌋As the Republican *reported in this article on the first running, the event was viewed as a dramatic and epic symbol commemorating hard work and heavy expense plus great expectations for the future.* Missouri Republican *(St. Louis, December 3, 1852).*

The Iron Horse has been harnessed on the west side of the Mississippi, and yesterday morning, at 7 o'clock, his first loud and shrill whistle was heard. It was a cheering sound to those who, for years, have desired to see a commencement in Internal Improvements in Missouri. Long and eagerly have they looked for this period, and at last it has come. Probably we entertain a more lively feeling in regard to the event than others; but to every well-wisher of our country—to every one who desires to see the wealth of our State developed, and our city rise to the importance and eminence which it is destined to occupy—this occasion will be one of rejoicing and gratification. It is true, that it is only a commencement, but it is the "beginning of an end" which we cannot foresee or foretell.

The Pacific Railroad has been commenced, and has so far progressed, that the locomotive, with burden and freight trains, are running upon it. True, only a few miles are yet in use, but who can predict how long or short the period when the locomotive will start from the Mississippi and terminate its flight on the shores of the Pacific? Yesterday morning, a beautiful, and we trust a favorable omen, was presented at the starting of the train. The locomotive, with the tender, had been backed down nearly to

Fourteenth street, and after three heavily-laden cars of iron and ties had been attached—just as the shrill whistle announced an onward movement—the sun, previously invisible from the mist that hung over the horizon, suddenly burst forth, showing his full round disc through a smoky atmosphere. At the moment, a facetious friend remarked, "Old Sol is disposed to give us a race for the Pacific—we can't beat him to-day, for our track is not in order; but we will give him a right show for it in a short time."

The opening of a short distance of this road, so far as any immediate result is involved, is unimportant, but it affords gratification from the fact, that it is the first railroad, with a locomotive running on it, west of the Mississippi. It is the opening of a new era, not only in our city and State, but to the vast territory which lies west of the Father of Waters. Imagination is lost and bewildered in every attempt to look into the future of which this is but the pioneer movement. We could indulge in many pleasing speculations on the Consummation, but it is not necessary. There are those now in active life, and who were startled from their slumbers yesterday morning, by the clear, shrill whistle of the locomotive, who will live to see all the hopes and expectations of the most sanguine among us realized—in a Railway communication between St. Louis and the Pacific ocean.

3 | The Shift from Water Transport to Rails

Throughout the mid and late nineteenth century, the United States was preoccupied with growth, first that associated with commerce, and later with industrialization. Rows of raw statistics—demonstrating population increase, the rise in retail sales, expansion of manufacturing capacity, or changes in transportation—provided a shorthand method for expressing the dimensions of this progress. What today would be printed in small type, buried deep within the financial section of a major metropolitan daily, was feature news in the nineteenth century. The first American urban historians understood the importance of these rows of statistics, and in their encyclopedic histories, they reprinted previously published sets of figures and compiled their own data to provide their readers with a quantitative picture of the changes occurring in the city. J. Thomas Scharf, who published the first multivolume history of

St. Louis in 1883, furnished his readers with a variety of quantitative sets. The two tables that follow are from his history. Table 4 displays the number of boat arrivals at St. Louis and their combined tonnage between 1865 and 1882. This table shows that, although there were some fluctuations from year to year, the river trade was essentially stable. Given the enormous growth occurring in the Mississippi Valley during this period, the steamboat arrivals and the tonnage figures should have been increasing rapidly. Table 5 demonstrates where the increase was occurring. It contains the statistics for cotton arrivals by water and by rail between 1865 and 1880. Cotton, which was a heavy commodity

TABLE 4
Arrivals and Departures for Eighteen Years

	ARRIVALS				DEPARTURES		
Years	Boats	Barges	Tons of Freight Received	Registered Tonnage	Years	Boats	Tons of Freight Shipped
1882	2537	1310	802,080		1882	2487	769,905
1881	2426	1525	852,410		1881	2340	884,025
1880	2871	1821	893,860		1880	2866	1,038,350
1879	2360	1471	688,970		1879	2392	676,445
1878	2322	1291	714,700		1878	2348	614,675
1877	2150	660	644,485		1877	2156	597,676
1876	2122	683	688,755		1876	2118	600,225
1875	2201	743	663,525		1875	2223	639,095
1874	2332	951	732,765		1874	2364	707,325
1873	2316	1020	810,055		1873	2303	783,256
1872	2346	1485	863,919		1872	2322	805,282
1871	2574	1165	883,401		1871	2604	770,498
1870	2796	1195		1,166,889	1870	2782	
1869	2789	1240		1,225,443	1869	2786	
1868	2338	1133		1,055,795	1868	2579	
1867	2478	947		1,086,340	1867	2588	
1866	2972	1142		1,227,078	1866	3096	
1865	2767	1141		1,229,826	1965	2953	

TABLE 5
Receipts of Cotton at St. Louis, by River and by Rail,
During the Past Fourteen Years

Cotton Year Ending August 31st.	By River	By Rail	Total
	Bales	*Bales*	*Bales*
1866	53,506	1,921	55,427
1867	18,712	1,066	19,779
1868	38,804	220	39,024
1869	16,614	82	16,696
1870	17,034	1,484	18,518
1871	15,582	4,688	20,270
1872	30,018	6,403	36,421
1873	26,577	33,132	59,709
1874	27,538	76,203	103,741
1875	11,750	122,219	133,969
1876	19,620	224,978	244,598
1877	6,650	211,084	217,734
1878	9,998	238,858	248,856
1879	15,012	320,787	335,799
1880	32,279	464,291	496,570

shippable either by water or rail, was increasingly entering St. Louis by the latter mode. (The fluctuations of the late 1860s reflect the problems of southern cotton growers in the years immediately after the Civil War.) In microcosm, the two tables illustrate the story of railroad and inland water carrier competition. The railroads, with their ability to overcome geography, came to dominate freight carrying. In the process, the business of all inland waterway ports declined relative to the total. St. Louis, which was heavily dependent on the Mississippi trade for revenues, faced a severe adjustment when other midwestern cities extended railroads into what St. Louisans perceived as their city's natural hinterland. Scharf, History of St. Louis, *vol. 2, pp. 1133, 1218.*

4 | The St. Louis–Illinois (Eads) Bridge:
Symbol for an Industrializing City and Transportation Center, 1874

Seven years were required to build the Eads Bridge. When it was completed in 1874, St. Louis gained a distinctive and auspicious civic symbol, a visual proclamation of the city's growing industrial status and its long-term position as a transportation crossroads. Tourists traveling merely to see the sights or engineers who came especially to examine the structure were rightfully impressed, for there was much to admire. The four-pier, triple-span bridge had been pronounced an engineering impossibility by some when its plans were revealed. The piers alone were a triumph in design. Under the direction of James Buchanan Eads, the project's chief engineer, the associated engineers and contractors worked out a system of air locks which allowed the bridge's expanding caissons to be eased down through the soft mud on the river bottom. The tallest pier extended 197 feet from its skyward tip to the bedrock below. Above the water, the 520-foot center span, with a 50-foot clearance above normal river flow, arched gracefully over the main body of the stream and was the largest span in the world. Even the cost of the structure was impressive. More than $6,500,000 was spent on the project over seven years. Comparatively, the city of St. Louis in 1870 collected total revenues of only a little more than $1,000,000. It is fitting that this document is by L. U. Reavis. He was for more than two decades the city's chief booster. With what was for him a minimum of hyperbole, Reavis summed up the significance of the bridge. L. U. Reavis, A History of the Illinois and St. Louis Bridge (St. Louis: Tribune Publishing Company, 1874), pp. 1–2, 16–17.

Each age and nation produce their own great works of art, some as trophies of ambition, others to subserve useful purposes, according as the people have advanced in art and civilization. The early Jews erected the tower of Babel, a monument of folly and mental weakness. The ancient Egyptians erected the pyramids, a monstrous exhibition of tyranny and ambition. The Greeks built the Parthenon and temple of Diana, evidences of intellectual and moral growth. The Romans built the Colosseum and the great acquiducts [sic], evidences of personal regard and pleasure.

Modern civilization, affording a wider range of thought to the human faculties, demands a more useful order of mechanical structures to subserve the wants and purposes of the more advanced peoples of the world.

Stepping into the new era of use and greatness, we find the greatest work of mechanical art that the world has yet beheld is the Crystal Palace of the nineteenth century. It combines in one grand masterpiece of art, and one glow of associated beauty, the highest civilization and progress of man.

The leading feature of the present age is the strife for commercial dominion. In this department of civilization is enlisted more capital, talent and men than in any other. All the rapid strides of the race are made in its interest—whether in the achievement of art, of science, or of genius. The wild billows of the Atlantic have been defied by steam and electricity, and the two great continents of kindred shores united by these subtle agents; and now with one steady, grand march, does civilization, carried by the tides of men, continue its journey to the West—to the high mountains, and the broad and calmer waters of the wide Pacific Ocean. With these great movements, come the masterworks of mechanic arts.

Since the invention of the steam engine, the railway may be regarded as the greatest aid to civilization the arts have produced, on account of the rapid intercommunion of men and ideas and the exchange of products. But a great railway without bridges to cross the streams lying along its track, would be comparatively impracticable. And yet, notwithstanding the usefulness of bridges, the greater the structure demanded, the greater the difficulties to be overcome for its accomplishment. . . .

That the trade of the central portion of the Mississippi Valley, which centers in St. Louis, and advances every year with such gigantic strides, was not sufficiently provided for by the present arrangements for transportation across the broad stream which separates Missouri and Illinois, or, to speak more correctly, the true East and West of the United States, has been known and seen by every one for many years. Nor could it be, without a great bridge at St. Louis, the central city of the continent. . . .

Although not so great in length as the Victoria bridge over the St. Lawrence, which is nearly two miles long, nor the bridge over the Nebudda [Narbada], in India, which is one and a half miles long, nor the bridge from Bassein to the main land, which is over three miles long, yet its magnificent spans and stately piers place it far above these bridges in character and structure. And now that it is built, it is grander than the Colossus at Rhodes, grander than the Pharaohs at Alexandria. It will vitalize the commerce of the Mississippi Valley, and unite the great railway chains between New York and San Francisco, the Lakes and the Gulf. It will place the name of its builder, Capt. James B. Eads, with those of Telford, Smeaton, Stephenson, and other distinguished engineers of the world. . . . To him, and to the enlightened, public-spirited citizens who pledged their capital and influence to sustain the enterprise, will justly belong the glory that surely attaches to the Illinois and St. Louis Bridge.

5 | "The Central Continental Metropolis," 1897

By the mid 1890s, St. Louis had made the transition from a commercial city dependent on the river to a mature and diversified industrial metropolis. During the period encompassed by that transition, American magazines matured as well. Respectable monthlies and journals of current opinion became a regular feature of intellectual life. The American Magazine, *from which this document is excerpted, became a muckraking journal after 1900, but as this article indicates, in the late 1890s it still was devoted to high-quality feature articles. In describing the transformation from commercial city to industrial metropolis, the writer also lays out accurately how in the course of that massive change, St. Louis' economic and social geography was altered. What in the 1820s was a compact and relatively integrated community by 1897 had become a city which had large, discrete industrial and residential sections as well as satellite cities in its metropolitan region. Charles T. Logan, "The Central-Continental Metropolis; St. Louis, the Fourth American City After Greater New York's Consolidation,"* American Magazine, XLIII (March 1897), pp. 337–48.

The consolidation of New York and Brooklyn has caused St. Louis to change positions with the latter in the relative standing of American cities, and instead of remaining fifth, she jumps to fourth place, while Chicago and Philadelphia remain second and third respectively. The importance of this sudden rise has had its effect on the people, and the fight is now on for holding to what is in hand. There appears to be no danger of any other city over-taking St. Louis, though it would be no surprise to see this central-continental metropolis in a brush with the Quaker City for honors before another decade rolls away. Predictions made a quarter of a century ago of what St. Louis ought to be were slow in fulfilling, because the people thought they would fulfill themselves. Twenty years ago they saw their mistake, and since then they have en-deavoured to make prophecy for themselves. How well they are succeeding is told in the story of St. Louis as herewith presented.

A careful study of St. Louis from every possible standpoint must convince the most skeptical that the city is prosperous to an unusual degree, wide awake at all times, and abreast with the spirit of progress in its deepest meaning. . . . Scarcely a week goes by that the local papers do not herald the opening of a new industrial enterprise of some sort, and the city has so rapidly run ahead of Eastern manufacturing centres that she now leads Boston by $50,000,000 a year, and Newark, N.J., by over $100,000,000. It will also fall like an explosion of dynamite to be told that the St. Louis shoe market is now larger than that of Boston—not in goods manufactured, but in sales made of Eastern and home manufacture combined. Three hundred million dollars represents the present output of the city's total manufactured product yearly, of which $12,000,000 is in shoes. The difference in freight rates from the East placed a prohibitive tariff upon Western products, so St. Louis went into the manufacturing business from necessity. The trademark, "Made in St. Louis," is now almost as famous in America as "Made in Germany" was at the [Chicago] World's Fair. No city in America is without St. Louis-made goods of some form, while the English markets eagerly buy shoes and many other articles from this central-western city. Of late years, also, St. Louis has opened up a big volume of business with Mexico, the Central American states, and with many of the South Ameri-can republics.

Prior to 1870 . . . the business district was located between Wharf (the levee front) and Fourth Streets, a distance of five short blocks, and extending about one mile north and south along the river. The introduction of railroads after 1870 produced a most rapid change in this business district, and within three years it had widened out to Broadway (Fifth Street), Sixth and Eighth Streets, and on Washington Avenue to Ninth Street. This caused a rapid rise in realty values west of Fourth Street, and a corresponding decrease east toward the river. The westward movement caused heavy losses in the old district; but when the causes were fully known, and the fact that it would not occur again, confidence was restored, while from that date, or say within the last twenty-five years, St. Louis has done her real work of development. That it has been phenomenal, considering the fact that no "boom" period of any kind ever prevailed, goes with the mere statement of the fact. Throughout all its many financial storms, St. Louis has never shown aught but a feeling of conservative methods, with the result that while Chicago, the modern wonder, went ahead under booms, borrowed capital and other like influences, St. Louis plodded along, not slowly, but with more certain purposes and entirely on her own resources.

The steady increase in population, and the magnificent suburbs which year by year are being opened for settlement and made accessible by the enterprise and capital of the street railway companies, have inspired the confidence of investors. It is a common expression that no one can lose on a real estate investment in St. Louis at present prices, no matter where the property is located. The great panic of 1893, and the terrible depression of 1896 did not cause a dollar's reduction in St. Louis values. This steadiness and upward tendency make the city a most inviting field for investment or speculation. The president of the Real Estate Exchange is authority for the statement that money in large or small sums can be more easily borrowed on property in St. Louis than in any other city in the country.

The prime factor of the municipal growth of St. Louis, however, is better represented in the population increase. [In] 1880, 350,518; . . . [in] 1897, 650,000.

If to these figures be added the legitimate population of East St. Louis and various other smaller municipal suburbs, the present population of St. Louis is not far from 900,000 souls within a radius of twenty miles. It will be no task for the population in this territory to pass the million mark by 1900, and by 1907 or 1908 St. Louis proper ought to go beyond a million. . . .

Notwithstanding the remarkable financial crash which began
to sweep over the world in 1890, covering the American continent in 1893, St. Louis has never shown the mark of the depression to an appreciable extent. There was never a "run" on a
St. Louis bank in all these long four years of unsettled conditions.
It is almost inconceivable that no serious results of the panic
were brought about, and it can be attributable to the fact that
St. Louisans own a clear title to themselves; they are not bonded
and mortgaged to the East. . . .

One of the most striking points of value noticeable in St. Louis
is the study of economics practiced in nearly all branches of commercial life. Competition with the East, and a desire to prevent
encroachments upon the legitimate trade boundaries of the city,
led the thoughtful business men to delve deeply into the problems
of self-protection, so that today the great metropolis is ensconced
within her own fortress, and most happily the position is well-
nigh impregnable. New York or Chicago can no more trench upon
the legitimate preserves of St. Louis than can Kalamazoo. The
introduction of scores and scores of manufacturers which were
formerly located in the East, has made the city a power in the
land. The $300,000,000 of St. Louis manufactures is as large a
volume of business now as was the total annual commerce fifteen
years ago. This latter item now runs up to the enormous sum of
$1,250,000,000. With cheap fuel (coal being $1.00 to $1.25 per
ton), and splendid facilities for transportation both by rail and
water, the lines reaching to every point of the compass, there
was everything in favor of St. Louis goods. A sense of justice on
the urgent appeals of the various commercial bodies caused the
railroads to do away with all discrimination against the city, so
that the interests of St. Louis were placed on an equal footing with
Chicago and the East in every sense. These things, with an unusual amount of business acumen, have brought the city forward
until it is no longer a question of possible greatness, but greatness
achieved. Perhaps no more remarkable compilation of the real
suggestiveness of St. Louis' achievements within twenty years was
ever made of any city than the following, from the Business Men's
League:

"As compared with the world, St. Louis has the largest railroad
station, hardware house, drug house, woodenware house, tobacco

factories, lead works, brickyards, and stove and range factories. As compared with the United States, St. Louis has the largest brewery, shoe factory, saddlery market, street-car factories, hardwood lumber market, shoe output, and finest street-cars and botanical gardens.

"St. Louis is the largest shoe distributing point in America, and the third largest dry-goods, clothing and grocery market. It has 346 miles of electric street railroad. It was the first city to run electric street railroad. It was the first city to run electric mail cars, to sprinkle its streets by municipal contract, and to light its streets and alleys uniformly by electricity. It is the only city in the world which has held 14 consecutive, annual, self-supporting expositions."

6 | Gottfried Duden's "Report"

A massive emigration of Germans to the United States began in the second quarter of the nineteenth century. As with the earlier English movement, potential immigrants were stimulated by a promotional literature that proposed colonization to solve domestic problems in the mother country and provide new opportunities for the settlers. Among the more influential German propagandists were Gustav Körner, who described Illinois, Friedrich Koch, who wrote about Michigan, and Gottfried Duden, who promoted Missouri. Duden visited Missouri between 1823 and 1827, so his writings had the authority of personal observation, although his enthusiasms occasionally distorted realities. Like Thomas Malthus, Duden was concerned that overpopulation would cause mass impoverishment and threaten the social order in Germany. His solution was to settle the vast, fertile lands along the Mississippi and Missouri, which he likened to his native Rhineland. He hoped that in the new Vaterland, *an essentially Germanic state could be established within the political framework of the United States. Duden obviously was a man with the right message at the right place, and thousands of Germans came to settle in Missouri, with St. Louis being their principal stopping point while shopping for a farm or deciding to move on. Thousands more, many of whom were artisans in the leather trades and brewing, came to settle in St. Louis itself. The city that the French had established under rights of colonization and the Spanish had obtained by treaty, the*

Germans came to dominate by numbers. "Gottfried Duden's Report, 1824–1827," trans. by William G. Bek, Missouri Historical Review, XIII (January 1919), pp. 174–80.

A moderate amount of property, good guidance, medical aid for the first two years of residence, and the presence of friends from the Fatherland—these are the true conditions of successful immigration. . . .

If a little city could be founded, for the purpose of making it the center of culture for the Germans in America, then there would soon arise a rejuvenated Germania, and the European Germans would then find in America a second Fatherland, just as the British have it. Would that in Germany a lively interest might develop for this project. No plan of the present time promises so much to the individual and to everyone as a plan of founding such a nursery for German culture in western North America, and especially in the lands west of the Mississippi. It would make the new world at once a home to the German, and would add to the gifts of nature those things which must always emanate from man himself. There is no cause for fear that any kind of political hindrance or envy on the part of the Americans would oppose such an enterprise. German immigrants are always welcome here, and as soon as they have entered upon the new continent they are regarded equal to the citizens,—barring, of course, the political rights, which are dependent upon a residence of five years, and at first are more of a hindrance than a help to him. . . . Even a foreigner may acquire land in the state of Missouri.

How many men there are in Germany who have a capital of from four to six thousand Thaler (a Thaler is about seventy-five cents) without having any prospect of using it except to consume it by and by! Such a sum, however, is more than abundant for the happy life of a whole family on the banks of the Missouri, even tho eight hundred to a thousand Thaler should be deducted as traveling expenses—provided that proper guidance is not wanting. With the above sum an immigrant could purchase two adult slaves, a man and a woman, which would cost him twelve hundred Thaler, and could establish himself in such a manner that he could live happier, and especially more carefree in view of the future lot of his numerous posterity, than he could in Germany with six times that amount. . . .

... Hitherto I have spoken, almost exclusively, of the prospects of agriculture, which are so splendid that during the whole of the present century they cannot become worse, even after the immigration of millions. It is of course manifest that in a country which rests upon such a physical basis as this one does, the other trades must also prosper, provided only that legislation remains passive and avoids foolish interference. There are but few trades which do not prosper here. The prospects are most favorable for tanners, skilled mechanics, joiners, masons, carpenters, saddlers and blacksmiths. To the tanners I wish to say that hides and dyeing materials are extremely cheap, while, on the other hand, leather is expensive. The saddlers I wish to note, that in this country no one goes on foot. There is a great lack of glass factories. A common flask costs twelve and a half cents in St. Louis. Earthenware, too, is very dear. There is no lack of good clay, and since private ownership does not hinder in its utilization and in the selection of sites where it may be obtained, finer varieties of clay, suitable for finer and more delicate vessels, will doubtless soon be discovered, and indeed, perhaps, in the proximity of navigable rivers and near dense forest. Beer brewers would quickly become rich on the Missouri, tho they would have to see to the raising of hops and barley themselves, since little attention has been paid to the cultivation of these two crops. St. Louis derives its beer from Pittsburg, and even from the Atlantic coast. The manufacturers of chemicals and of medicines would find in all the western states enticing opportunities for their business. I need hardly add that master builders are always welcome in this land of ceaseless town building.

7 | Lutheran Parochial Schools

Germans were slow to shed their loyalties either to their culture or to each other. The sense of ethnic community was heightened by the manner of the crossing. The first German Lutherans, like early Puritans, made a compact while on board ship to establish a community which would center around church and school. The result was a proliferation of parishes and parochial schools which not only was characteristic of nineteenth-century St. Louis but has continued to the present. As this document points out, even those who lacked religious inclination or were hostile to the churches still sent their children to German-language parochial schools in order to maintain ties to their heritage. Churches and schools were only one form of ethnic identity. The Germans created hundreds of associations centering on music, sports, culture, crafts, and town or region of birth. The result was a vital and independent German society that distinguished and characterized St. Louis from the 1830s until well into the twentieth century. Thomas Graebner, The Lutheran Church Guide of St. Louis, Missouri *(St. Louis: Concordia Seminary, 1916), pp. 166–67.*

The Lutheran parochial schools of this city were founded in the year 1838 in mid-Atlantic. The Saxon emigrants who were the founders of the St. Louis Lutheranism left Bremen, Germany, in November of that year on several vessels. The trans-Atlantic journey lasted 64 days, and during this time a parochial school was organized on board ship. Whenever the state of the weather permitted, regular school hours were held. In the months of January and February, 1839, four New Orleans steamers landing at the St. Louis levee brought about 700 emigrants to St. Louis, then a city of 16,000 inhabitants. The greater number of these emigrants soon left St. Louis again to settle in Perry County, Missouri. Those remaining in St. Louis, together with a few that later returned from Perry County, soon after organized the first German Evangelical congregation, and at once established a parochial school. When in 1842 Trinity Church, the first Lutheran house of worship, was built, the basement of the church was utilized as a schoolroom. Soon afterwards a new school was built in another part of town. Trinity congregation then had two parochial schools, four teachers and 310 pupils. There are today [1916] in St. Louis 45 teachers, instructing 2,400 children.

There is a marked change in the relation of the non-churchgoing German element to the parochial school. The German immigrant of twenty-five and thirty years ago, as a rule, sought Lutheran church connections, especially if he came from a farming district of Germany. He would send his children to the parochial school. Even members of the irreligious majority—for even at that time the preponderance of free thinkers among the German immigrants was very large—would enter their children at the parochial school for the sake of the language. As a result more than a third, in some congregations fully two-thirds of the pupils were children of parents indifferent to the church. At that time immigration from Germany to America rose to 250,000 a year. A few years ago it had fallen to about 25,000. Naturally there was a corresponding drop in our school enrollment, more so because those who still came were to a most amazing degree indifferent to the church, indeed, hated it with a most cordial hatred. Such children as they had they would, as a rule, refuse to send to a parochial school, because they disliked to be told that their children were going to a religious school.

Yet our schools exist and flourish.

What does this mean?

It means that we are no longer dependent upon immigration for the continued existence of our schools. Those who attend them now are, to an extent of at least 90 per cent, the children of those who are themselves parochial school product[s]. In other words, the Lutheran parochial school is a fully Americanized institution, supported by native Americans and attended by children almost exclusively of American parentage. The language of our country has, to an increasing degree, become the exclusive medium of instruction. Until a year or two ago German was still the prescribed medium of religious instruction. Trinity discontinued the use of German as a medium of instruction in the religious branches a few years ago, Bethlehem followed this year, and the day may not be far distant when our schools will not only be thoroughly American in management and spirit—they are that now—but entirely English in language as well. And why should they not be, if they but hand down to our children undiminished and untainted the precious heritage we have received from our fathers: the doctrine of Christ and his apostles?

8 | German Cultural and Intellectual Life in St. Louis: An 1874 Report

Few visitors failed to report on the pervasive German influence in St. Louis after 1850. It was easy to locate German entertainments, institutions, or German-named businesses. Seldom did nineteenth-century visitors venture to explore the unique con-

tribution made by St. Louis Germans to American intellectual history. However, Edward King, a well-known journalist of the period, not only examined the customary cultural contributions but delved into St. Louis' German-influenced intellectual element as well. His report explains how Americans became familiar with important currents in European thought through the mediation of William Torrey Harris, a transplanted Connecticut Yankee educator and philosopher, who discovered Hegel and German idealism through contacts with the local German intelligentsia. In the pages of The Journal of Speculative Philosophy, *which Harris introduced in 1867 in St. Louis, some of the earliest writings of John Dewey and William James joined with extracts and interpretations of Hegel, Fichte, and Kant to elevate significantly the quality and broaden the range of American thought. Edward King, "The Great South. Some Notes on Missouri: The Heart of the Republic,"* Scribner's Monthly, *VIII (July 1874), pp. 263–66.*

On Saturday evenings the street life is as animated as that of an European city. In the populous quarters the Irish and Germans throng the sidewalks, marketing and amusing themselves until midnight; and in the fashionable sections the ladies, seated in the porches and on the front doorsteps of their mansions, receive the visits of their friends. . . . At the more aristocratic and elegant of the German beer gardens, such as "Uhrig's" and "Schneider's" the representatives of many prominent American families may be seen on the concert evenings, drinking the amber fluid, and listening to the music of Strauss, of Gungl, or Meyerbeer. Groups of elegantly dressed ladies and gentlemen resort to the gardens in the same manner as do the denizens of Dresden and Berlin, and no longer regard the custom as a dangerous German innovation. The German element in St. Louis is powerful and has for the last thirty years been merging in the American, giving to it many of the hearty features and graces of European life, which have been emphatically rejected by the native population of the more austere Eastern States. In like manner the German has borrowed many traits from his American fellow-citizens, and in another generation the fusion of races will be pretty thoroughly accomplished.

There are more than fifty thousand native Germans, from beyond the Atlantic, now in St. Louis, and the whole Teutonic population, including the children born in the city of German parents, probably exceeds one hundred and fifty thousand. The original emigration from Germany to Missouri was from the thinking classes—professional men, politicians condemned to exile, writers, musicians and philosophers, and these have aided immensely in the development of the State. The emigration began in 1830, but after a few hundreds had come out it fell off again, and was not revived until 1848, when the revolution sent us a new crop of patriots and statesmen whose mother country was afraid of them. Always a loyal and industrious element, believing in the whole country, and in the principles of freedom, they kept Missouri, in the troublous times preceding and during the war, from many excesses. The working people are a treasure to the State. Arriving, as a rule, with little or nothing, they hoard every penny until they have enough with which to purchase an acre or two of land, and in a few years become well-to-do citizens, orderly and contented. The whole country for miles around St. Louis is dotted with German settlements; the market gardens are mainly controlled by them; and their farms are models of thorough cultivation. In commerce they have mingled liberally with the Americans; names of both nationalities are allied in banking and in all the great wholesale businesses; and the older German residents speak their adopted as well as their native tongue. At the time of my visit, a German was president of the city council, and bank presidents, directors of companies, and men highly distinguished in business and society, who boast German descent, are counted by hundreds. . . .

German social and home-life has, of course, kept much of its original flavor. There are whole sections of the city where the Teuton predominates, and takes his ease at evening in the beer garden and the arbor in his own yard. At the summer-opera one sees him in his glory. Entering a modest doorway on Fourth street, one is ushered through a long room, in which ladies, with their children, and groups of elegantly dressed men are chatting and drinking beer, into the opera-house, a cheery little hall, where very fashionable audiences assemble to hear the new and old operas throughout a long season. The singing is usually exceedingly good, and the *mise en scène* quite satisfactory. Between the acts the audience refreshes itself with beer and soda-water, and the hum of conversation lasts until the first notes of the orchestra announce the resumption of the opera. On Sunday evenings the opera-house is crowded, and at the long windows of the hall, which descend to the ground, one can see the German population of half a dozen adjacent blocks, tiptoe with delight at the whiff of stolen harmony. The "breweries" scattered through the city are gigantic establishments, for the making of beer ranks third in the productive industries of St. Louis. Iron and flour precede it, but a capital of nearly four millions of dollars is invested in the manufacture, and the annual productive yield from the twenty-five breweries is about the same amount. Attached to many of these breweries are concert gardens, which are scrupulously respectable in all their attributes, and are frequented by thousands weekly. The Germania and Harmony Clubs, and a hundred musical and literary organizations use up the time of the city Germans who are well-to-do, while their poor brethren delve at market gardens, and are one of the chief elements in the commerce of the huge and picturesque St. James Market, whither St. Louis goes to be fed. The Hibernian is also prominent in St. Louis; he has crept into the hotel service, and the negro has sought another field of occupation. . . .

The operation of the German mind upon the American has been admirably exemplified in St. Louis by the upspringing in the new and thoroughly commercial capital of a real and noteworthy school of speculative philosophy, at whose head, and by virtue of his distinguished preeminence as a thinker, stands William T. Harris, the present superintendent of the city public schools. Mr. Harris, during his stay at Yale, in 1856, met the venerable [Bronson] Alcott, of Concord, and was much stimulated by various conversations with him. At that time he had studied Kant a little, and was beginning to think upon Goethe. The hints given him by Mr. Alcott were valuable, and sometime afterwards, when he settled in St. Louis, and came into contact with Germans of culture and originality, his desire for philosophical study was greatly increased and strengthened. In 1858 he became engaged in teaching, for eight years conducting one of the graded schools. The first year of his stay in St. Louis he studied Kant's "Critique of Pure Reason," without, as he says, understanding it at all. He had been solicited and encouraged to these studies by Henry C. Brockmeyer, a remarkable and brilliant German, and so enthusiastic for Kantian study that he awoke a genuine fervor in Mr. Harris. They arranged a Kant class, which Mr. Alcott on one occasion visited, and in a short time the love for philosophical study became almost fanaticism. A number of highly cultured Germans and Americans composed the circle, whose members had a supreme contempt for the needs of the flesh, and who, after long days of laborious and exhaustive teaching, would spend the night hours in threading the mysteries of Kant. In 1858 Mr. Harris claims that they mastered Kant, and between that period and 1863 they analyzed, or, as he phrases it, obtained the keys to Leibnitz and Spinoza. The result of this long study is written out in what Mr. Harris calls his "Introduction to Philosophy," in which he deals with "speculative insights." Everyone, he claims, will have the same insight into Kant, Leibnitz and Spinoza as he did, by reading his "Introduction." He already has a large number of followers, many of whom apply his theories, according to his confession, better than he does himself: and his *Journal of Speculative Philosophy,* started boldly in the face of many obstacles, has won a permanent establishment and gratifying success. . . . The publication is gaining ground in this country, and has won a very wide and hearty recognition in Germany and among thinking men throughout Europe.

9 | An Irish Celebration, 1869

After the Germans, the Irish were the second-largest foreign-born group in the city. Irish-born constituted 13 percent of the city population in 1850 and nearly 16 percent a decade later. Germans were spread throughout the city, although their principal concentration was on the south side. The Irish also were scattered, although their principal concentrations were in two sections located northwest of the business district. These were designated Kerry Patch and Vinegar Hill. As a group, the Irish were less affluent than the Germans, and their social life reflected the difference. One day of the year, however, the St. Louis Irish made their presence obvious. An 1867 English visitor to the city captured the tone of the event as the Mound City Irish celebrated St. Patrick's Day. John Chester Greville, Transatlantic Sketches in the

West Indies, South America, Canada and the United States *(London: Smith, Elder & Co., 1869), pp. 243–45.*

St. Patrick's Day occurring during my stay at St. Louis, I had the opportunity of seeing the great demonstration of the Irish upon that occasion. The various Irish societies met, and after mass and sermon marched round the city, visiting the principal convents and churches on their route. A programme had been prepared by "Grand Marshal Quinlivan," and the societies were set in motion by him and his deputy marshals, who, though somewhat seedy-looking gentlemen, rode a-cock-horse with great intrepidity, displayed their scarfs and rosettes, and brandished their truncheons as if they had been genuine field-marshals from babyhood. There was the "Hibernian Benevolent Society," with 150 members, and the "Emmett Band," all wearing green scarfs, and carrying "appropriate banners;" and the "Total Abstinence Society of our Lady of the Assumption," led by Mr. T. Moloney, marshal; and the "United Broghers of Erin;" and the "Shamrock Benevolent Society," dressed "in white regalia," and commanded by Alderman Hogah, and several other organizations while round them and about them were crowds of sympathizing friends, each wearing a bit of green ribbon, or a harp, as a badge of distinction. The church was densely crowded. At mass a "Panegyric of the Life of St. Patrick" was pronounced by the Rev. Father Phelan, a fair handsome young Irishman, whom I heard eulogized by an admirer as a *"splindid Praste."* And a "splindid Praste" he was, and preached a "splindid" sermon, though unhappily, the Panegyric of St. Patrick merged into something very like blasphemy against St. George for the latter part of the discourse was of the "accursed coils of St. George and the Dragon," which I then learned for the first time, on the authority of Mr. Phelan, were emblazoned on the bloodstained banner of England. However, the sermon was rich fun, the only take-off being that, as I was in church, I could not laugh out as I wished.

After service the procession re-formed and started on their weary tramp. The unhappy members were kept on their legs from eight in the morning till dusk. It made my heart ache to see how sad and subdued and changed the majority of the men appeared. Scarce a smile was visible upon any countenance, and they had the air of men performing a stern, unpleasant duty. Another noticeable point was the characteristic tolerance with which their proceedings were regarded by the American spectators. A procession, which would have driven Mr. Whalley and the Dean of Ripon, and any number of old ladies at Clapham, mad with rage, was looked on with, may be, some contempt, for in truth, as a show, it was mean enough, but with the most perfect equanimity. The feeling was, that if people liked to amuse themselves with scarfs and banners, their predilection should be respected. People generally are much more tolerant in the States than they are in England, and in all matters connected with religious ceremonies far less superstitious.

10 | The Burning of the Mulatto McIntosh: Racial Disorder in the Nineteenth-Century Urban Society

By the mid 1830s, St. Louisans liked to regard their city as one of urbanity and civility. But like larger eastern cities, St. Louis experienced a number of incidents when the thin line between order and bloody violence was crossed. Numerous duels, a "medical riot," and heavy property damage and shootings during labor strikes are examples of breaches in public order. No issue held more potential violence than relations between blacks and whites. Codes regulating the behavior of blacks in St. Louis were first passed by the Spanish governors. Stiff regulation continued after American takeover. During the 1830s and 1840s, as St. Louis experienced its first population boom, earlier ordinances were reenacted and elaborated.

Roughly 10 percent of the population were slaves and less than 3 percent were free blacks in 1835, when Elijah P. Lovejoy, a white abolitionist newspaper man, came to St. Louis and began publication of The Observer, *which editorialized against slavery and labeled slaveholders as cruel oppressors. The response was public outrage. Determination to control the city's black population led such prominent citizens as former Mayor William Carr Lane and Missouri Senator Thomas Hart Benton to support the creation of vigilante groups to maintain the peace against possible uprisings.*

This document, a dramatic illustration of the breakdown of

*urban order, is the recounting of the burning of a mulatto, Francis
McIntosh, by a vigilante mob after he had murdered a policeman.
The account is taken from Lovejoy's newspaper. Parenthetically,
Lovejoy's criticism of the mob that burned McIntosh caused an-
other mob to burn his press, forcing him to move to Alton, Illinois.
In 1837, an Alton mob murdered the unrepentant Lovejoy, who
had continued his abolitionist writings.* The Observer *(St. Louis,
May 5, 1835).*

On the afternoon of Thursday, the 23th ult. an affray between
two sailors or boatmen took place on the steamboat [ferry] landing. Mr. George Hammond, Deputy Sheriff, and Mr. William
Mull, Deputy Constable, in the discharge of their official duty, attempted to arrest the boatmen, for a breach of peace. In so
doing they were set upon by a mulatto fellow, by the name of
Francis J. McIntosh, who had just arrived in the city as cook on
board the steamboat Flora from Pittsburg. In consequence the
boatmen escaped, and McIntosh was arrested for his interference
with the officers. He was carried before Patrick Walsh, Esq., a
Justice of the Peace for this county, and by him committed to jail
and delivered to the same officers to be taken thither. On his way
he inquired what his punishment would be, and being told that it
would not be less than five years imprisonment in the States Prison,
he immediately broke loose from the officers, drew a long knife
and made a desperate blow at Mr. Mull, but fortunately missed
him. Unfortunately, however, a second blow, aimed with the same
savage violence, had better success, and struck Mr. Mull in the
right side, and wounded him severely. He was then seized by the
shoulder by Mr. Hammond, whereat he turned and stabbed him in
the neck. The knife struck the lower part of the chin and passed
deeply into the neck, cutting the jugular vein and the larger ar-
teries. Mr. H. turned from his murderer, walked about sixty steps,
fell and expired! Mr. M. although dangerously wounded, was
able to pursue the murderer who had fled, until his cries alarmed
the people in the vicinity. —They turned out, and without much
difficulty secured the blood thirsty wretch and lodged him in jail.

The bloody deeds of . . . McIntosh . . . [became known]
through the city; and crowds collected at the spot, where the body
of Mr. Hammond lay weltering in its blood. The excitement was

intense; and soon might be heard above the tumult the voices of a few exhorting the multitude to take summary vengeance. The plan and process of proceeding were soon resolved upon. A mob was immediately organized and went forward to the jail in search of their victim. The Sheriff, Mr. Brotherton, made some attempts to oppose their illegal violence. Apprehensive for the fate of his family, who occupied a portion of the jail building, he then retired taking them along with him to a place of safety. Another of our fellow-citizens courageously attempted to reason with the angry mob, and to stay them from their fearful proceedings. When, however, "he saw that he could prevail nothing, but that rather a tumult was made" and being himself threatened with violence he was compelled to retire from the place and leave the enraged multitude to do their work. All was done with the utmost deliberation and system, and an awful stillness pervaded the scene, broken only by the sound of the implements employed in demolishing the prison doors. Men spoke to each other in whispers, but it was a whisper which made the blood curdle to hear it, and indicated the awful energy of purpose with which they were bent upon sacrificing the life of their intended victim. —Armed persons were stationed as guards to protect those engaged in breaking down the doors.

At length between eight and nine o'clock at night, the cell of the wretch was reached. Loud shouts of execration and triumph rent the air, as he was dragged forth, and hurried away to the scene of the burnt sacrifice! Some seized him by the hair, some by the arms and legs, and in this way he was carried to a large locust tree in the rear of the town, not far from the jail. He was then chained to the tree with his back against its trunk and facing to the south. —The wood, consisting of rails, plank, &c., was then piled up before him, about as high as his knees, shavings and a brand were brought, and the fire kindled!

Up to this time, as we have been informed, McIntosh uttered not a word; but when the fire had seized upon its victim he begged that someone in the crowd would shoot him. He then commenced singing a hymn and trying to pray. Afterwards he hung his head and suffered in silence until roused by some one saying that he must be already out of his misery. Upon this, though wrapped in flames, and though the fire had obliterated the features of humanity, he raised his head, and spoke out distinctly, saying, "No, no; I feel as much as any of you. I hear you all; shoot me, shoot me." He was burning about twenty minutes, before life became extinct.

But the tale of depravity and woe is not yet all told. After the crowd had somewhat dispersed, a rabble of boys who had attended to witness the horrid rites, commenced amusing themselves by throwing stones at the black and disfigured corpse, as it stood chained to the tree. The object was to see who should first succeed in breaking the skull!

Such, according to the best information we have been able to obtain, is a faithful description of the scene that has been transacted in our midst. It has given us pain to record it; but in doing so, we feel, deeply feel, that we are fulfilling a solemn duty which as one of its members we owe to this community, and as an American citizen to our country at large. Let no one suppose that we would lightly say a word in derogation of the character of the city in which we live; on the contrary we have, as is natural, a strong desire to sustain and vindicate its reputation. But when constitutional law and order are at stake, when the question lies between justice regularly administered or the wild vengeance of a mob, then there is but one side on which the patriot and the Christian can rally; but one course for them to pursue.

We have drawn the above gloomy and hideous picture, not for the purpose of holding it up as a fair representation of the moral condition of St. Louis—for we loudly protest against any such conclusion, and we call upon our fellow-citizens to join us in such protest—but that the immediate actors in the horrid tragedy may see the work of their hands, and shrink in horror from a repetition of it, and in humble penitence seek forgiveness of that community whose laws they have so outraged, and that God whose image they have, without his permission, wickedly defaced; and that we may all see (and be warned in time) the legitimate results of the spirit of *mobism,* and whither, unless arrested in its first out-breakings, it is sure to carry us. In Charlestown it burns a Convent over the head of defenceless women; in Baltimore it desecrates the Sabbath, and works all that day in demolishing a private citizen's house; in Vicksburg it hangs up gamblers, three or four in a row; and in St. Louis it forces a man—a hardened wretch certainly, and one that deserved to die, but not *thus* to die—it forces him from beneath the aegis of our Constitution and Laws, hurries him to the stake and burns him alive!

It is not yet five years since the first mob, within the memory of man, (for the French settlers of this city were a peaceable people, & their descendants continue so), was organised in St. Louis. They commenced operations, by tearing down the brothels of the city; and the good citizens of the place, not aware of the danger, and in consideration of the good done, aside from the *manner* of doing it, rather sanctioned the proceeding, at least they did not condemn it. The next thing was to burn our Governor in effigy, because in the discharge of one of the most solemn functions belonging to his official character, he had not acted in accordance with the public sentiment of a part of this community. The next achievement was to tear down a gambling house; and this was done last winter. The next and last we need not again repeat.

And now we make our appeal to the citizens of this community, and wherever else our voice can be heard, and ask, and ask with the most heartfelt anxiety, is it not time to *stop?* We know that in a case like the present, it is difficult to withdraw our thoughts and feelings from the great provocation to violence, to be found in the murderous atrocity of the wretch who has so fearfully atoned for his crime. But we do say, and insist, that these considerations must not be permitted to enter at all into our reasoning and practice on this point. We *must* stand by the Constitution and Laws.

11 | Colored Teachers for Colored Schools:
A Petition for Blacks to Instruct Blacks

Even when legislation was enacted to establish equality for blacks, it was difficult to implement. After 1865, when state laws mandated that schooling should be extended to blacks for the first time, whites resisted. In the face of this hostility, black leaders rarely considered integration. Instead, they sought to make the best accommodation possible within a segregated system. The public manifestation of this attempt was the development of an early "black power" movement, in which blacks, especially parents, pressed for teachers from their race to teach black children. While the parallels with the programs proposed by contem-

porary black activists are evident, this document, a petition by black teachers to the all-white school board, is not militant. Despite protests and the threat of organizing as a voting bloc, blacks lacked the leverage to force the community to acknowledge their rights. St. Louis Daily Globe-Democrat *(March 14, 1877).*

From the St. Louis Educational Council, St. Louis, February 26, 1877. To the Honorable President and officers of the St. Louis School Board:

GENTLEMEN—Whereas, in the Public Schools of the City of St. Louis, separate or class education prevails; and

Whereas, the objection to mixed education obtains against one peculiar class only, viz., those tinctured with African blood; and

Whereas, we, your petitioners, are of the said objectionable class, and subjected to all the embarrassment and disadvantages obtaining from such fact:

Now, therefore, we as representatives of the whole class so proscribed in the City of St. Louis . . . ask that you will favorably consider the claim we shall present, and grant our petition.

We call the attention of your honorable body to the following facts:

That in the City of St. Louis there are established certain public schools known as the white schools of said city, where all classes of American citizens may have the advantage of public instruction, except those known to have African blood *coursing through their veins;* and

Whereas, there are certain public schools in the said City of St. Louis set apart for the use of that class in whose veins African blood is known, or supposed to be, where they may obtain public instruction, separate from the class first named, and such separation being contrary to any wish on the part of the class proscribed; and

Whereas, in the second as in the first of the above named instances, white teachers may and do find employment, and colored teachers, though possessing equal qualifications, are refused employment, though sought for in the second instance mentioned only, and request made on their behalf by a majority of said proscribed class,

Now, therefore, in view of these facts, we, your petitioners, are *greatly aggrieved,* and respectfully ask that your honorable body remove these objectionable barriers; and, so long as we, your petitioners, are compelled to have separate or class schools, we respectfully ask that you will give us teachers of color over them, where they possess the requisite qualification to teach.

And, as a further reason for such request, we, your petitioners, have found that, as a rule, by reason of many beliefs in which they have been schooled, white teachers are not the best teachers for colored schools.

2 | That certain false and wicked ideas, the outgrowth of theories invented to justify prejudice, have been widely spread and so long unchallenged that their influence have become pernicious in the work in instruction, by limiting education, by checking aspiration, and by shutting off opportunities for development and promotion.

3 | That the prejudices of a large proportion of the white citizens of St. Louis are so great that, as a rule, the white teachers who are best qualified and would probably do all in their power to educate and refine their pupils, will not engage to teach a colored school on account of the *social stigma attached* to such a position.

Therefore, the advantage to us, your petitioners, of your employing qualified colored teachers in colored schools may briefly be stated thus: Their association with parents and children causes them to know better the wants of their pupils and how to supply them. They are free from unfavorable social surroundings, and become objects of greater respect and esteem thereby increasing their zeal and power for good.

And, as a further advantage, we would ask your honorable body to consider—

That competent colored teachers, such as your petitioners propose to present for examinations and employment should our petition meet with favor, will, by their example and intercourse, have a tendency to elevate and refine our social as well as intellectual condition.

12 | The St. Louis Residential Segregation Referendum, 1916

At mid-century, when slavery still existed within St. Louis, blacks were recorded as living in every ward in the city. Even then a few black enclaves existed, all of them located at the edge of the cen-

tral business district. Unlike the poor Irish, with whom they often shared social space at mid-century, blacks did not diffuse residentially during the next fifty years. As their numbers increased, pressure mounted to confine their homes to set districts. The residential history of blacks in St. Louis after the Civil War, therefore, was one of increasing segregation. With the black population increase, especially after 1890, new residential locations had to be found. The characteristic process was the amoebalike movement of the black ghetto, outward from the city center through old middle-class residential corridors.

This situation paralleled that of other cities around the turn of the century. The growth of the ghetto posed a threat to whites in neighboring areas who feared for property values and objected to living with blacks. In the first decade of the twentieth century, whites increasingly organized protests, pressured real estate operators, and even resorted to violence to stem the incursions of blacks into their neighborhoods. Beginning in 1910, white neighborhood associations and real estate dealers pressed for a municipal ordinance legitimating segregation. Following the example of such border and southern cities as Baltimore, Atlanta, and New Orleans, St. Louis passed such legislation in 1916 and thereby prohibited blacks from establishing additional residences on blocks that were at least 75 percent white. During the months in which both sides appealed to the voters, the support in opposition—which included numerous church groups, most of the press, and many important civic leaders—seemed overwhelming. Yet when the votes were counted, segregation was voted by a three-to-one majority. The segregation ordinance had two ironic twists: it was the first issue to have been decided by the progressive reform innovation of the initiative-referendum method for passing local ordinances, and a similar Louisville ordinance was struck down by the Supreme Court on the grounds of denial of property rights, making the St. Louis referendum a dead letter before it went into effect. This document is an editorial from St. Louis Labor, *a Socialist weekly, which had opposed the ordinance, attempting to explain why the measure had passed.* St. Louis Labor *(March 4, 1916).*

The two ordinances providing for negro segregation in St. Louis, voted on last Tuesday under the initiative provision of the City

Charter, were adopted by majorities of more than 34,000. There were 52,220 votes for and 17,977 against the ordinances. Even a capitalist paper like the *Post-Dispatch* comes out editorially with comment like this:

"The opponents of segregation suffered an honorable defeat in Tuesday's election. They stood for principle against overwhelming forces of power, interest and prejudice. A minority with right on its side is better than a majority supporting wrong. It will be justified in the long run. The forces backing the segregation movement were so powerful that they were able to control newspapers and induce them to abandon their principles. That they should mislead for a time a large number of voters is not a matter of wonderment."

Of the 17,977 votes cast against segregation we may safely say that fully 75 per cent came from the negro voters and from the Socialists. Never before has the writer of these lines felt more proud of the Socialist Party than last Tuesday. . . .

The St. Louis negroes got one of the worst deals from their old Republican party machine that has ever been handed out to any class of people. It is true, the Republican City Central Committee had to operate under the pretext of being opposed to segregation and Mayor [Henry] Kiel even made speeches against it. But it was in the strong Republican wards where segregation received the overwhelming vote. In the Ninth, Tenth and Eleventh Wards, for example, the few hundred of anti votes came almost exclusively from the Socialists. . . .

More than ever before are we convinced of the gross injustice done to the negroes of this city. With segregation accomplished, the politicians and their masters may proceed to disfranchise the colored people politically by some cleverly concocted scheme of gerrymander. If it is right and just to drive the negroes of St. Louis into certain corners or districts, it must be right to segregate them in the county, in any county, or to drive them into a certain corner of the State. Last Tuesday, while passing a Chouteau avenue polling place, we contemplated: Here are the negroes, born and raised in this country, native Americans. Their ancestors came to this country not by their own free will, but were imported, bought like an inanimate commodity. Today, fifty years after the Civil War, we are confronted by this queer situation: Ignorant people from Asia Minor, from Turkey, from Italy, from every Southeast European country, driven from their homes by hunger and misery, come to our American shores. Some of them come to St. Louis. Within one year they are permitted to vote. Some negro-haters start a segregation campaign. They appeal to prejudice, to ignorance, to the "beast of property." Alas, there come the newly-made voters from the backwoods of the Old World, still ignorant of American life and condition, ignorant of the language and customs of this country—but they go to the polls and vote in favor of segregating the colored race, the citizen born and raised in this country! And the hypocrites and fanatics of segregationists applaud them! What a disgrace on our free institutions! We sincerely hope that the St. Louis Segregation ordinances may be declared unconstitutional.

13 | The Teaching of Urban Discipline and Industrial Skills

The rapid growth of St. Louis during the middle of the nineteenth century placed enormous stress on community relations. The problems inherent in making the city work as a social organization were well understood by William Torrey Harris, superintendent of schools from 1868 to 1880. Harris was highly conscious of the revolution in social organization that was taking place as America became more urban and industrial. His annual reports were read with care throughout the United States and Europe by those who were concerned with preparing urban citizens for life in the industrial city. Believing that a new kind of behavior was necessary in order to transform a rural population into an urban one, Harris saw the schools as the key instrument for insuring that St. Louis and other cities would have the kind of citizen necessary for future progress.

By mid-century, the public school had become the major educator of urban children. This condition represented a dramatic change in the traditional patterns of socialization, where instruction of the young was left to the family, church, or privately organized institutions. Since moral education had always been an essential ingredient in the instruction of the young and since the churches for centuries had considered it one of their prerogatives, Harris felt pressed to prove that public schools could produce moral citizens. In Harris's defense of the city system, he outlined a new kind of secular morality in which the catechism was replaced by the roll book. Great emphasis was placed on producing well-behaved and disciplined children, and the most important values that the schools imparted were punctuality and regularity. Indeed, virtually the only way a child in the St. Louis schools could win an award was by regularly coming to school on time. The Nineteenth Annual Report of the St. Louis Public Schools for the Year Ending August 1, 1873, *pp. 77–80;* The Seventeenth Annual Report of the St. Louis Public Schools for the Year Ending August 1, 1871, *pp. 31–32.*

Necessity of Public High Schools

During the past twenty years, there has been an unparalleled growth in wealth and population, and still greater possibilities of commanding the services of nature. The construction of seventy thousand miles of railroad means a most radical change in society; it means the creation of a myriad of cities, where there were only villages before. It means the extension of urban life into the vast regions of country where before was only patriarchal simplicity. . . . There is another phase of this influence of the railroad still more important. The railroad is the creation of commerce. Its most immediate influence on the country population is to stimulate them to division of labor and to exchange of products. It comes to pass that a mutual interdependence of the individual upon society grows up quite rapidly. . . . By this means a given amount of human industry accomplished far more than before, and the wealth of society increases proportionately. This explains the immense growth of cities during the present century. Manufacturing has doubled once in seven years. Increased transit facilities have so abated the friction of exchange that the raw material has risen in value while the cost of the manufactured product to the consumer has decreased in the same ratio.

Certain well-marked social and political effects have resulted from this. Where each individual lives in comparative isolation from his neighbor, relations are very simple, and very little governmental influence is required. The political government is consequently very simple in a country where urban life has not been developed. After the railroad system has become a network over the country, relations of each to all have so multiplied, and rights have become so complex and intertwined, that the political government is a very delicate and difficult problem to adjust and solve, requiring the greatest insight and practical skill.

In the modern (urban) status of society, new vocations continually arise, one after the other, based upon the necessities of unity in the organism which society has become. . . . A demand upon a highly educated class of laborers is occasioned by these complex relations which come into existence through the changes in the relation of the individual to society. . . . Manifold vocations —some being commercial, some having for their end protection of society, its culture, 'or its amusement—have arisen from this source, and have come to demand immense stores of directive intelligence. . . .

In fact, in the former simple, patriarchal state of society it was not essential that the individual be educated to any considerable degree. If he could read and write, and understood a little arithmetic, he was educated beyond immediate necessities; for there was little to read, little to write, and not much arithmetical calculation required. Neither did he find much need of a disciplined will and habits of regularity, punctuality, and attention. When it rained, or after the harvest was cared for, he could lounge about the village store and exchange gossip over the trivial affairs of his neighborhood. But with the new country life all is different. The railroad reduces all to rhythm. There must be regularity, punctuality, attention, and systematic industry. More than this, there must be an education far above the "three R's" in the great army of men who exert the directive power required to manage all the manifold complex relations that come to exist as a consequence of this instrumentality. Hence we see that modern society, resting, as it does, on the union of the country and town, or on the elevation of the country into a direct participation in urban life, demands as its necessary condition a system of popular education widely different from that required under its former status. Indeed, if the question be asked as to whether the modern State and modern civil society, constituted as it is, and is becoming to be, can exist without a system of public education, including High Schools, we are ready at this point to answer with a prompt and emphatic no. . . . The closely organized society that grows into existence with the instrumentalities of commerce and inter-communication, finds popular education simply an indispensable provision.

School Discipline

The pillars on which public school education rests are BEHAVIOR or deportment, and SCHOLARSHIP. The first requisite of the school is ORDER: each pupil must be taught first and foremost to conform his behavior to a general standard. Only thus can the school as a community exist and fulfil its functions. In the outset therefore a whole family of virtues are taught the pupil, and these are taught so thoroughly, and so constantly enforced, that they become fixed in his character. The method of this moral training is, like that which rules everywhere in the practical world, one of division and repetition. The duty of being a well-behaved pupil is not a vague generality. It divides into specific, well-defined duties. (1) PUNCTUALITY: the pupil must be at school in time. Sleep, meals, play, business, indisposition—all must give way to the duty of obedience to the external requirement of time. Punctuality does not end with getting to school. While in school it is of equal importance. Combination cannot be achieved without it. The pupil must have his lessons ready at the appointed time, must rise at the tap of the bell, move to the line, return; in short, go through all the evolutions with equal precision. (2) REGULARITY is punctuality reduced to a system. Conformity to the requirements of time in a particular instance is punctuality; made general it becomes regularity. Combination in school rests on these two virtues. They are the most elementary ones of the moral code—its alphabet. . . .

The community submits to regulations patiently, but it may be doubted whether their importance is fully appreciated. This age is called *the age of productive industry*. It is the era of emancipation of each and every member of society from the drudgery of slavery to his natural wants. The emancipation is effected through *machinery*. Machinery during the past fifty years has quadrupled the efficiency of human industry. . . . Achievement in this direction has but begun. In the future hovers the picture of a humanity so free on the side of its natural wants that its time is its own for spiritual culture. But there is one general training especially requisite for the generations of men who are to act as directors of machinery, and of business that depends upon it—this training is in the habits of punctuality and regularity. A human being may wait for the arrival of another, a machine will not make any allowance for subjective whims, or caprices, or failures in obedience to the laws of time and space. The fact that so much labor depends upon machinery makes itself felt throughout all occupations of life. The necessity of conformity to the time of the train, to the starting of work in the manufactory, fixes the times for the minor affairs of life with absolute precision. Only by obedience to these abstract external laws of time and place may we achieve that social combination necessary to free us from degrading slavery to our physical wants and necessities.

14 | The Social Benefits of Kindergarten

The concern for behavior became greatest when the poor were considered. While children of all classes attended school for at least three to four years in the second half of the nineteenth century, school professionals believed this time insufficient to help the poor overcome the negative influences of the street and deficient home environment. Since it was assumed that such children could not be kept in school beyond age twelve, when most went to work, the kindergarten was introduced in the preschool years as a means for prolonging the beneficent influences of schooling. Like other parts of the school system, the kindergarten was not designed initially to encourage spontaneity and individuality. Rather, it was a means for creating disciplined urban citizens. Begun as an experiment in 1873, kindergartens quickly spread in St. Louis. About 8,000 students attended them by 1880. St. Louis was the first city to sponsor a successful, large-scale, public effort to reform urban children. The Twenty-second Annual Report of the Board of Directors of the St. Louis Public Schools for the Year Ending August 1, 1876, *pp. 79–82.*

The importance of reaching all of the population of the community, and of subjecting it to the beneficent influences of the school, presses itself upon the educator. More than all is he concerned for the children growing up in poverty and crime. Living in narrow, filthy alleys, poorly clad and without habits of cleanliness, the "divine sense of shame," which Plato makes to be the foundation of civilization, is very little developed. Self respect is the basis of character and virtue; cleanliness of person and clothing is a sine qua non for its growth in the child. The child who passes his years in the misery of the crowded tenement house or an alley, becomes early familiar with all manner of corruption and immorality. The children thus unhappily situated are fortunate if they are placed at work even in their tender years, and taught habits of industry, though deprived of school education. The unfortunate ones grow up in crime. But if they can receive an education at school besides the education in useful industry they are more than fortunate, their destiny is in their own hands.

In my report for 1870–71 I [Superintendent William T. Harris] urged this point:

"The average duration of the school-life of a child in manufacturing districts is only three entire years. Commencing at the age of seven, he completes his school education at ten. If he could be properly cared for in school at five years of age his school-life would last five years. This period would suffice to make a durable impression on his life."

"The exclusion of pupils under seven years of age, to which I have alluded in former reports, still continues, but not to such an extent as formerly. In certain sections of the city where the influences are corrupting to the children, they being obliged to play on the street, it is decidedly better to have them in school at an early age, and to so far modify the tasks imposed on them as to prevent overstraining their delicate organisms. The Kindergarten system of culture for the young is justly receiving much attention from educators everywhere. To it we must look for valuable hints on the method of conducting our instruction in the lowest primary grades." The establishment of an experimental kindergarten was accordingly recommended.

In my report for 1871–72 I again called attention to the provision for the education of the younger children:

"The regime of the school (more general than that of the family) is needed to prevent arbitrariness and caprice, and to secure the growth of proper respect for elders and for moral and civil ordinances. That three-fold reverence, that Goethe speaks of as the basis of all higher life—reverence for superiors, for equals, and for inferiors—is very difficult to inculcate if the child remains too long under that influence, without the training of the school. School discipline is found to be far more potent when applied at the age of five than at the age of eight years."

In my report for 1872–73 I alluded again to the increase in our schools of the number of pupils under the age of seven years, and urged its importance:

"We do not look so much to the gain in intellectual possessions as to the training of the will into correct habits, during the years previous to the seventh. After his third year, the child becomes social and hungers for companionship. In the school he can secure this with less danger to him than on the street. Such careful training in habits of regularity, punctuality, industry, cleanliness, self-control, and politeness, as are given in the ordinary primary school, and still more efficiently in the well-conducted kindergarten, are of priceless benefit to the community. They lessen the number of rough, ungovernable youths whose excesses are the menace of the peace of society.

"The formation of habits of cleanliness and politeness is marked and successful. But the development of the intellect in making quantitative or mathematical combinations is more surprising. Geometry and arithmetic seem to unfold simultaneously in the minds of the pupils. They are trained to exercise their faculties in recognizing form, shape, and numbers, as well as in designing combinations with them. This training in the exact and quantitative is counterbalanced and compensated by a discipline of the phantasy and imagination. Manipulation, in various ways—drawing, folding paper into artistic forms, embroidering, construction with sticks and softened peas, modeling in clay—so as to train the hand and eye, is practiced. It would seem as though Froebel had especially in view the education of a race of industrious and useful people."

15 | Education of Immigrant Children, 1880

Like so many boomtowns in the American past, St. Louis was a city with a small native population and an overwhelming majority of newcomers. The need to assemble children from different backgrounds in schools that would create a sense of community and

TABLE 6
Birthplaces of White Children Ages 6–16 and Their Fathers,
1880, by Percentage

Birthplace	Children	Total	Fathers	Total
Native born		93.9		25.3
Missouri	78.6		7.4	
U.S. outside				
Missouri	15.3		17.9	
Foreign born		6.1		74.1
Germany	3.4		46.2	
Ireland	1.6		16.0	
Other Europe	1.1		11.9	
Unknown	0.0	0.0	0.5	0.5
Total	100.0		100.0	
	(6,141)		(6,141)	

harmonize different cultural strains within an American tradition was not a theoretical problem but a pressing reality. The difficulties presented by this goal are evident in the above table, which is based on demographic data culled from the manuscript census of 1880. The largest proportion of school-age children, 94 percent, were born in the United States, but only 25 percent of their fathers were native-born Americans. Three times as many fathers were European immigrants, with the largest group, 46 percent, from Germany, followed by 16 percent from Ireland. Reinforcing the immigrant character of the community was the small number of fathers, only 7 percent, who were native to Missouri if not to St. Louis, while two and a half times that amount, 18 percent, were drawn from virtually every section of the country. On the other hand, 79 percent of the children were Missourians. St. Louis educators were attempting to build a system for first-generation Americans in the largely European-born community in which Germans were the dominant group. Selwyn K. Troen, The Public and the Schools: Shaping the St. Louis System, 1838–1920 *(Columbia: University of Missouri Press, 1975), p. 58.*

16 | The Street Arabs of St. Louis, 1878

St. Louis possessed its share of what were called "the dangerous classes"—criminals, streetwalkers, and vagabonds. However, it was the presence and behavior of undisciplined and uncared-for children who populated the city's streets that most excited the interests of nineteenth-century reformers. As the following report by two newspapermen reveals, the best efforts of city officials and philanthropists at devising institutions and legislation still proved inadequate in controlling and reaching street youth. The source for this document is one of the numerous exposés of "the underside" of nineteenth-century city life. Joseph Dacus and James Buel, A Tour of St. Louis or, The Inside Life of a Great City *(St. Louis: Western Publishing Company, 1878), pp. 410–12.*

The Street Arabs of both sexes in St. Louis are divided into tribes or clans, and susceptible of a classification into the working Arabs and the thieving, heathenish class. Among the first-named class may be reckoned the boot-blacks, newspaper peddlers, and the corps of boys who hang around to do chores about houses, stores, shops, stables, etc. Among the female Bedouins are to be found match-sellers, dealers in pins, needles, combs, etc., and peddlers of fruits and flowers. There are few flower sellers in the city. As for the vendors of fruits and nuts, the dark-eyed daughters of sunny Italy almost monopolize the business.

Then we meet another class of Arabs, namely, the idle and vicious ones, who neither seek nor wish to find employment. These are the juvenile pariahs, and are most numerous in the neighborhood of Almond, Poplar, Plum, and a portion of Third Street, and in the neighborhood of Seventh and Eighth streets, from Wash Street to O'Fallon Street, and in the whole region of the town east of Broadway and north of Cherry Street. "Kerry Patch" is celebrated for its bands of young Bedouins.

In a portion of the Seventh and Eighth Street district, mentioned above, there is a very populous region peopled altogether by people of color, most of them of a low and degraded character. The darkey Arab is a genius, and can not be classed with any other clans of wanderers through the desert streets and alleys of the great city. They constitute a class by themselves. The lives led by all classes of the Arabian population of the city is characteristic of the people from among whom they have come out. How can they live? Who can tell?

The bad boys and girls of St. Louis live much in the open air. During the hot summer days, they repose on the shaded side of buildings, lumber piles, and in old outhouses. In the summer evenings the street tribes are in their glory. Then they come forth and fill the streets and the vacant lots, and the various throngs fill the air with their fearful clamor. Profanity and obscenity early become a part of the Arabian character. Such cries, such foul language, such volleys of oaths, such shouts and boisterous laughter as ascend from thousands of strong-lunged children and youth of both sexes, from every vacant lot and old lumber-yards, are seldom heard or dreamed of, away from the city and its tribes of Arabs.

Their gambols and noise is kept up to a late hour—midnight often stealing over the city ere they become still.

For lodging places, in the summer time, the street boys are at no loss. They crawl into basements, go into lumber yards, find beds under old sheds, and often even sleep on green sward of some vacant lot. Every night will find them at a different lodging-place from that which they occupied the night before. Girls and boys are often found scattered around indiscriminately through the vacant spaces of lumber yards.

In the winter season, the condition of the Arab is certainly not enviable. Some of the tribes of this class have established their headquarters in caves, which they have excavated in some vacant lot; some take possession of untenanted buildings and establish themselves in the cellars, where they crowd together thick enough to keep themselves warm. The police know of more than half a dozen caves excavated in favorable situations by these street boys, which are capable of accommodating from twelve to twenty-five boys each. Into these subterranean dens the boys crawl through a small aperture, and, once within the grimy cavern, the coldest weather may be defied.

It has happened that a dozen or more masculine Arabs have secured a cavernous abode, and taken a girl of fourteen from her wretched home to play the role of housekeeper for the tribe. Such an establishment was broken up not a great while ago.

Sometimes two clans of street boys will disagree, and a feud between them be the result. Severe fights take place between them, and very often serious wounds are received and inflicted by the combatants. Such feuds are perpetuated for years sometimes.

Stealing is practiced as a fine art by a large section of the Arabian tribes. Gambling is a vice indulged in by all. It is the delight of the Arab, when an opportunity is offered for him to get into the gallery of one of the variety theatres. The genus make excellent claquers, to render famous the latest star clog dancer, or the most abbreviated, dressed female danseuse of the variety boards. The applause they indulge in is perfectly deafening.

The problem of rescuing the street boys and girls from their career of vice and crime, has often engaged the attention of the philanthropic people of the city. Sometimes such good has been accomplished among them by the efforts of friends who have established Mission Sunday-schools especially for their benefit. The Newsboys' Home is one of the permanent institutions established in their particular interest.

17 | The "Social Evil" Experiment

Like children, adults had to be disciplined. Some St. Louisans waged constant struggles to regulate or suppress drinking, gambling, and prostitution, which were considered the most extreme and visible forms of public misconduct and improper behavior. In the 1870s, the city embarked on a novel way of dealing with "the great social evil," or prostitution. In the first, and one of the few, experiments at regulating prostitution in the United States, the city government began to register and license prostitutes and ordered the city's health department to begin compulsory medical inspections to reduce the incidence of venereal disease. In defending the ordinance from its critics, William Barrett, the city's chief health officer, asked St. Louisans to suspend moral judgments and view prostitution as a health problem. William Barrett, Prostitution and Its Relation to the Public Health *(St. Louis, 1873), pp. 1–3, 13–14.*

It is undoubtedly the duty of a good and wise government to provide for the health and morals of the community, especially when the consequences of unrestrained action are serious and visible. The "liberty of the subject" is a precarious trust; but the absence of law to meet the case of the infected prostitute is in reality *license for evil,* since no precaution is taken to prevent most grievous infringements of the rights of others.

It is certainly an overstrained delicacy on the part of legislation to shrink from interference with a class which causes so much private misery, open violence, and public expenditure, as the records of our prisons, lunatic asylums, poor-houses and hospitals, can amply attest.

For the maiden who in a moment of passionate love renders up the jewel of her chastity, there may be some commiseration; but what excuse or palliation can be offered for the woman who abandons her body to every comer, for money? Infamy has attached to the latter among all people and in all ages.

Should not the Board of Health, aided by the police . . . suppress prostitution as much as possible, and confine it in the limits compatible with public morals, security and health?

The control and restriction of prostitution is a law of self-defense. Why let it raise its head in the sunshine of the "let alone policy" and pursue unmolested its fearful ravages? Such conduct is incompatible with the welfare of the community. Shall a fearful malady that is stalking madly over the country be ignored, houses of prostitution given full swing, young girls be delivered over without a single effort to save them, to dens of vice? To prevent and relieve, is the special effort of the authorities under the present law. That it has accomplished much good, none familiar with its action doubt, or who view its workings with an unprejudiced eye, can fail to perceive. . . .

As soon might we hope to bail the ocean dry, to touch the stars with our fingers, as to inhibit prostitution. The vice is as ancient as history and a universal and incurable evil, that must be tolerated, and should be, as far as possible, palliated. Do we not quarantine to prevent the spread of volatile contagious disease, and is it not productive of much good, though some cases do escape? Is it not then logical to conclude that the ravages of syphilis, the most fearful in its consequences of all diseases—a disease communicated by contact, and that too immediate, may be mitigated by surveillance? . . .

We do not suppose our registration is, or even will be, perfect, or that every woman of easy virtue can be controlled by law; nor is it desirable it should be so, for, as has been truly stated, "it is a great mistake to class all fallen women together under one sweeping censure of contempt, as if they were absolutely vile and irredeemable," or all equally guilty.

We confess to inexperience in the management of the vice of prostitution. . . . Ours is the first attempt in the United States to control it. . . . but we do contend that our experience, so far as it goes, and more extensive experience in foreign countries, demonstrates with unmistakable clearness the correctness of the principles on which regulation and license systems are predicated. Our experience to the present time proves the enforcement of regulation to be economical and humane, that it is efficient in the promotion of morals and prevention of disease. This is all its most sanguine advocates claimed or expected. It is an ample vindication of the experiment made, and an unanswerable reason why the experiment should be continued until the ultimate result is fully and conclusively settled.

18 | The Suppression of the "Social Evil"

St. Louisans did not suppress moral judgment on prostitution for long. In 1874, the "social-evil" ordinance was repealed, even though prostitution continued to flourish with the toleration of the police in segregated districts near the downtown. The presence of brothels was a continual affront to some citizens, and there were periodic campaigns to pressure the police into enforcing municipal ordinances. Between 1910 and 1920, reformers were so successful that they claimed St. Louis to be one of the most proper of American cities. The many reasons for invoking the full weight of the law are outlined in this document. The physical health of the public was the last item on the list; the primary issue was the moral well-being of the community. Committee of One Hundred for the Suppression of Commercialized Vice in St. Louis, Brief in Support of Citizens' Memorial to the Board of Police Commissioners of St. Louis, Missouri on the Illegality and Inexpediency of Segregating Commercialized Vice in St. Louis *(St. Louis, 1914).*

More than twenty-five years ago St. Louis had a segregated district in which vice was licensed by law and where the keeper of a house of prostitution displayed her name over her place of business and solicited her trade like any other merchant. But this was in the day when unenlightened men thought that public prostitution was a "necessary evil" not only to be recognized but to be licensed and regulated by the state.

This shameful partnership between law and crime, between government and lust was many years ago dissolved not only in this city but throughout the civilized world.

In place of a licensed social evil St. Louis, like many other cities, substituted a "tolerated" district. Under the scheme of "toleration" the entire traffic is illegal and the keepers and inmates of bawdy houses are criminals before the law, but the police, for effective administrative purposes, as they aver, "tolerate" or "wink at" such offenses as are committed within the boundaries of a district which they have set apart for this traffic. . . .

Under the last administration and under the present chief of police the policy of toleration, coupled with strict regulation, was adopted. Today there is one tolerated red light district in St. Louis.

The Fallacy of Segregation

1 | The Failure of Segregation as a Solution of the Social Evil.

Segregation means to isolate, to set apart. It means separation. As applied to the policy of controlling prostitution it has been distorted into meaning toleration and protection of an open "red light district" where vice is supposedly confined. . . .

[It] actually foster[s] . . . this.

2 | Segregation Does Not Segregate.

It is a fact well known to the police and to all social workers that segregation does not segregate, but on the contrary actually increases immorality throughout the entire city.

3 | Conditions Improve After Abolishing Segregated District.

Abolishing the segregated district does not scatter the traffic. It drives it out of the city. Commercialized vice can not live under a policy of continual repression. Its patronage being frightened away, it exists, if at all, in the occasional "street walker" and the "clandestine house" where the inmates are few and where the temptation to the young men of the community is not nearly so great as in an open district operating under police protection.

4 | The "Open House" Worse than the "Clandestine House".

Even if the "clandestine house" were the alternative of closing up the segregated district (which we have shown it is not) it is much to be preferred to the "open house" which does a hundred fold more harm, which invites the uninitiated and uninformed by its open door and which requires fresh young girls every year to increase its patronage and enrich its keepers.

5 | Social Vice is Sapping the Life Blood of Our Civilization.

The segregated district, with its brood of crime and disease, is a standing menace to our civilization. Adultery, murder, theft and blackmail reach out their tentacles from such a district to entrap and destroy our young men, and indirect infection of innocent wives and children from diseases contracted there lower the birth rate and impair the vitality and health of future generations.

6 | Segregation Makes Possible the White Slave Traffic.

The argument which has usually driven the segregationist to surrender is the startling fact now abundantly proven that without a segregated district there would be no white slave traffic. That is, where there are no public houses to be filled with young girls for whose services the keepers enrich themselves by exorbitant charges, there is no market where the white slaver can dispose of the unwary victims of his hellish devices.

7 | What Becomes of the Inmates When a Vice District is Closed?

In no instance has the closing of a district in any city resulted in an epidemic of suicide, and there is no record of a single one perishing in the streets, as frequently predicted by apologizers for present conditions.

. . . Adam Smith in his "Wealth of Nations" has shown that capital and labor flow into profitable and out of unprofitable channels, and the business of prostitution should be made unprofitable so that the ranks of the prostitutes shall not be increased but diminished throughout the country.

8 | Segregation Unjust and Undemocratic.

. . . Our less fortunate neighbors . . . in the crowded portions of the city, with fewer constructive forces for good and with the many destructive and tempting forces of evil, should not have this great social evil "segregated" in their midst to defile their children and to add its poison to the many handicaps upon a clean and decent community life. . . .

9 | Segregation Makes the Citizen who Endorses it Responsible for Its Influence.

There is no escaping the conclusion that the toleration of crime in a certain district is an invitation on the part of the city for the individual to commit that crime in that district and the citizen of any city who endorses such an invitation is responsible for the consequences.

10 | Segregation Corrupts the Police Department.

There is no charge that the St. Louis Police Department or any member thereof is corrupt. But the evidence in other cities where the department has been under investigation discloses the fact that the red light district furnishes a very rich source of graft to patrolmen and even a temptation to officers high up. . . .

11 | The Segregated District a Hotbed of Venereal Diseases.

Leading physicians and surgeons for many years have warned the public that many of the serious operations performed on women and many of the serious diseases of childhood have been due to infection from husbands and fathers who had carelessly transmitted the germs of disease, peculiar to this social evil, to their loved ones at home. While we quarantine against even the simple diseases of children, shall we tolerate this source of wide-spread infection in our midst?

19 | The Proper Functions of the Police Force, 1868

Like the public schools, the police forces of American cities were created to enforce numerous ordinances regulating public behavior as well as to combat more serious crimes. As the previous document revealed, some police cooperated with, rather than suppressed, those who offended public morality. The police issue was complicated by the fact that since officers superintended elections, they often played a crucial role in determining election results. Political factions, therefore, sought to control the police. With the dangers of the Civil War pervasive, in 1861 the Missouri General Assembly followed the lead of New York City in creating a metropolitan police system to combat the threat of the politicization of police. With this act, the St. Louis police force was taken out of the mayor's and City Council's control and was placed instead under the supervision of a Board of Police Commissioners who were appointed by the governor. The mayor of St. Louis sat on this board only as an ex officio member, and the various elected city government officials had no control over the organization. The new state-controlled board did not remove corruption from the police department, as this document indicates. The 1868 investigation reported here was carried out by a Special Committee of the Missouri General Assembly. At the time, the Assembly was largely from one party while city officials were predominantly from another. The investigation thus had a political setting. The document is important for two reasons. First, even though the report is largely a "whitewash," it examines some of the issues involved in the discretionary authority that police necessarily exercise. Second, the report airs a common and continuous complaint: that too few police were available to do an adequate job, and that the court system was too lax on criminals after the police apprehended them. Report of the Joint Committee of the General Assembly Appointed to Investigate the Police Department of the City of St. Louis *(St. Louis, 1868).*

The police force number in all, officers and men, only about two hundred and sixty-seven—a number that to us seems inadequate for the demands of a city of two hundred and forty thousand inhabitants, and with the extended area of the great city of St. Louis. To us it is a wonder that the present force has been so successful in giving security to public and private property, to the lives of citizens and strangers, and to the other varied interests of the city. During the time that we have had an opportunity to observe the conduct and character of the police force, we have been favorably impressed toward its members. We have seen them when called out in companies, and we have visited them on their beats, and the result of our observations has been a conviction of an efficiency that cannot easily be excelled. The Board of Police Commissioners has not only done its duty in the selection of men of integrity and sobriety (having made but a few mistakes), but deserves special approbation for employing such men from the discharged loyal soldiers. It is safe to conclude that the men who resisted rebellion during the late war are proper guards to society now.

Certainly no fraud on the part of the present Board has been detected by us, or cause for suspecting it disclosed, by the examination and the evidence taken. The same remarks apply to the charges of "corruption;" we think that nothing of the kind is fairly suggested by the evidence. However, as the whole evidence is submitted to you, and is before the public, we ask that it be read by those interested. . . .

Beer-Jerking Saloons—Gambling-Houses

In examining the charge made by the Mayor that the Board had failed or neglected to suppress gambling-houses and beer-jerking saloons, we obtained evidence of the existence of only one beer-jerking saloon in the city, and that one was first licensed upon the recommendation of the Mayor; and it further appears from the evidence that . . . it is one of the worst dens in the city, [and] the proprietors have . . . managed to get the advantage of the law. . . . As to gambling-houses, it was shown that frequent raids had been made upon them, and it is admitted by the Mayor that they are pretty effectually suppressed.

"Sunday Law"

It may readily be perceived with what ease distilled liquors may be dealt out at the same bars with beer, and how difficult for policemen to detect the violation of law. By the testimony of Mayor [James] Thomas and others, it was shown that the law has been violated, and it is deplorable that these places of vice occupy so many prominent corners in our great city, but it is not in evidence that the policemen or Police Commissioners ever neglected or refused to enforce the law when informed of its violation.

These are salient points in the charges presented; the failure of proof on the others is as entire as on these, and we believe that a careful analysis of the evidence will satisfy an impartial reader of the accuracy of this statement. The present and past members of the Board, upon whom such grave charges have been made, are gentlemen of high character and standing, and above just suspicion of seeking other than the public good in the discharge of their official functions. Nothing short of positive proof of "corruption" could damage the reputation of these men, and this, we think has not been produced. . . .

In reply to the charges of the Mayor, the Board of Police Commissioners charges that the Mayor has neglected his duty as President of the Board by attending but few sessions of the Board, thereby failing to become acquainted with its action and purposes; by seeking ill of the Department from discharged policemen; by withholding valuable information from the force; by seeking to injure and defame the Police Department instead of aiding it to an efficient discharge of its duties; and by pardoning criminals and vagrants, or granting stays of execution after conviction, thereby returning outlaws upon the citizens; and that the Mayor himself has violated both the laws of the State and of the United States.

We find that thousands have been liberated from the Workhouse by the Mayor in the exercise of the pardoning power, and it is in evidence that some of those liberated are so encouraged as to become impudent and defiant toward the Police Department. This power of the Executive undoubtedly works against the efficiency of the Police Department, and we are of the opinion that it should be limited by further legislative action.

20 | The Organization of the Western Sanitary Commission in St. Louis, 1861

Catastrophes often stimulate important innovations and reforms. The devastating cholera epidemic that St. Louis experienced in 1849, for example, catalyzed the development of hospitals and relief societies, as well as extensions of the water system and installation of the city's first sewer system. The Civil War produced a crisis of a different scale. As this document indicates, although the Northern states had prepared for battle, they had not prepared for casualties from the fighting. The Medical Department of the Army was so ill prepared that it welcomed the assistance of volunteers. In 1861 St. Louisans organized the Western Sanitary Commission. Its first responsibility was to furnish new hospital space for casualties from western battlefields. Under the leadership of James E. Yeatman, a Tennessee-born banker who had immigrated to St. Louis around 1850, the organization carried out its first mandate by fitting out a five-hundred-bed hospital, which not only tended sick and wounded soldiers but also received supplies gathered privately in other parts of the country and distributed them to hospitals in and near St. Louis. During the 1860s, the Western Sanitary Commission became the largest single charitable endeavor in nineteenth-century St. Louis. It raised more than $4,000,000

*during the war decade. The commission soon broadened its re-
sponsibilities from hospitals to caring for all those who were in
distress or need as a result of the war, including freedmen, who
benefited from grants to start schools in order to ease the transition
from slavery to freedom. The initiatives of the war period became
a permanent legacy, as the work of the commission was taken over
by private groups or public agencies. For one brief decade, however, there was widespread community action that was not to be
realized again until the organization of the United Fund-type campaigns in the twentieth century.* Report of the Western Sanitary
Commission on the General Military Hospitals of St. Louis *(St.
Louis, 1862), pp. 3–5.*

The General Military Hospitals of St. Louis, Mo.

The history of the Military Hospitals in St. Louis . . . constitute[s] . . . an important part of the history of the civil war in
Missouri. The whole nation felt that the contest would rage fiercely
in the Border States, and commenced to prepare for the *struggle,*
but did nothing to alleviate the evils which must necessarily ac-
company it. The clash of arms was soon heard in various sections
of the land; sick and wounded combatants were now and then
met with, but no provision was made for their relief. . . .

Post Hospitals were established in different parts of the State,
and General Hospitals in St. Louis. The first opened here was the
General Hospital at the *New House of Refuge,* on the 1st of
August [1861]. It was fitted up in haste, and soon filled beyond its
capacity, chiefly with sick suffering from the severity of climate,
and the diseases incident to camp life. But after the battle at
Wilson's Creek, (August 12th) the wounded began to arrive. All
the available wards in the *St. Louis Sisters* and *City Hospitals*
were taken, and were also soon replete to overflowing.

About that time, the *Western Sanitary Commission* was organized, and duly commissioned by the Commander of the Department, Major-General [John C.] Fremont. This body was to be
auxiliary and advisory to the Medical Director. They were authorized to assist him in organizing and furnishing hospitals, and
to see that the wants of the sick were properly cared for.

The people responded heartily to the frequent appeals of the Western Sanitary Commission for aid, well knowing that the General Government could not have made adequate provisions for this gigantic war. They undertook also the laborious task of hiring suitable nurses for the hospitals: especially were they instrumental in introducing female nurses in them—a system not recognized in the Army and Hospital Regulations of the United States, but which, thanks to the advocacy and influence of that noble philanthropist, Miss [Dorothea] Dix, found favor with the then Secretary of War, Mr. [Simon] Cameron, and was approved by the President.

A wise and a very opportune measure. The inestimable value of woman at the bedside of the sick is universally appreciated. Thousands of our soldiers had never missed the daily greetings of mother, wife, sister or daughter, until this war called them from their midst, and threw them among strangers, but *brothers* united in one holy cause. While in the constant exercise of their military duties, absent woman could only be *remembered* by them, but she was painfully *missed* when they were prostrated on the sick bed, and tended only by comparatively rough male hands.

The women of the land volunteered to emerge from the seclusion of domestic life, in order to perform both a patriotic and a philanthropic work. Thousands of them left their quiet, comfortable homes to follow, tend and nurse those who had willingly offered themselves on the altar of their country. The dangers to which these good women exposed themselves were equal to those of the men in the field, breathing, as they do, the atmosphere in rooms where hundreds of sick and wounded are confined. The extraordinary labors, constant vigils, the anxiety and care for those they have taken under their charge, are exceedingly exhausting. Women-nurses are true heroines. When the one will be remembered for valor in the field, the other will be spoken of for her assiduity, self-sacrificing devotion and unremitting kindness to the sick soldier. It would be difficult to select for praise the most worthy female nurse in our hospitals. They all did well. The surgeons, the soldiers, the whole nation unite in their gratitude to them.

21 | Organizing Charity in the City:
The St. Louis Provident Association, 1863 and 1902

In colonial St. Louis, charity was an individual event, characteristic of small villages and towns. Despite the growth of St. Louis through mid-century, the giving of charity still remained largely an individual transaction. Before 1850, charity was organized or administered by volunteer civic groups or through churches, usually only after some disaster or catastrophe elicited large-scale need. As St. Louis became more industrialized and experienced greater diversity among its inhabitants, those persons engaged in philanthropic activity saw the need to systematize their operations. The St. Louis Provident Association, founded in 1860, was typical of the charitable societies that appeared in cities throughout the United States and Great Britain after mid-century. It was a citywide umbrella organization which had about fifty affiliates, including Catholic parishes, Protestant churches, orphanages, industrial homes, immigrant aid societies, and hospitals. Two beliefs are implicit in the first document from the Provident Association Report for 1863: that most individuals should overcome their difficulties through "self-help," and that poverty and distress were usually the fault of those in difficulty. For these reasons, the Provident Association suggested that charity be dispensed carefully to insure that only the worthy poor received it. These attitudes remained unchanged at the turn of the century, even though charity work was becoming more professionalized and "scientific." This underlying continuity is illustrated by the second document, which reports on the work of the Provident Association at the turn of the century. The essential difference is that formerly trustees or donors personally screened applicants, while modern scientific charity hired professionals to impose standards of suitability. The two reports have wider significance. They illustrate the roots of the modern-day welfare movement: today professionals working for government perform the tasks formerly done privately, then by volunteers, then by professionals hired by volunteers. Moreover, they show the escalation in the number of social problems defined as within the realm of charity. Third Annual Report of the St. Louis Provident Association for the Year 1863 *(St. Louis, 1863), pp. 3–4;* St. Louis Directory of Charitable, Philanthropic and Humane Societies *(St. Louis, 1902), pp. 7–11.*

Statement of Philosophy, 1863

To be poor may or may not be an evil. To some it is a blessing. Many will never be otherwise than poor. Being poor does not necessarily imply the need of receiving fuel or food from the stores of others. Sickness, old age, misfortune, inability to work, or to obtain work, are the only grounds which justify us in helping the poor. To help them at other times, or to help them unwisely then, is to break down that feeling of self-respect which prompts to active exertion for the supply of their own wants, and of those dependent upon them, and which scorns to receive aid from others until compelled by necessity. To break down, in any breast, that feeling of independence and self-respect which God has implanted, is to commit a great wrong against that individual and society. That wrong may be committed by either societies or individuals seeking honestly to help the poor. Against this we cannot be too guarded; but just as great a wrong is it when any fellow man is suffering, or likely to suffer, not to render delicately and wisely needed aid, and in the most judicious form, seeking at the earliest period to place them in the natural position of self-dependence.

There is a large class who have been unable to lay up any of their earnings, and who by honest industry earn their daily bread. Failure of employment, accident, sickness, or other misfortunes, stop the supply in its accustomed channel. For just such cases, needing temporary aid in time of necessity, organizations like ours have been instituted. They were never intended to be the sole means of support to whole families or to single persons, nor to aid the wilfully vicious and indolent. Their object is not by almsgiving to encourage beggary, which so often ends in pauperism; but by judicious and discriminate relief in a time of need, to save families from the degradation of the poor-house or of sending out their children to beg from door to door.

When by experience we find a family that *cannot* be elevated, that manifest a determination to receive permanent help, they cease to be proper subjects for expenditure by an organization like ours, and become proper subjects for the poor-house.

What To Do with Applicants For Charitable Aid, 1902

A long acquaintance with the innumerable schemes that are "worked" on the benevolent public warrants us in saying that it is never advisable to give to unknown persons soliciting alms, money, or aid of any kind, without an investigation of their affairs. . . . If you cannot make this investigation yourself let the Provident Association do it for you. If you will refer such cases to the association it will undertake to relieve immediate and apparent needs and make you a prompt written report on the case. . . . Applicants should, wherever possible, be sent directly to the Central Office. . . . If this course seems unadvisable, communicate with the association by telephone or by mail. Immediate information can usually be given. *Names and addresses are of importance. . . .* There are many cases where enough is known of the circumstances to warrant relief. We enumerate below some of these, offering suggestions as to the best method of treating such cases.

SICKNESS.—WHERE HOSPITAL TREATMENT IS NECESSARY. If it is a case of injury by accident, or otherwise, proper for the City's care, telephone to the Health Department or City Dispensary.

Provident Association visiting nurses are subject to call for emergency aid in providing doctors and temporary care for the indigent, and may be reached by telephone to Central Office.

BURIALS.—The City Health Department provides for the burial of poor persons who are not able to pay funeral expenses. If the family has any church connections aid can often be obtained by consulting the pastor. Reasonable prices for funeral expenses can be obtained from a number of reputable undertakers. The Provident Association does not undertake burials, but can often give advice which will save expense. Below we give minimum prices which may be obtained in cases of poor persons.

	For an Adult	*For a Child*
Coffin	$10.00	$ 5.00
Carriages, each	5.00	5.00
Ambulance (in lieu of hearse)	5.00	5.00
Hearse	10.00	10.00
Grave	5.00	3.00
Box	5.00	3.00
Sending box to cemetery	2.50	2.50

POOR HOUSE CASES.—The City provides maintenance at the Poorhouse for residents who are unable, by reason of old age, or other infirmity, to make a living and have no means of support. Permits are granted by the Health Department at Old City Hall, 11th & Market streets, where applications should be made.

INSANE PERSONS.—The indigent insane are also provided for by the City at the Insane Asylum. Application should be made to the Health Department, as above.

The City provides no "out-door" relief, or relief in the homes. Its aid is limited to inmates of the public institutions and medical treatment at its three dispensaries, which latter are located as follows: Main Dispensary, 11th & Market streets. Branch No. 1, 3618 N. Broadway. Branch No. 2, 3562 S. Broadway.

HOMELESS MEN.—If these apply after night, asking the "price of a bed," send them with a reference card to the Provident Association. Twilight or night applicants are always to be suspected. "Saturday afternoon" cases are often found to be fraudulent. It is at these times that professionals make their most urgent appeals and reap their greatest harvest. Few persons who deserve aid will defer their applications till after night. The association doors are open every week day from 8 to 6 o'clock.

APPLICANTS FOR CLOTHING can also be referred to same office. In proper cases of able-bodied men a work-test is required, and in other cases relief is given as the circumstances seem to require. Special attention is given to children that should attend school. Much of the clothing given to applicants at private residences finds its way immediately to the second-hand or pawn shops for drink-money, while the applicant still holds onto his rags.

CHILD BEGGARS should always be investigated and the Provident Association will take great pains to prevent the use of children for such purposes. Always consult with the association by telephone or get names and residences and send them to Central Office. The demoralizing effects of child-begging are serious and far-reaching, encouraging idleness in the parents, depriving children of school privileges and educating them to mendicancy.

Other cases, not enumerated above, of whatever kind, may be referred to the Provident Association with a confidence that they will receive prompt and necessary attention.

22 | Causes of Disease: A Report on Public Health, 1885

A prime motivation for improving the quality of life in St. Louis stemmed from the public health movement. Investigations of urban sanitary conditions, combined with the fear generated by periodic epidemics, alerted the public to the many health hazards that confronted them. In St. Louis, these investigations resulted in the creation of an active municipal health department after the 1876 charter gave the agency greater powers. Beginning with the task of cleaning up household water, successive health commissioners worked for the filling in of ponds; effective refuse removal; the paving of streets; a systematic and careful inspection of dairies, meatpackers, and ice venders; and rigid enforcement of laws dealing with sanitary problems. In the process, the city developed a new bureaucracy which, through an enlargement of traditional municipal police powers, worked to eliminate the odors and unsightliness that were the norm in cities for centuries. This document, a paper presented by Dr. Robert Luedeking, who served as clerk of the St. Louis Board of Health, to the American Public Health Association for 1885, assesses the overall sanitary conditions in the city. Robert Luedeking, "The Chief Local Factors in the Causation of Disease and Death," in George Homan, ed., A Sanitary Survey of St. Louis. *Reprinted from the* Transactions of the American Public Health Association, Vol. X, for the St. Louis Local Committee *(Concord, N.H., 1885), pp. 35–37.*

One of the most striking peculiarities of the city of St. Louis is the large area over which its population is distributed. . . . In the year 1883 the density was computed at 9.8 persons to the acre, the greatest density being 90 persons to the acre in the tenth ward, and 0.2 persons to the acre in the twenty-fifth ward.

This is indeed a low density compared with that of most metropolitan cities: that of London, for instance, is given at 52.5 to the acre in 1883. And yet we find the annual rate of mortality per thousand in London in 1883 to have been but 20.4, while that of St. Louis was 21.35. With such a variance existing in the relative densities, and a rate of death in favor of the city of greater density, it must needs force itself upon our conviction that inherent faults in our sanitation must be the cause. On scrutinizing the table of the distribution of our mortality in 1883 by wards, . . . we find that the lowest rate of 17 per thousand is found in the second ward, with a density of 65 persons to the acre, and that the highest mortality prevails in the twenty-first ward, being 26 per thousand, with a density of four persons to the acre.

In this twenty-first ward having the highest mortality, we have an area of 1,012 acres; and reference to the sewer and water-pipe map shows that not more than half a dozen blocks are sewered and supplied with water, while, on the other hand, in the second ward, 233.8 acres is perfectly drained and supplied with water; and yet this ward, together with the fourth, tenth, twelfth, and fourteenth wards, contains the greatest number of tenement houses and habitations of the poor. Each and every block of the territory mentioned, however, is supplied with an abundance of water from the municipal water-works, and nearly every house is connected with a district, private, or public sewer. The result is most striking in that the rate of mortality does not exceed the average, in fact is but 21.2, while the density is 75 to the acre. This very striking contrast demonstrates beyond question the utility of a perfect drainage and water-supply in lowering the mortality of large cities.

[Our figures] show the sanitary disadvantages of the thinly populated districts without sewerage and water-supply, as against the densely populated districts that are well provided for in this regard. Low, marshy ground along the river bank, and some of the western districts that abound in ponds and sink-holes, have high mortalities. . . .

A most potent factor in the causation of sickness and death is to be found in the slight efforts put forth by the city of St. Louis in the direction of preventive measures.

The health commissioner, only in the past summer, with cholera prevalent in southern Europe, was by the municipal assembly refused the paltry sum of $15,000 to defray the expenses of a complete house to house investigation of the city. Yet a work of this character has never been done in our city, and once done might have made the basis of preventive operative measures for years to come. . . . As it is, our health department today presents the anomaly of being without a corps of sanitary inspectors.

And in many other regards St. Louis has reason to be ashamed of its neglect of precautions and safeguards that every civilized community should observe. Notwithstanding that our milk-supply is notoriously bad, and that adulterations of food are common, there is no provision whatsoever in our charter or ordinances for a chemist, or for a corps of inspectors of milk or meat and other provisions. Our public markets should be specifically regulated by ordinance, and a systematic supervision by a competent officer is imperative.

Another most glaring defect in our legislation is the absence of a law governing plumbing, and providing for competent inspection of our house drainage. In the Eastern cities private corporations undertake to make intelligent and competent inspection, at given intervals, of the plumbing, drainage, heating apparatus, and ventilation of private dwellings for moderate compensation. We in St. Louis do not, so far, enjoy the satisfaction of such a necessary luxury.

Further sanitary measures of a preventive nature, that are poorly provided for, is our system of street and alley cleaning. Only a pittance is allowed for this most important work. The failure to provide amply no doubt costs many a life. Our method of removal of refuse and garbage, and the removal and disposition of dead animals, should be extended, improved, in fact entirely changed.

All of these points are intended to convey the fact that in point of public sanitation much must be done in St. Louis.

Our control of cow and other stables, of rendering establishments, and other offensive trades, is insufficient. In fact, the whole *modus operandi* for the abatement of nuisances, even the simple and every-day kind, is too cumbrous and clumsy. If an offender be refractory, it takes a month to remove a *bona fide* abominable nuisance.

The management of contagious diseases is pretty well provided for. At any rate, notification of all cases is demanded; and exclusion of all children, that may convey contagion, from the public schools is practised.

In summing up, I desire, therefore, to state emphatically that the chief factor in the causation of disease and death in St. Louis is the disregard of nearly all those measures that have been so ably and eloquently advocated . . . by the members of this association. It is to be hoped that the citizens of St. Louis will become aroused to the incalculable benefits to be derived from the ounce of prevention. No representatives should be chosen to the municipal assembly but such as have learned that all things municipal should be made subservient to that greatest factor in the promotion of welfare, the *public health.*

23 | Trying to Clean Up Smoky St. Louis, 1895

St. Louis had a "smoke problem" which dated from the 1820s, when the local government allowed fire clay kilns to dry brick in newly developing residential areas. As population and industrialization increased in the city, the smoke grew thicker. While mid-nineteenth-century St. Louisans knew little about the scientific aspects of smoke, they recognized that it was dirty and smelled bad. By the latter part of the century, the darkness of a smoky skyline conjured up two opposite images for city residents: it was a symbol of economic prosperity but it also was a filthy nuisance. St. Louis' first response to smoke was to try to let the winds blow it away; hence, in 1867, the city passed an ordinance requiring that smokestacks be at least twenty feet higher than adjoining buildings.

In 1876, the Engineers' Club of St. Louis, the largest professional society of its kind in any American city, began a systematic investigation of the smoke problem and explored means for its abatement. The work of this organization bore fruit in 1892 with the enactment of an ordinance declaring the emission of "black smoke" (a very untechnical definition of what constituted pollution) as a public nuisance. With the cooperation of industry and the education of the public, the St. Louis smoke cloud was reduced by about 75 percent over the next few years. Some companies refused to comply, however, and succeeded in having the ordinance overturned by the courts. New legislation was passed in 1901, but as this document illustrates, the Civic League's campaign was doomed to failure for three reasons: first, St. Louis' most readily available and cheapest form of energy was soft, heavy-sulphur-content coal; second, the press for production during World War I encouraged a reneging on the abatement program; and third, the fin de siècle *generation lacked sufficient scientific knowledge about the constituent elements in air pollution,*

*the economical methods for diminishing smoke, and the connec-
tion between smoke and sickness. Thus, despite much turn-of-the
century agitation, of which this 1906 report by the Civic League
is one part, St. Louisans continued to suffer under an oppressive
pall of smoke until more effective reforms were instituted during
the 1940s. The Civic League of St. Louis,* The Smoke Nuisance;
Report of the Smoke Abatement Committee of the Civic League
(St. Louis, 1906), pp. 4–10.

To the Executive Board, The Civic League of St. Louis:
[*From the Smoke Study Committee*]

Injurious Effects of Smoke

The damage which smoke inflicts on this community every year
is not merely sentimental and aesthetic. While the actual money
loss cannot be calculated, the destruction of merchandise, the
defacement of buildings, the tarnishing of metals, the injury to
plant life, the greatly increased labor and cost of housekeeping,
and the deterrent effect which smoke has on well-to-do families
who are seeking desirable homes, express losses which amount into
the hundreds of thousands of dollars annually.

Merchants everywhere must add a considerable sum to their
expense account because of the deteriorating effects on all kinds
of merchandise of smoke and soot.

A leading retail merchant . . . [states]:

". . . It costs twice as much to keep a store clean in St. Louis
as it would in an eastern city. Our porter and cleaning bill runs
about $17,000.00 a year and much of it would be unnecessary
were it not for the extra dirt due to smoke. This sum would be a
direct loss even if merchandise were preserved undamaged."

A book and stationery company says:

"We would say that in our opinion a very conservative estimate
of the damages due to smoke would be $10,000.00 annually. We
employ three boys whose sole duty it is to keep the stock clean
and they are kept busy continually brushing off dust caused by
smoke."

The Librarian of the Public Library estimates the damages by
smoke to the books belonging to the public at $10,000.00 an-
nually.

Damage to Plant Life

The enormous damage to trees and shrubbery is evident even to the most casual observer. Only hardy and smooth leaved trees will grow on our streets. The Director of the Missouri Botanical Gardens, Dr. Wm. Trelease, was asked to furnish the committee with a statement showing the effects of smoke on plants and trees.

Dr. Trelease says:

"The smoke nuisance is a very serious one to us. . . . We can no longer grow the evergreen conifers, with the exception of the Dwarf Junipers and the Austrian Pine. It is not possible to cut a flowering branch from a Spiraea or Crab without having one's hands made filthy by the operation. While we grow a good many roses, it is only the hardiest that stand the present smoke, and varieties that are beautifully grown only a short distance from St. Louis are impossible in the city."

History of Smoke Abatement in St. Louis

. . . From the time the city became a manufacturing center of importance to the present day the problem of smoke abatement has been under discussion. Years ago the Engineers' Club appointed a standing committee on this subject which made frequent reports to the Club. . . . In 1891 Mayor [Edward A.] Noonan appointed a committee. . . .—all members of the Engineers' Club —to investigate local conditions and make recommendations looking to an abatement of the nuisance. As a result of their exhaustive investigation two ordinances were passed by the Municipal Assembly—one declaring smoke to be a nuisance, the other providing for the establishment of a Smoke Abatement Commission which should canvass the whole situation, make tests of smoke preventing devices and suggest practical methods for solving the problem.

The First Ordinances Invalid

At about the same time the Citizens' Smoke Abatement Association was formed, which later became the Smoke Abatement Committee of the Civic League. The association and the expert commission worked in close harmony in the effort to arouse public sentiment in favor of smoke abatement. Many manufacturers and owners of smoke making plants indicated an entire willingness to comply with the ordinance to equip their plants with effective smoke appliances. But when the attempt was made to enforce the law against the recalcitrant smoke makers, the validity of the ordinance was tested before the courts, and in the well known Heitzberg case, the Supreme Court of the State in 1896 declared the ordinance invalid on the ground that the municipal legislature had exceeded its authority in declaring smoke a nuisance *per se*. This decision made it necessary to prove in each case that the particular smoke complained of had caused special and individual damage. The difficulty of proving damages in each case practically nullified the ordinance. Early in 1901 the Citizens' Smoke Abatement Association prepared the draft of an act to be introduced into the State Legislature giving to cities of over 100,000 inhabitants the right to declare smoke a nuisance and to provide for its regulation. This act was finally passed and became a law, but with an undesirable proviso which gave the offender the chance to escape a fine if he could "show to the satisfaction of the jury, or Court trying the facts, that there is no known practicable device, appliance, means or method by application of which to his building, establishment or premises, the emission or discharge of the dense smoke complained of in that proceeding could have been prevented."

. . . The present ordinances of the city . . . prohibit the discharge of dense smoke from any building, establishment, or premises (including brick kilns), steamboats, tugs or other water crafts, or from any locomotive engine; and give the chief smoke inspector and his deputies all the necessary authority to enter buildings and premises in the discharge of their duties. These ordinances have now been in effect four years and their validity affirmed by the highest court in the State. The city has had in its employ a chief smoke inspector and five deputies for four years and has spent more than $35,000.00 in the maintenance of the smoke abatement department.

In view of all of this agitation, education, legislation, and the expenditure of so considerable a sum of the city revenues, it is not strange that the people are clamoring for results and a more marked abatement of this nuisance.

Kinds of Fuel Used in St. Louis

. . . It is obvious that soft coal is and must continue to be the chief fuel of this city. Within a radius of fifty to one hundred miles to the east in Illinois are vast deposits of bituminous coal. Nine miles east of St. Louis, coal of a good quality is found and large mines are in operation. Along the lines of fourteen railroads within a radius of fifty miles are located more than one hundred mines with shafts tapping deposits of vast extent. Soft coal of a good quality for manufacturing purposes is delivered in car load lots by contract to the plants for $1.55 to $1.90; while hard coal of a relatively equal quality delivered to a few plants costs by contract $7.60 to $7.85 per ton. Soft coal is retailed at $3.50, while hard coal is retailed at $8.50.

But in spite of these conditions and facts; namely, the large and increasing number of manufacturing plants, the rapid increase in number of buildings of all kinds and the necessity of using a smoke producing coal, the abatement of the smoke to a minimum is entirely possible as shown by a score of boiler plants in actual operation in this city, by the experience of other cities, and by the statements of able scientists based upon the physical laws governing proper combustion of fuels.

24 | St. Louisans Try to Beat the Tenement, 1908

Investigations of the city's sanitary conditions inevitably focused on the environment in which the poor lived. Reformers, therefore, moved naturally from cleaning the water and air to eliminating or reforming tenements, the cheap multiple-unit housing of the poor. Although the slums of St. Louis were not as crowded as those of New York City's Lower East Side, they were nevertheless a civic problem. The Civic League, which was active in most early-twentieth-century campaigns to clean up the city, whether physically, socially, or politically, led in tenement reform. In 1908, the famed reformer and muckraker Jacob A. Riis, who had been making war on tenements in New York City for nearly three decades, examined the housing of St. Louis' poor by commenting on the Civic League's Tenement House Report and its plans to overcome the evils of poor housing. The solution that the St. Louis group proposed—the building of cheap model tene-

*ments with low rent—unfortunately was based on a number of
misconceptions. The Civic League and Riis held a simplistic be-
lief in common—that tenements continued to exist because land-
lords charged exorbitant rents to make even more outrageous
profits. In fact, the tenement was a far more complex problem. It
was a building exploited by both landlord and tenant. The landlord wanted large profits and usually made the most minimal of
repairs. Under most local taxation policies, however, to make
any improvements meant that the value of his investment would
increase, and he would be charged higher taxes. He, therefore,
would have to charge higher rents. The tenants of the slum dwellings, meanwhile, also exploited the building. They overcrowded
their dwelling units in order to pay their rent; some did this to
maintain subsistence, while others accepted tenement life in order
to accumulate savings so they could move from the slum district.
Exploitation of a tenement building was a factor in more than one
family's move to the middle class. Jacob A. Riis, "The Plight of
St. Louis,"* Charities and Commons, *XX (1908), pp. 213–16.*

Hear the report of the housing committee of the Civic League,
just made. It deals with that district between Seventh and Fourteenth streets, Lucas avenue and O'Fallon street, comprising
forty-eight blocks, where the poor live in neglected rear tenements,
sometimes two, and in one case three, upon the lot beside the front
house:

> The lower rooms of these houses might, for all the sunlight they
> receive be at the bottom of a well. . . . Dilapidation, misery and
> dirt reach their depths in the rear buildings. The people who live
> in them are poorer, more sickly, less cleanly and generally of lower
> standard in every way than those who live in the front.

. . . The slum in St. Louis does not rear itself in many storied
tenements as it does in New York. It hugs the soil closer, seldom
rising over two, or at most three stories. The typical house is the
old one-family dwelling which has been made over into a tenement in its decrepit old age and now houses three or four times
the people it was built to shelter. . . . The old houses are still the
worst, being wholly unfit for the purpose to which they have been
put, and those from which imminent danger always threatens, for

no winter passes without an attempt in the legislature to withdraw them from under the tenement house law. There is a bill there now to that effect. Eternal vigilance is still the price of liberty. In St. Louis there are yards and, at first glimpse, air and sunlight in plenty; and back alleys between the streets, intended for the decent removal of refuse, I suppose, but landlord greed has packed the yards with frame tenements, of the kind to which "no repairs are ever made;" the alleys have become streets where the people and the largest rats I ever saw burrow together in the filth, overflowing into dark cellar and basement rooms of which, the committee declares, from forty to sixty percent would be declared nuisances under any health law. Nearly half of the six hundred and odd yards inspected were drained wholly by surface drainage. Over half of the yards were marked "dirty," "very dirty," or "filthy." Here is a picture:

> Life would be easier for the people crowded together in these closely packed yards and alleys, if they could get rid of the rubbish and refuse. The methods of getting rid of them begin half with yard fights, especially, of course, among the women, and the whole yard combines in fighting the "garbage gentlemen." And what to put the garbage in? Buckets, baskets, pans, piano boxes, bureau drawers, wash-tubs, hat boxes, trunks, baby carriages, anything of any material, size and shape. Of course everything leaks, and what of the contents does not fall out is dragged out and fought over by stray dogs and fierce cats and the immense rats that come out of the sewers.

"They eat the cats," adds the report. I don't doubt it. As a matter of fact I saw very few cats there.

That in 280 rear buildings, housing 2,479 persons, only one bath tub was found—that in the house of a landlord—is hardly surprising. We could do worse in New York and did in the old days. Out of 13,233 persons, the report shows that 96.26 percent had no chance to bathe. The hydrant in the yard was the only water supply.

If in the winter it is frozen, so what are the people to do?

"The children's clothes have all been sewed on for the winter, and a washing of the visible parts is all the school authorities require." I suppose there are people who, reading this, will turn up their noses at "the great unwashed," and dismiss the matter with the verdict that they won't keep clean. . . .

Things enough are suggested by the housing committee's report to set a town less wide awake than St. Louis to thinking. Poking about among the alleys I saw piles of banana stalks, bakers' tools and supplies, and other things that spoke of home work. And this was what the report said under that head:

> The most immediately deadly thing connected with the home industries in St. Louis is the dirt that is poured, baked and frozen into the food-stuffs manufactured in the dwelling houses. It is difficult to imagine the dirt in which wholesale and retail milk, butter and ice cream businesses are carried on. The milk is kept in damp cellars, the floors muddy from spilled milk and the water dripping from the iceboxes. These boxes are never aired—seldom drained, and are unbelievably unclean. Milk can be bought, late in the day, sometimes at three cents a quart. This does not sour either,—in the regular way—by next morning. It seems somehow to rot, if that is possible. The bakeries are in the cellars and alley houses are beyond description.

Mostly, says the report, when an old woman lives in such a cellar or basement, she takes in washing, and asks pertinently, "Yours?" The question ought to sink in. . . .

After this to find a family of three in O'Fallon street sharing their two rooms with two women and twelve men lodgers, and two rooms in another street housing sixteen sleepers by night is not surprising, to me at all events, for I heard of such things in Los Angeles where, of all places, I did not expect it; and then, St. Louis has no law definitely regulating tenement house crowding, it appears. . . .

The people of St. Louis,—for so I identify the real backing of the Civic League, ask many things to make their city what its founder dreamed it would one day be. They ask first, and justly, for laws which shall set a barrier against the slum and enable them to fight their battle to win. They ask from the state legislature these powers: To close houses unfit to live in; to limit the space a tenement may occupy on the lot to sixty-five per cent of it; to abolish cesspools and interior dark rooms, one as bad as the other; to exact 600 cubic feet of air space for each sleeper in a tenement; to compel the lighting of dark hallways; to prohibit bakeries, butcher shops, sweat shops, etc., from stables and tenements. This is all elementary sanitation and it is not to be doubted that every demand will be granted, now that the city no longer is "suffering from a lack of definite information as to its living conditions," or the state either. What is set forth in the housing committee's report is sufficiently definite on every point, and certainly the Civic League has shown cause why St. Louis should bestir itself with all speed. And here upon my table, just brought in by the postman, lies the evidence that it is about to bestir itself, in the shape of the St. Louis Tenement House Association's prospectus. "Tenement House Association" has not the sweetest of sounds, but there are two points about this one that take the sting out: the first that it advertises its proposed work as "investment philanthropy," and backs up the statement with the declaration that dividends to its stockholders shall never exceed two per cent, all the rest of its earnings being set aside for the extension of its work, which is good and quite compatible with low rents and all improvements in St. Louis as elsewhere. For in its essence the whole tenement house question resolves itself into one of what you will take. If five per cent, there is no tenement house question, and the slum is beaten; if twenty-five, then both loom large.

The second point in favor of the Tenement House Association is that Dr. William Taussig, who is truly the embodiment of all good citizenship and civic virtue in his city, as he has been these many years, is its president. His eighty odd years sit lightly upon him because they have been filled with good works. . . . I have word from him that the association, which proposes to invest $300,000 in its initial venture at giving the wage workers "at low rents, clean, healthy rooms and a high standard of living accommodations," has recently reorganized its board and resolved to go ahead energetically as soon as the financial conditions improve. So, upon the solid basis of an awakened civic conscience and of a rescued home, the city of Pierre Laclède Ligueste can move on hopefully toward the proud destiny he prophesied for it.

25 | An Invitation to Move to the Suburbs, 1866

During the 1850s, thousands of acres of land, both contiguous

*to the built-up area and far removed from it, had been subdivided
in anticipation of a burgeoning suburban movement in the next
decade. The physical expansion of the city was retarded during
the Civil War years, but it picked up after 1865. After subdivision,
a lag of several years often occurred before a settlement company took over the project and promoted its development. The
advertisement presented in this document for the Mont Cabanne
addition is typical of nineteenth-century suburban merchandising.
At the time Mont Cabanne was opened, it was beyond the city
boundaries, but it was laid out in anticipation of the city's further
expansion. In 1876, this subdivision would be brought under St.
Louis' political jurisdiction. Meanwhile, this advertisement remains an excellent example demonstrating the range of amenities
offered by mid-nineteenth-century subdividers to attract upper-
class residents away from locations closer to the city center.* The
"St. Louis West-End Improvement Company," Organized December 22nd, 1866 *(St. Louis, 1867).*

THE SAINT LOUIS WEST-END IMPROVEMENT COMPANY has
purchased at "MONT CABANNE," over twelve hundred building
lots, fronting more than six miles, on avenues from eighty to one
hundred and sixty feet in width, running east and west, with north
and south avenues eighty feet wide.

This extensive and valuable property is bounded on the east
by King's Highway, on the south by Olive street, on the west by
Union Avenue, and on the north by the estate of James H. Lucas,
to the St. Charles Rock Road, on which avenue the horse cars
are running (to within half a mile of Mont Cabanne) in connection
with the Franklin Avenue cars.

This suburb, directly west of the centre of St. Louis, within
five miles of the court house, is located in a neighborhood remark-
ably free from fevers and epidemics and all nuisances so common
in the southern and northern suburbs of the city.

It is elevated over one hundred feet above the Mississippi river,
commanding beautiful and extensive views of the city and the
surrounding country.

The general level of the plat is from thirty to thirty-five feet
above the stream that passes through the western half of the
grounds, with a rapid descent, into the river Des Peres, half a

mile to the south of "Mont Cabanne," affording unusual advantage for a thorough and perfect system of drainage, so important to the health and comfort of the inhabitants of a town or city, and which cannot be too highly prized, especially in seasons of epidemics. . . .

[From] the well known "Cabanne spring," on this property, flows an abundance of pure sand-rock water to supply a large population. A suitable tower, with a reservoir will be erected early next spring, with machinery to give this water a head of over fifty feet above the highest part of the plat, with suitable pipes for its distribution into the buildings erected early in the season, into their upper stories. The value of pure water and the danger of using impure water from hydrants, wells or cisterns in large cities, is too apparent to need illustration.

It is also proposed to erect gas works the coming summer, to light the streets and buildings, also to grade the avenues and make sidewalks, plant shade trees and lay down sewers and culverts for drainage, and include the whole cost of these improvements in the price of lots, leaving only the ordinary county and State taxes to be paid by the purchaser. An efficient police force and fire department will also be provided by the Company, free of expense to the inhabitants, until Mont Cabanne becomes a portion of the city.

The erection of convenient and comfortable dwellings, for sale or rent, on moderate terms, providing a meat and vegetable market and a provision store, depots for building materials and for fuel, at a small advance upon the wholesale price will be a marked and novel feature in this new enterprise, and will remove many of the objections so common to suburban towns without these advantages. It will have unusual suburban facilities, in the frequent and rapid communication with the city, by cars drawn by locomotive power, on the "ST. LOUIS WEST-END RAIL ROAD," the stock of which road, ($50,000) was subscribed last month by responsible parties, and is now located from Grand Avenue to Union Avenue, between Olive street and the St. Charles Rock Road, and the right of way for an independent track—to be fenced on both sides, with cattle guards at the street crossings—is nearly secured for the whole distance.

A contract has been made between the Rail Road Company and this Company, for the accommodation of persons on the route and those residing at Mont Cabanne and its immediate vicinity.

In short, every improvement that capital, skill and experience can command will be introduced to make this suburb a desirable home, including the early introduction of churches, universities, colleges, schools, libraries and reading rooms. A post office and telegraph line will be established as early as July, 1867.

An offer of twenty arpen[t]s of land at "MONT CABANNE," has been made for the site of the "ST. LOUIS CENTRAL UNIVERSITY," and was accepted by the Board of Trustees last month. . . .

. . . Can there be a doubt in the mind of any intelligent and observing citizen of St. Louis, that an enterprise of this character, rightly inaugurated, skillfully projected and energetically carried forward under a joint stock association, with ample capital, faithfully and prudently expended, must soon create a first class suburban town, yielding satisfactory dividends to its share holders and contributing greatly to the comfort of its citizens, and the rapid growth of the city.

26 | Private Places in St. Louis

While St. Louisans fared no better in eliminating slums than residents of other cities, they developed a unique residential design at the upper end of the economic spectrum. That solution was the "private place." While the idea was attempted in the city before the Civil War, it did not reach its full articulation until later. The "places" were designed as exclusive residential areas. They featured elaborate gates which could be opened and closed by a watchman. These gates had a twofold purpose: they discouraged through traffic and they symbolized elegant privacy. In order to build in one of the places or purchase a home there, an owner had to sign a restrictive deed which required membership in an association of homeowners and the erection and maintenance of a house in conformity with the high-class standards of the enclave. The associations also made regular assessments for the maintenance in common of trees, park strips, gates, and the watchman's salary. In addition, the association usually maintained the streets and streetlights. When first built, the places were away from the contiguous, built-up area of the expanding city, but their chief design features anticipated the outward movement. The technique worked well, and most of the private places, now special island communities surrounded by usually inferior types of urban development, not only continue to exist, but remain an attractive alternative for families who otherwise probably would choose suburban living. John Noyes, "The 'Places' of St. Louis," The American City, XII (March 1915), pp. 206–8.

OUT-OF-TOWN visitors to St. Louis are probably more impressed with the beauty of the homes and the residential sections of the city than with any other thing. If they are of an enthusiastic nature, and particularly beauty-loving, they usually go into raptures when passing through some of the more finished "Places," where many of the best homes are to be found. Vandeventer Place, Westmoreland Place and Portland Place seem to impress the visitor most of all. If the visitor has traveled over the country much, he doubtless wonders why a scheme so simple and practical, and yet so rare, should not have been adopted in other cities long ago.

The first "Place" of any importance was Vandeventer, laid out some forty years ago by Mr. Julius Pitzman, the originator of the idea. Mr. Pitzman, familiar with the success of Baron Haussmann in Paris, and the resulting attractiveness of the streets where building restrictions had been imposed, was fired with a resolve to give St. Louis one at least that would be the equal of any residential street in the country. His idea became so popular that it was not long before he was engaged to lay out many other "Places" throughout the city. Portland Place, Westmoreland Place and Flora Boulevard, mentioned elsewhere in this article, were all laid out by Mr. Pitzman.

To-day there are dozens of them of one sort or another in this city. Some are nothing less than good-sized subdivisions of several streets, similar to the subdivisions of Cleveland, New York, Boston and other cities. Vandeventer, Portland and Westmoreland Places are simply straight, single streets, and to my mind it is only to such as these that the name "Place" should be applied. . . . Flora Boulevard (for homes costing $4,000 or more) was laid out as an approach to the main gate of the Missouri Botanical Garden, hence the name "Boulevard."

The cooling breezes in summer are mainly from the south in

St. Louis, making the lots that run north and south, and the streets that run east and west, the popular ones for residences. So it is that these "Places" run east and west, almost without exception. They are usually several blocks in length, with the intersecting north and south streets left out wherever possible, thus leaving them nearly intact their entire length. The different "Places" vary in width, but are essentially the same in plan, the avenue between the north and south row of lots being divided into a central parking, with a roadway, a turf strip and sidewalk on either side. Flora Boulevard has a central parking 50 feet in width, with a 28-foot roadway, a 6-foot turf strip and a 6-foot sidewalk on either side. The lots are about 150 feet in depth, with a frontage of not less than 50 feet in any case.

The "Places," as a rule, are well planted. The turf strip is usually occupied by a row of trees, and the central parking has similar rows in keeping with those on the turf strip. Informal beds of shrubbery and perennials are also planted on the central parking, and in some of the "Places" an occasional formal garden, a fountain or a piece of statuary is found, lending an added interest and a variety to what otherwise might be a monotonous repetition. The grounds about the homes are usually planted in accordance with the general planting scheme.

The residences in the better class "Place" are, almost without exception, beautiful, and although there is a great variety in the architectural styles used, the ensemble is very pleasing, especially in combination with the foliage.

One of the most distinctive features of those that are privately owned is the gateways marking the entrances. They are altogether in keeping with the spirit of the "Place," usually very attractive and dignified, and strongly impress the visitor with the privacy of the territory within.

The building restrictions for the different types of course vary considerably in detail. In the true "Place," private, one-family residences only are allowed, with a stable, garage or outhouse, if of fitting design, and only one residence to each lot is permitted. A building line of usually not less than 25 feet from sidewalk edge is enforced. There is, of course, a minimum cost limit on the residence.

It must indeed be a pleasure to live in these "Places" if one must live in the city. It is certainly a great pleasure to ride or walk through them, a fact that most of the beauty-loving citizens of St. Louis recognize.

27 | Forest Park, 1875

St. Louis was slow to begin a public parks movement. Since the countryside was so close, parks were intentionally neglected until the 1840s. Then St. Louis officials began to secure land for open space and improve it. By the mid 1870s, St. Louis had nearly 2,700 acres of parkland ˎacquired either through donations by public-spirited individuals or through purchase. These areas ranged in size from Gamble Place, with little more than an acre, to Forest Park, which, with nearly 1,400 acres, was one of the largest urban nature preserves in the country. In the 1870s, Tower Grove was the most heavily used park, with 277 magnificently landscaped acres and eight miles of drives. Forest Park, however, would have the greatest long-term significance for the city. Between 1870 and 1874, a fierce fight raged over its acquisition. Since it was not connected to the city either by horsecar lines or by paved roads, it was inaccessible to most citizens. Some, therefore, argued that only the wealthy would benefit by the nearly one-and-a-half-million-dollar expenditure necessary for its purchase and development. Another criticism concerned the amount of open space already existent in St. Louis: until World War I, St. Louis had sufficient greenery to necessitate maintenance of a city forestry service. From today's perspective, the criticisms were shortsighted, for Forest Park now not only provides excellent recreational possibilities, but houses major civic, cultural, and educational facilities. This document, written by one of the city's major boosters, gives a sense of how distant and distinctive the area four miles from the downtown was a century ago. L. U. Reavis, Saint Louis: The Future Great City of the World *(St. Louis: Gray, Baker and Co., 1875), pp. viii–xiii.*

Forest Park lies immediately west of the center of the city, in the direct line of its greatest growth and progress, and in full view of the elegant mansions of its wealthiest citizens. To Hiram W. Leffingwell [an important, early real estate dealer] the city of St. Louis is indebted for the conception of her grand park. He first proposed a park containing about three thousand acres of land, lying in the same general direction from the city as Forest Park. His plan was in advance of the wants, condition and population of St. Louis, but it was afterward modified so as to embrace only the present boundaries of the park. A bill for its establishment was prepared, passed by the Legislature, and approved March 25, 1872. Some of the property owners resisted the act, and upon appeal to the Supreme Court of the State, it was declared to be unconstitutional. Mr. Leffingwell still earnestly advocated the enterprise, and in January 1874, at a meeting of the friends of Forest Park, Andrew McKinley was requested to take charge of the new bill, and attempt to pass it through the Legislature. . . .

Forest Park is the center of the grand system of the parks of St. Louis and lies four miles west of the Court-house. It is far larger than any other. Lindell Boulevard and Forest Park Boulevard, each about two miles in length, the former one hundred and ninety-four feet, and the latter one hundred and fifty feet wide, are parallel to each other, and lead directly from the park to the heart of the city. Four grand boulevards bound the park on the north, east, south and west, the narrowest of which is one hundred and twenty feet wide. The "Boulevard Bill," passed by the Legislature at the session of 1875, provided for connections with the other parks. With as much natural beauty as distinguishes any portion of St. Louis county, the grounds are especially adapted, by rare and manifold advantages, to minister to the enjoyment and recreation of the denizens of a great city.

An area of the Park, of at least eleven hundred acres in extent, is covered by the original forest, and hence the title by which it is designated. Black, white, post and water oak, gum and horse chestnut, blackberry, elm, butternut, ash and tulip trees are found in great quantity, and are the principal trees of large size; while among the smaller growth is found the red-bud and other flowering trees, which, grotesquely festooned here and there by the wild grape-vine, make of the park, at the appropriate season, a rare scene of beauty and enchantment.

A feature of the Park is the little stream known as the River Des Peres, which traverses it diagonally from the northwest to the southeast. Meandering for a distance of four miles, now through quiet valleys and slopes, and again under high and precipitous bluffs, it furnishes sites for extensive lakes, which may be constructed with but little labor and expense. The soil is light and extremely fertile, and the famous blue-grass being indigenous, needs only exposure to light and ventilation to insure a fine sward.

The general level of the park is about one hundred and fifty feet above the level of the Mississippi River, but at some points it rises much higher. From these, views of the city and country for many miles can be had, and present beauties and attractions rarely combined.

It is strange, indeed, that this large body of land, so much of which is now in the same state as when the savage roamed through it, should have been preserved to form the principal pleasure grounds of a great city. Art, with its magic power, is tracing paths and constructing carriage drives through its whole extent; is arranging its original growth into fanciful groups; transforming its rugged and diversified surface into beautiful slopes and terraces, and generally making it "a thing of beauty," which will be "a joy forever."

28 | The Association between Reform and the Coming of a World's Fair

The movements to improve the quality of urban life in St. Louis, which had grown more powerful from the 1870s onward, coalesced in 1896 in the organization of the Civic Improvement League. This organization, by itself and with other organizations, worked for a host of improvements, including better health care, recreational facilities, transportation, education, and government. The catalyst for these activities was the desire to prepare the city for hosting the Louisiana Purchase Exposition of 1904. During the eight-year tenure of Mayor Rolla Wells (1901–1909), the city demonstrated the positive effects that could occur when long-held reform goals were joined to dominating civic purpose. This document, which appeared in a national reform magazine in 1913, points out the critical importance of the world fair as a catalyst for reform generally, as well as the interconnections between the movements for rooting out physical and political corruption. Louis Marion McCall, "Making St. Louis a Better Place to Live In," The Chautauquan, *XXXVI (January 1903), pp. 405–9.*

St. Louis . . . is preparing for a World's Fair . . . to commemorate the centennial of the Louisiana Purchase. The discussion of
such a project naturally called the attention of all good citizens
to the prime necessity of making the city itself a striking feature
of the show proposed for the nations of the earth, and this necessity was the more strongly borne in upon the people by the fact
that, for years, the municipality had been governed by about as
incompetent and corrupt a set of cheap politicians as ever were
produced in any place in the world. The city was "out at elbows
and down at the heel". . . .

A few persons studied the general subject of the City Beautiful.
A few got together and prepared some circulars which were sent
to the officers of every organization that might possibly be interested in such a movement. Copies of the pamphlets, papers and
other literature indorsed and prepared by the American League
for Civic Improvement were circulated—were placed in the hands
of those who were thought likely to favor the idea of a city beautiful. This had its effect, especially as the newspapers kept lively
on the subject. It was evident at last that enough people had
been interested to justify the calling of a meeting to organize for
work. The meeting was held, and the attendance was moderately
good, while the enthusiasm was fine. Organization was promptly
effected, and in a short time the Civic Improvement League was
actually working. Its platform was promulgated, and the workers began to gather in more members. The response to the movement was most gratifying, and continues to be so. The doings of
the league are regular features of the papers, whenever there are
any doings, and there is always "something doing". The officers
of the league are not above the task of preparing statements of
the league work for the press, and delivering it to the papers at
the right time. The league has striven for publicity. It has been
getting it slowly, but effectively. The people have begun to wake
up. Business men are glad to pay annual dues for such a cause;
in fact, everybody takes to the idea kindly, as soon as it is made
clear that the league is not in partisan politics in any sense whatever. This helps the league, too, with the partisan papers. They
don't see a scheme of "the other man" behind it, and so they don't
hesitate to push it. The league, furthermore, prints a monthly
Bulletin that briefly explains what is being done, and what we

hope to do. People actually take a liking to the brochure, and demand copies to send to their friends. . . .

The new head of the city government, the mayor [Rolla Wells], early took an interest in the league, and kept in touch with its officers. He has done everything he could to give effectiveness to league ideas in the city government. Moreover, the police force has been bent to the service of the league and of all citizens in this respect, through the lively, personal interest of the president of the police board in our work. The police have been instructed to *enforce* the ordinances that make for cleaner streets and alleys, compliance with the building laws, the abolition of protruding street signs, the repair of streets and sidewalks after excavation by contractors, etc. The police have actually begun to arrest and petty [i.e., City Court] judges to fine men for littering the streets with scraps of paper. League receptacles for waste paper will soon be placed. Official action and public clamor have enforced the better collection of garbage, and the league has taken up sanitary inspection, in cooperation with the health officer. The league pays the salary of women inspectors, charging the health department a fixed price for inspection. Music in the parks, that had been discontinued in order that its cost might go to the pockets of "gangsters", was reintroduced. Street sprinkling and street sweeping are better done than ever before. The mayor has appointed three members of the league on a commission to determine how most effectively to make a great road, Kingshighway, a fine and impressive boulevard according to modern ideas. The agitation remotely begun by the league was responsible for the observance of a cleaning-up week all over the city; the newspapers took up the idea so strongly that the clean-city topic became the fad, and householders really began to see that they had better keep their own premises in order, if they did not desire to be criticized as backward by their neighbors. . . .

Some of the effectiveness of the general discussions is to be seen in the fact that the most recently erected police stations have been made really model buildings of their kind and ornaments to the locality in which they are placed, while the new fire-engine houses are also conceived with some regard for something more than mere utility. The value of beauty as an asset is recognized even by great commercial institutions, and at least four of the St. Louis trust companies and banks have put up buildings that attract visitors, and, presumably, deposits, by their outer and inner graces of architecture.

The leaven is working in St. Louis. One can see it and feel it everywhere. The World's Fair project is regarded as a blessing simply because it affords a reason, appreciated by all, why the city should be promptly put in its best shape to receive visitors from all the world. The property owner, the real estate agent, everybody, in fact, is beginning to see that beauty is a city's asset that can be realized upon in a splendid manner. It is gradually dawning upon everyone that a nice, clean, well-kept city is "money in the pocket" of everyone who lives in that city. Gradually the question of suppressing dust and smoke is being more carefully considered. We find the merchants, manufacturers and real estate owners gladly coming into our organization to help that cause along. Even the coarser sort of politicians are beginning to realize that it makes for their personal popularity to be in favor of improvements such as we urge, and that they may even strengthen themselves by reason of appointments they may get for their friends on the forces that may be set to work to clean up the town.

There is less protest than ever about the taxes involved in better streets, alleys, and sewers, in better lighting, in tree planting, and in the general improvement of the town, to the eye alike of the casual visitor and the native.

All these things have come about, not solely as the result of the work of our organization, but to some extent at least from that cause. It was the discussion begun by the agitation of the few who first took up the idea that brought the matter to general attention. That discussion has broadened in scope, until the desire for "a better city to live in" finds expression in agitation for free public baths, for a park on the city's river front, for one boulevard through the city east and west, and another north and south, innocent of street car tracks, and appropriately paved for riding and driving. It has intensified the impression of the importance of a supply of clearer water, either by filtration of the Mississippi fluid, or the impounding of the clear, unpolluted water of the Meramec Springs, at a point eighty miles from the city, and its delivery in the city by gravity. In short, there is such an incipient renaissance in the staid old city of St. Louis as is to be found nowhere outside of the national capital with its stupendous and colossal scheme of beautifying the city of magnificent distances. It touches everything in the city's life. It moves the people to demand the suppression of steam railroad tracks; it urges the Terminal Association, controlling all the railroad entrances and exits, to abandon the smoky tunnel, to use it only for freight transportation.

And finally the agitation of the things for which the St. Louis branch of the American League for Civic Improvement stands has been not a little instrumental in causing a MORAL AWAKENING, which has resulted in the indictment, trial and sentence of three alleged official corruptionists, and the flight of several others to parts unknown. It is all part of the "New St. Louis movement" that began with a few people agitating in the press and in private talk and letters for such principles and objects as the American League represents.

29 | "Meet Me in St. Louis"

Forest Park was the location for the Louisiana Purchase Exposition of 1904, which, with nearly twenty million visitors and with exhibits from sixty-two nations and numerous cities, was one of the great world fairs of the period. In large measure, the exposition celebrated the progress that St. Louis' development exemplified. In the various halls, the genius of late-nineteenth- and early-twentieth-century industry and technology were viewed by as many as one hundred thousand visitors per day. In addition, there were architectural, educational, and cultural presentations which attempted to demonstrate the progress of civilization. The enormous attention that focused on St. Louis was celebrated in Andrew B. Sterling's and Kerry Mills' song "Meet Me in St. Louis, Louis." The idea for the lyrics came to Sterling in a Broadway cafe when a customer asked a waiter, whose name was Louis, for a glass of St. Louis beer. "Another Louis, Louis!" called the customer and thereby gave inspiration for the song. Millions sang it at the fair, and it was later revived by Judy Garland in the 1944 movie Meet Me in St. Louis. *For millions it captured the excitement and enterprise of turn-of-the-century St. Louis. From "Meet Me in St. Louis, Louis," words by Andrew B. Sterling and music by Kerry Mills. Original publication date, 1904. Copy-*

right MCMIV F. A. Mills, assigned MCMXXXV to Jerry Vogel Music Co., New York, N.Y.

Meet Me in St. Louis, Louis

When Louis came home to the flat,
He hung up his coat and his hat.
He gazed all around, but no wifey he found,
So he said, "Where can Flossie be at?"
A note on the table he spied,
He read it just once, then he cried.
It ran: "Louis, dear, it's too slow for me here,
So I think I will go for a ride."

> "Meet me in St. Louis, Louis,
> Meet me at the fair,
> Don't tell me the lights are shining
> Any place but there.
> We will dance the Hoochee Koochee,
> I will be your tootsie wootsie,
> If you will meet me in St. Louis, Louis,
> Meet me at the fair."

The dresses that hung in the hall
Were gone; she had taken them all.
She took all his rings and the rest of his things;
The picture he missed from the wall.
"What! moving?" the janitor said,
"Your rent is paid three months ahead."
"What good is the flat?" said poor Louis. "Read that."
And the janitor smiled as he read:

> "Meet me in St. Louis, Louis,
> Meet me at the fair,
> Don't tell me the lights are shining
> Any place but there.
> We will dance the Hoochee Koochee,
> I will be your tootsie wootsie,
> If you will meet me in St. Louis, Louis,
> Meet me at the fair."

PART THREE

From City to Region:
Growth and Dispersal, 1910-1975

1 | The Geography of the St. Louis Trade Territory, 1924

After World War I, St. Louis businessmen advertised their city as the "49th state." This term was employed to delineate the trading area of which St. Louis was the center. Since the city encompassed large sections of Missouri, Illinois, Kentucky, Tennessee, and Arkansas, the notion of the "49th state" was not merely the expression of the creative imaginings of local boosters, but a valid reflection of the regional importance that St. Louis played in the economic life of the Midwest. Lewis Thomas, drawing on his doctoral dissertation at the University of Chicago, presented this thesis in a feature article in the city press in 1924. Viewed one way, this document illustrates how boosterism changed from the nineteenth century, as boastful amateurs were replaced by more scientifically oriented professionals. The goal still remained the same: merchandising the attractive qualities of a particular city. From another standpoint, Thomas's writing tells how the railroad, automobile, truck, and airplane allowed the establishment of other regional capitals in what previously had been perceived as St. Louis' trade territory. Lewis Thomas, The Geography of the Saint Louis Trade Territory *(St. Louis:* St. Louis Globe-Democrat, *1924), pp. 5–7, 21–22.*

The territory involved in this discussion occupies a central position in the Great Central Lowlands of the United States. The limits of the area have been determined by the author after many consultations with men of general business experience, . . . manufacturers and the advertising managers of the daily newspapers which serve this city and vicinity. . . . The line includes in the area Sedalia and Hannibal, Missouri, and Springfield, Illinois; . . . Louisville, Kentucky; Nashville and Memphis, Tennessee; Little Rock, Arkansas; and Springfield, Missouri.

. . . At the beginning of the era of railroad expansion in the Middle West and Great West, Saint Louis held a dominating position in the commerce of those regions and was truly the "Gateway to the West." As evidence, Saint Louis was the base of operations of most of the exploratory expeditions which opened up the Western Territories.

As transportation facilities increased in number and extent, this vast area has been occupied by competing cities which have cut in on the widespread sphere of influence of Saint Louis so that it is no longer St. Louis' "own." The influence of Chicago has, by numerous railroads, covered most of the Upper Mississippi Basin, even dominating a portion of Northern Missouri.

Kansas City, Denver and Omaha have become important trade centers for the Great Plains and Mountain States. If, in the opinion of some people, these cities are dependent upon larger commercial and industrial centers, then Saint Louis must share this position with Chicago and even New York City.

The influence of Saint Louis never extended very far to the eastward because of the importance of Cincinnati, Indianapolis and Louisville. These cities have maintained their dominance in their respective regions.

The Southwest has been the particular pride of Saint Louis merchants. However, the easy and cheap connections between the Gulf cities and the Atlantic Coast cities have steadily increased the commercial prestige of Mobile, New Orleans, Galveston and Houston. As a consequence, the battle line of competition has been pushed northward through the cities of Nashville, Memphis, Dallas and Fort Worth.

There remains an area which is truly and indisputably under the influence of Saint Louis and the above-mentioned cities. Beyond this zone, Saint Louis offers keen competition in many lines of business because of her strong national and economic foundations in those lines. . . .

The limits which have been described for the Saint Louis trade territory gain in significance when one considers the areas covered by the business districts allotted to various fundamental, everyday commodities which make up the bulk of the volume of business. Note the limits of the Eighth Federal Reserve District and its branch banks. Examine the districts allotted to Saint Louis by companies which distribute nationally automobiles, agricultural implements, hardware, packing-house products, groceries, clothing, shoes, furniture and many other widely used articles. Furthermore, notice the areas covered by the great morning daily newspapers which are published in the large cities of the Mississippi Basin. These papers cater to the commercial, industrial and financial interests of their respective spheres of influence and reflect their success in their circulation territories.

It might seem from the foregoing that Saint Louis should have shriveled and fallen by the wayside in growth and prosperity. On the contrary, Saint Louis has forged ahead in size and significance. From a far-flung and attenuated sphere of influence she has turned her attention to the intensive development of her immediate territory. Her progress is an indication of the wealth of resources which has made her present position possible. . . .

Summarizing the activities of the regions, the wide range of activities and their substantial geographic foundations make it quite evident that the Saint Louis trade territory has the basic elements of prosperity. Agriculture has crop cultivation of great variety, fruit growing and stock raising as its principal phases. Lumbering is prevalent in the hardwoods, pines and cypress timber regions. Mining is based on both metallic and non-metallic minerals. Growing out of these activities there are several other activities of great importance.

Most of the materials which have been mentioned on the foregoing pages need alteration before they are ready for the consumer. These materials furnish abundant raw materials for manufacture. Coal is abundant and cheap for industrial purposes. One of the major petroleum pipe lines passes through the territory. Labor has been attracted to the territory in large numbers. As a consequence, flour and feed mills, meat-packing plants, tanneries, cooperages, smelters, paint factories, lead works, iron foundries, enamelware factories, lime and cement plants, clay-products plants and glass factories are a few of the important manufactures of this type. The activities add to the significance of the population in the way of wealth and buying power.

The activities thus far enumerated are fundamental to the resources of the territory. The population thus supported is a valuable market. Consequently, there have been attracted to this territory many manufacturers which cater to such a demand: shoes, clothing, tobacco, furniture, automobiles, tools, machinery, parts, printing, chemicals, soap and food products using materials from other regions. These manufactures bring to the territory a large group of skilled and common laborers. They constitute a valuable market in themselves.

The buying and selling of the commodities produced in the territory, both in raw or primary states and in manufactured forms, constitute an important activity and engage a large class of administrators, clerks, salesmen, and merchants. They handle in addition to the commodities already mentioned, wheat, corn, hides, skins, wool, cotton, horses, mules and lumber. These activities add another element to this already great territory.

From the beginning of travel, exploration and trade in this part of the United States, this territory has played an important part. The rivers provided the easiest means of travel. The Ohio-Missouri rivers made up a well-used east and west route. The Mississippi river provided a north-south route. These routes cross in this territory. The trading posts grew to towns, then to cities. These towns naturally attracted the railroads when that means of transportation began to develop. The major rivers and the smoothness of the plains surfaces made the building of railroads easy. Saint Louis being the largest city in this general region, attracted the most. Today there are twenty-six railroad lines centering on

St. Louis. They radiate, like the spokes of a wheel, to all points of the compass.

The extraordinary facilities for transportation of commodities have made Saint Louis one of the great distributing centers of the United States. Branch houses handling every article of trade have been established. Some of the more important ones are drugs, barbers' supplies, candy, photographic plates, shoes, hats, millinery, and machinery. Not only are all places in the trade territory within one day's service, but the railroads cover a wide area in the Middle West. The Saint Louis merchant "ships from the center and not from the rim" of a great trade territory and market.

2 | The Geographic Landscape of Metropolitan St. Louis, 1927

The integration of St. Louis into the national economy in the late nineteenth and early twentieth centuries had important consequences for the spatial development of the metropolis. During most of the nineteenth century, St. Louis was fairly compact, with relatively short distances separating industry and high-quality residential areas. In the twentieth century, there was increasing spatial differentiation, abetted by the development of mechanically powered transit after the mid-1880s and by the introduction of dependable trucks and automobiles running on paved highways. These transportation modes offered new possibilities for metropolitan expansion. In 1927, Lewis Thomas defined the metropolitan region as covering 125 square miles. St. Louis City, with its 61 square miles, contained slightly less than half of this total. Since the means of transportation did not serve all parts of the region equally, the edges of this metropolis were uneven. Corridors extended west into St. Louis County and east from the river in Madison and St. Clair counties in Illinois. In the process of regional expansion, functions tended to become differentiated in space with single functions occupying discrete land areas. While this phenomenon is characteristic of land-use patterns in "modern" American cities, the numerous hills, valleys, and rivers of the St. Louis region make its perception clearer than in cities with less remarkable physiognomies. Lewis Thomas, "The Localization of Business Activities in Metropolitan St. Louis," Washington University Studies, *I (October 1927), pp. 2–10.*

Metropolitan St. Louis comprises an irregularly-shaped area of some 125 square miles in extent. About 75 square miles are on the Missouri side of the Mississippi River, and about 50 square miles are on the Illinois side. . . . Although the Mississippi River separates the two parts of Metropolitan St. Louis, the constriction [of the river] makes it possible for the centers of activities in the two parts to be close together.

East St. Louis and other cities on the Illinois side of Metropolitan St. Louis are on the floodplain of the Mississippi River, while St. Louis and other cities on the Missouri side extend onto the adjacent upland of the St. Louis Plain. The layouts of the various urban units on the two sides of Metropolitan St. Louis are in marked contrast, in keeping with the dissimilar topographic features. St. Louis proper and its suburbs have grown up on undulating uplands of smoothly rounded hills and broad shallow valleys. These uplands rise gradually toward the west from the river, and have a relief slightly more than 300 feet. Where the uplands come close to the Mississippi River, they are truncated by slopes, the steepness of which depends upon the recency of impingement by the river. The valleys of several small streams mark off the heights into more or less separate city sections. The railroads which follow these valleys have tended to accentuate the division of the city into sections.

East St. Louis and its associated cities have sprung up opposite St. Louis on the west central portion of the essentially smooth, broad surface of the American Bottoms. These bottoms are approximately thirty miles in length from north to south, and vary from three to ten miles in width. Their eastern border is marked by loess-capped limestone bluffs which rise more or less precipitously one hundred-fifty to three hundred feet above the general level of the bottoms. Since only a small part of the floodplain, that is directly opposite St. Louis, has witnessed urban development, there is ample room for growth and expansion of the Illinois cities of Metropolitan St. Louis. . . . The Metropolitan area east of the Mississippi River is graded alluvial plain, almost flat, save for a few abandoned meander channels and a few mounds [built by the Indians].

In delineating the boundaries of the geographic sections, one recognizes easily the adjustment of their distinctive activities to topography. One accessory to the activities of the several sections is railroads. Because the valley floors of the West Side of Metropolitan St. Louis present lower gradients and fewer construction difficulties than the uplands, most of the railroads of that side are located on the floodplains. Some of them reach into the heart of the city along the floodplain of the Mississippi River, others along the bottoms of its tributaries. In order to be near a railroad many factories have located in the valleys. Thus, because the valleys are largely devoted to railroad and factory uses, the residence and business sections, for this and other reasons, are situated on the adjacent or intervening uplands. As a consequence, the activities of St. Louis are sharply localized in distinct units. The sixteen sections on the West Side are an index to the varied economic adjustments to diversified topography, while the one section in the East Side connotes the simplicity of its topography.

A brief resume will show the type activities of the West Side Sections. The *North Broadway Industrial Section* is dominated by large lumber yards and woodworking factories, which have evolved from the simple log yards and saw mills of the days when the principal supply of lumber for St. Louis came, by river, from logging areas in the forests along the Upper Mississippi River and its tributaries. In addition, there are several grain elevators, foundries, and one large meat packing plant. These industrial plants together with the yards and shops of the Wabash, the Chicago, Burlington and Quincy, and the Missouri, Kansas and Texas railroads spread out over the southern portion of the smooth surface of the North St. Louis part of the Mississippi River floodplain. The *South Broadway Industrial Section* is characterized by smelters, chemical plants, and foundries, although a large acreage there is occupied by the yards and depots of the St. Louis, Iron Mountain and Southern Railroad. This section is not large, being the long, narrow, partly natural, partly artificial terrace between the South Side bluffs and the Mississippi River. The *Mill Creek Industrial Section* is given over so completely to railroad activities that it is sometimes referred to as Railroad Valley. . . . Warehouses and light manufacturing establishments are crowded close around the terminals [of the railroads]. . . . The *Oak Hill Industrial Section* is also given over chiefly to clay products. . . . The *Northwest Industrial Section* is devoted chiefly to extensive light manufacturing plants. . . . The *Downtown St. Louis Section* is located on an upland between the North Broadway and Mill Creek Industrial sections. Within its boundaries are found the principal retail, financial, wholesale, jobbing, and light manufacturing activities of Metropolitan St. Louis. The residential sections . . . occupy uplands, in most cases adjacent to or between the industrial sections.

Across the almost level floodplain of the East Side . . . the network of railroads provides efficient transportation facilities for every part of the East Side Section. As a consequence, mills and manufacturing plants are scattered along the main line tracks, switch tracks and terminal railroad tracks. . . . In East St. Louis, the manufacturing plants include steel foundries, smelters, refineries, chemical plants, flour and feed mills, and many mills, large and small, of miscellaneous types. . . . The growth of the East Side has been principally outward from an original area in East St. Louis. As a consequence, the peripheral areas are experiencing the present-day industrial expansion of the section, since the ever-widening terminal net makes more and more acreage available for heavy manufactures. Thus, the East Side Section will continue to expand over the American Bottoms.

The geographic sections of Metropolitan St. Louis which have been briefly described, are based on the distribution of activities as they are related to the features of their environments. These sections provide the keys to the distribution of business activities.

3 | The Labor Market, 1930

One important component of any successful industrial city is the availability of skilled and disciplined workers. St. Louis possessed such a population in abundance, although its ethnic and national character differed markedly from that of other major industrial cities. The essential difference is that between 1885 and 1920, little of the "new immigration," people from eastern and southern Europe, came to settle in St. Louis City. These newcomers, instead, tended to locate across the river in East St. Louis and in neighboring cities, where large, heavy industries requiring a low-skill labor force were located. St. Louis City continued to draw German and Irish immigrants, as well as native-born Americans from the Midwest and the South. In this document, the Industrial Club of St. Louis, a group organized within the St. Louis Chamber of Commerce, explains to industrialists from outside the city that these migratory trends have resulted in an attractive labor force—including cheap, female labor—and in lower wages than those paid to nearly all groups of workers in cities farther north and east. The Factory Labor Situation in the St. Louis Industrial District *(St. Louis: Industrial Club of Saint Louis, ca. 1930), pp. 1–6.*

Industrial workers are drawn not only from the district and surrounding rural sections, but also from the extensive labor reservoir southward to the Gulf of Mexico, there being no large manufacturing cities directly south of St. Louis on either side of the Mississippi River to attract ambitious labor, which naturally seeks large centers. In a survey of one industry in St. Louis it was found that 86.98% of 4,093 workers were born in the seven states of Missouri, Illinois, Arkansas, Tennessee, Kentucky, Indiana, and Mississippi, ranking in the order named. The survey showed that 26.66% were born in the St. Louis Metropolitan District. . . .

This labor supply includes an especially intelligent type of beginner, willing and quick to learn various factory operations. White common labor is very plentiful, the rural districts maintaining a constant flow of the hard-working classes. Colored workers are available here in considerable numbers, and, according to reports, are more intelligent, energetic, and a better type than those farther south, being especially useful for certain kinds of factory work. An adequate supply of skilled, semi-skilled and trained factory workers is well maintained in this district because of the regularity of employment. This regularity of employment is due to the diversification of industry, as no one line of industry employs more than 10% of the total number of factory wage-earners.

No other large industrial district is so well favored in respect to education of, as well as supply of, available workers. Proof of this statement is shown in the low percentage of illiteracy in St. Louis. Illiteracy among all classes is lower here than in any other large industrial city, and likewise is lower among the foreign born and negroes in respect to the total population. . . .

St. Louis has a greater percentage of native-born industrial workers than any other large city in the Middle West, and a much greater percentage than most eastern manufacturing cities, large or small.

United States Census figures show that only 13.4% of the residents of St. Louis are foreign born. Seventy per cent of the foreign-born residents in St. Louis come from the northwestern and west-central European countries, Germans predominating with 29%, Irish next with 8.9%. If Austrians and Hungarians were included with Germans, the German percentage would be 40%. . . .

Survey shows the percentage of foreign-born workers in large plants runs from 4% to 11.8%. A conservative estimate of foreign-born workers in all industries, large and small, would not be over 8%. . . . Survey and the foregoing figures prove that St. Louis has a greater percentage of native-born workers than any other large city, and the majority of the foreign-born population —small as it is in respect to the whole—comes from the most desirable and hardest-working races of Europe.

Some cities have an available supply of male workers for factory pursuits, but, unlike St. Louis, are lacking in industrially-minded female workers. . . . While the number of females varies according to the kind of industry itself, many machines ordinarily worked by men in other cities are operated equally well here by women. Jobs requiring accuracy and care, such as packing and weighing of moderately heavy materials, are performed here by women. Several large industries with plants in St. Louis and other cities report that in St. Louis 90% of the employees in these departments are women, while in other cities the percentage of women is not over 75%. They report that the work is done equally well and at a lower cost in St. Louis. Survey indicates that there is a large supply of industrially-minded female workers in this district willing to work in factories on machines and other jobs wholly or mostly performed by male workers in other centers. This statement is not made as a reflection on the male factory worker here, but is mentioned to show the availability of, and possible resulting economy in the use of, female workers in this district.

Skilled and trained factory workers earn good annual wages here because employment is regular. Ordinary skilled and semi-skilled factory mechanics are not paid as high an hourly rate generally as is paid in other large centers north and east of here. . . . Starting rates for beginners, both male and female, are likewise lower than in other large industrial centers, as the large available supply has a natural tendency to keep down the starting rate. . . . The better type of common labor here appears to be on a par with the same labor north and east of this district, where wage rates are higher because of increased living costs and other factors.

4 | The Education of the Labor Force

Shortly after the turn of the century, the St. Louis school board embarked on a number of related innovations that marked a significant departure in the history of American education. Between 1904 and 1920, it introduced the nation's first comprehensive high school, pioneered the junior high school, and introduced path-breaking programs in vocational instruction and guidance. The attractiveness of these programs, together with effective compulsory attendance laws, caused a doubling in the average amount of schooling for the city's youth. Teenagers stayed in school rather than enter the work force, as the high school, for the first time, became an instrument for the instruction of the mass of urban young. With the growing importance of schooling as a preparation for work, the modern, democratizing correlation between education and social mobility became firmly established. The key to these changes is the concern with teaching the skills necessary for personal advancement as well as the economic well-being of a mature industrial society. The following excerpts focus on the vocational objectives of the system. The first is a description of a program designed to make urban children aware of the opportunities for jobs in a wide variety of areas. The second, an oath recited by teenage girls, bears testimony to the lengths to which vocationalism was inculcated even among females. It was during this period that the mass of women began to find employment outside the home and in the city's offices and factories. Fifty-fifth Annual Report of the Board of Education of the City of St. Louis, Missouri for the Year Ending June 30, 1909, *pp. 43–45;* Sixty-sixth Annual Report of the Board of Education of the City of St. Louis, Missouri for the Year Ending June 30, 1920, *p. 114.*

Excursions into the City

[The city boy must be put into] direct touch with the physical

and social world itself. The thing that the country boy is in touch
with all the time the city boy many times passes by and does not
see. He really does not see the city because of the houses. . . .
The country boy is with nature and grown up folks. He just has
to know something very accurately about . . . how men work,
and what they do with the products of their labor. His life is more
nearly participation in the whole life about him. The city boy lives
apart from his father's life and in many cases from his mother's
life. . . . He is just clothed, and housed, and fed, and of course
loved, by his parents without getting into real touch with them. He
is kept a child in a child's world till suddenly he awakens to the
fact that he is shoved into the whirl of adult human activity and
that he does not know enough about it to help himself or others
well.

On the social side, the city gives a much more extended opportunity for seeing the range of men's interests and work, but the
city child cannot get at these things by himself as well as the
country child can get at the corresponding interests in his sphere.

The village smithy stands with wide open door and the boy and
the smith have no difficulty in getting acquainted and profiting by
the acquaintance.

The door of the city business house or manufactory is sealed
to the child, because nobody has thought that he can look in without disturbing the work. In the very place where human life should
be richest in its social contact, the child is more shut out than he
would be in the country. While this is the very natural effect of
city life on children if parents and teachers let them drift, it need
not be so. Men in the city do not wilfully push aside the children,
but they themselves are pushed and are almost forced to forget
that they are living while they live.

These contacts and experiences that come to the children by the
simplicity of social relations in the country must be brought about
in the city by some organized plan of parents and teachers to
take children into many places where men are engaged in their
daily work, that the children may know how each contributes to
his fellow's welfare, and that they may have some widened experience to serve them when they come to choose what they intend
to do as men. Excursions of classes for this purpose are welcomed whenever they ask for admission, and there is no surer

way of putting a child in sympathy with the life about him or of fitting him for intelligent participation in that life. A number of our schools have realized, during this year, the opportunity given by these visits to the industries of the city for arousing the genuine interest of the pupils and of broadening their experience.

The quarries have told them of the myriads of lives that animated the skeletons now compressed into stone, and of the changes through which this stone must still further go to serve the uses of man. The furniture factory has taken them in imagination back to the woods and has shown how the skill and art of man has made the trees minister to his comfort. At the weather bureau they have learned how dependent the business of the world is upon the conditions of the air. In the courts, and in the post office they have gotten some notion of the social institutions. In these and other ways, these schools have turned the seeming prison house of the city into a world throbbing with human interests and full of opportunity for him who will open his eyes and heart. A future development of this kind of study should be secured with the pupils of our high schools, especially those in commercial and manual training classes.

A Creed of Work for Women

I believe that every woman needs a skilled occupation developed to the degree of possible support.

She needs it commercially, for an insurance against reverses.

She needs it socially, for a comprehending sympathy with the world's workers.

She needs it intellectually, for a constructive habit of mind which makes knowledge usable.

She needs it ethically, for a courageous willingness to do her share of the world's work.

She needs it aesthetically, for an understanding of harmony [sic] relationships as determining factors in conduct and work.

I believe that every young woman should practice this skilled occupation up to the time of her marriage for gainful ends with deliberate intent to acquire therefrom the widest possible professional and financial experience.

I believe that every woman should expect marriage to interrupt

for some years the pursuit of any regular gainful occupation, that
she should pre-arrange with her husband some equitable division
of the family income such as will insure a genuine partnership,
rather than a position of dependence (on either side) and that she
should focus her chief thought during the early youth of her children upon the science and art of wise family life.

I believe that every woman should hope to return in the second leisure of middle age to some of her early skilled occupation,
—either as an unsalaried worker in some one of its social phases,
or, if income be an object, as a salaried worker in a phase of it
requiring maturity and social experience.

I believe that this general policy of economic service for American women would yield generous by-products of intelligence, responsibility, and contentment.

5 | East St. Louis Race Riot of 1917

*After the Civil War, St. Louis was a transit and receiving point
for blacks who escaped the southern countryside to seek the opportunities offered in northern urban-industrial centers. When
World War I created an enormous demand for labor, the migration northward assumed flood-tide proportions. In East St. Louis,
heavy manufacturing industries were insatiable in their demand
for laborers. The results were dramatic. In a single four-month
period—between January and April 1917—the black population
of the east-side city jumped from 12,000 to 20,000, the latter
figure amounting to more than 25 percent of the total inhabitants.
In a working-class city traditionally hostile to blacks, an influx of
such proportions was bound to cause frictions. Racial animosities
were aggravated when some of the companies hired blacks to take
the place of white workers striking for better conditions. When
white workers at the 1,900-employee Aluminum Ore Company
struck in the autumn of 1916, the company began replacing them
with blacks, and the stage was set for violence. In April 1917
another strike occurred, and black strikebreakers again were
brought into the plant. On July 2, a mass riot erupted which lasted
ten days. It required the intervention of the Illinois National
Guard to restore peace. This riot was not only a brutal event in
itself, but one of the largest of the eighteen that occurred be-*

tween 1915 and 1919. In this "first generation" of twentieth-century race riots, whites were the aggressors, and the official agents of order, both the local police and the national guard, failed to protect blacks and even participated in attacking them. The following selections are from eyewitness accounts reported in the St. Louis Post-Dispatch *(July 3, 1917). Some explanations as to the "cause" of the riots follow.*

Post-Dispatch Man, an Eye-Witness, Describes Massacre of Negroes

For an hour and a half last evening I saw the massacre of helpless negroes at Broadway and Fourth street, in downtown East St. Louis, where a black skin was a death warrant.

I have read of St. Bartholomew's night. I have heard stories of the latterday crimes of the Turks in Armenia, and I have learned to loathe the German army for its barbarity in Belgium. But I do not believe that Moslem fanaticism or Prussian frightfulness could perpetrate murders of more deliberate brutality than those which I saw committed, in daylight by citizens of the State of Abraham Lincoln.

I saw man after man, with hands raised, pleading for his life, surrounded by groups of men—men who had never seen him before and knew nothing about him except that he was black—and saw them administer the historic sentence of intolerance, death by stoning. I saw one of these men, almost dead from a savage shower of stones, hanged with a clothesline, and when it broke, hanged with a rope which held. Within a few paces of the pole from which he was suspended, four other negroes lay dead or dying, another having been removed, dead, a short time before. I saw the pockets of two of these negroes searched, without the finding of any weapon.

Rocks Dropped on Negroes [sic] Neck

I saw one of these men, covered with blood and half conscious, raise himself on his elbow, and look feebly about, when a young man, standing directly behind him, lifted a flat stone in both hands and hurled it upon his neck. This young man was much better dressed than most of the others. He walked away unmolested.

I saw Negro women begging for mercy and pleading that they had harmed no one, set upon by white women of the baser sort, who laughed and answered the coarse sallies of men as they beat the negresses' faces and breasts with fists, stones and sticks. I saw one of these furies fling herself at a militiaman who was trying to protect a negress, and wrestle with him for his bayonetted gun, while other women attacked the refugee.

What I saw, in the 50 minutes between 6:30 p.m. and the lurid coming of darkness, was but one local scene of the drama and death. I am satisfied that, in spirit and method, it typified the whole. And I cannot somehow speak of what I saw as mob violence. It was not my idea of a mob.

Crowd Mostly Workingmen

A mob is passionate, a mob follows one man or a few men blindly; a mob sometimes takes chances. The East St. Louis affair, as I saw it, was a man hunt, conducted on a sporting basis, though with anything but the fair play which is the principle of sport. The East St. Louis men took no chances, except the chance from stray shots, which every spectator of their acts took. They went in small groups, there was little leadership, and there was a horribly cool deliberateness and a spirit of fun about it. I cannot allow even the doubtful excuse of drink. No man whom I saw showed the effect of liquor.

It was no crowd of hot-headed youths. Young men were in the greater number, but there were the middle-aged, no less active in the task of destroying the life of every discoverable black man. It was a shirt-sleeve gathering, and the men were mostly workingmen, except for some who had the aspect of mere loafers. I have mentioned the peculiarly brutal crime committed by the only man of any standing.

I would be more pessimistic about my fellow-Americans than I am today, if I could not say that there were other workingmen who protested against the senseless slaughter. I would be ashamed of myself if I could not say that I forgot my place as a professional observer and joined in such protests. But I do not think any verbal objection had the slightest effect. Only a volley of lead would have stopped those murderers.

"Get a nigger," was the slogan, and it was varied by the recurrent cry, "Get another!" It was like nothing so much as the holiday crowd, with thumbs turned down, in the Roman Coliseum, except that here the shouters were their own gladiators, and their own wild beasts.

When I got off a State street car on Broadway at 6:30, a fire apparatus was on its way to the blaze in the rear of Fourth street, south from Broadway. A moment's survey showed why this fire had been set, and what it was meant to accomplish.

Fire Drives Out Negroes

The shed in the rear of negroes' houses, which were themselves in the rear of the main buildings on Fourth street, had been ignited to drive out the negro occupants of the houses. And the slayers were waiting for them to come out.

It was stay in and be roasted, or come out and be slaughtered. A moment before I arrived, one negro had taken the desperate chance of coming out, and the rattle of revolver shots, which I heard as I approached the corner, was followed by the cry, "They've got him!"

And they had. He lay on the pavement, a bullet wound in his head and his skull bare in two places. At every movement of pain which showed that life remained, there came a terrific kick in the jaw or the nose, or a cracking stone from some of the men who stood over him. . . .

Influx of Negroes Cause of Lawless Outbreak

A Post-Dispatch reporter today interviewed labor leaders and large employers of labor in East St. Louis for an expression of opinion as to the cause of the race riots, which have grown out of the large influx of negroes from the South in the last 12 months.

Michael Whalen, City Clerk of East St. Louis, and also president of the Central Trades and Labor Council there, stated that the riots are the result of a growing impression during the last year that the big employers of labor were determined to make East St. Louis "a negro town," and in so doing destroy labor unions.

"Last summer," Whalen explained, "4500 white men went on

strike in the Armour, Swift and Morris packing plants. Eight hundred negroes, imported from the South, took places in these plants as strikebreakers.

"The negroes came from the South in box cars and some in day coaches. Their work at the packing plants was the loading of box cars, the handling of crates of meat and lard, and pushing trucks.

"When the strike was ended, the 800 negroes remained employed at the packing plants and that many white men failed to get their jobs back.

"Since then negroes have been coming continuously from the South to East St. Louis. They arrive principally on Sunday nights, when three or four day coaches loaded with them arrive here. Many negroes bring their families."

Whalen asserted that among the big employers who had laid off white men and employed negroes were the Swift, Armour and Morris packing plants, the Aluminum Co. of America, the Missouri Malleable Iron Co., the American Steel Foundries, and the Cotton Seed Oil Co.

At least 2500 negro men, Whalen estimates, have come to East St. Louis from the South in the last year. Many of these, he pointed out, failed to obtain work. They lived with friends, he said, and then citizens began to experience frequent highway robberies, burglaries and similar crimes. Residents learned that many of the new arrivals brought with them, as baggage, only revolvers and razors.

"The people became exasperated at these conditions," Whalen declared, "and determined to drive these negroes out of town to protect themselves and their families."

Whalen said there was no difference in pay for white and the negro labor, being $2.50 a day for either for a 10-hour day. White laborers, he said, for a time had voiced no objection to working alongside the negroes in the industrial plants. The principal objection to negro labor, however, as stated by Whalen, is that the negro will not unionize and will not strike.

It was recalled by Whalen that about 20 years ago the East Side packers brought into St. Louis large numbers of foreigners as laborers. Many of these were Polish. Since then, he asserted, the Poles have become strong unionizers, have educated themselves and their families, have become good citizens, and always have led in the unions' demands for proper wages and hours. Now, Whalen insists, the packers are trying to supplant these foreigners with negroes.

Vean Morse, superintendent of the Armour plant, made a general denial of Whalen's statement that the packing plants had imported negroes from the South, or had authorized labor agencies to send them to East St. Louis.

R. F. Rucker, superintendent of the aluminum ore plant, declared that since the war began large numbers of foreign laborers had left East St. Louis to work in Eastern munitions plants at higher wages. The number of foreign laborers in East St. Louis, he estimated, had been cut in half in this way. As a result, he pointed out, negroes came voluntarily from the South. Upon arrival at East St. Louis they wrote their friends and relatives, telling of the opportunity of employment at good wages, with the result that other negroes followed. He thinks the negroes selected East St. Louis because it is one of the largest industrial cities on the Mississippi River and because negroes "always follow the Mississippi River in going North."

Rucker denied that labor agencies have been retained by large employers of labor to bring negroes to East St. Louis. He also insisted that negroes had not replaced white men at the aluminum plant, except during the strike, which was settled last week. At this time, he says, the number of negroes employed in the plant is no larger than it was before the strike.

6 | The Satellite Cities of St. Louis, 1912

The social tensions that characterized East St. Louis between 1910 and 1920 were present in other industrial suburbs that had recently sprung up outside such cities as Chicago, Detroit, and Cleveland. The initial justification for these communities was economic: large industries, seeking extensive tracts of cheap land for new or expanded plant sites, purchased thousands of acres and built modern manufacturing facilities. Pullman, Illinois, south of Chicago's built-up area, was considered by industrialists and contemporary critics alike a near-utopian experiment when it was created in the 1880s. Twentieth-century industrialists lacked such vision. Planning and installation of business or residences by the company were incidental. Only the minimal amenities necessary to attract workers were built, and often these were put up by private speculators who bought company land. Around the turn of the century, planners such as the Englishman Ebenezer Howard conceived of establishing more humane and orderly industrial suburbs outside existing cities, and several actually were built in England. Graham Taylor, a Chicago settlement-house worker and reformer, who was greatly influenced by these English examples, reported on the conditions in the United States. He hoped that his articles, which appeared in The Survey, *the leading reform journal of the period, would lead to an emulation of English practices. They did not. In the American setting, Howard's garden cities for industrial workers became "garden suburbs" for the middle and upper classes, as exemplified in Forest Hills Gardens, New York. Nevertheless, Taylor succeeded in coining the phrase "satellite cities," which served to characterize the working-class industrial suburbs of major American cities. Graham R. Taylor, "Satellite Cities,"* The Survey, *XVIII (February 1, 1913), pp. 582–93.*

The "East Side" has come to be almost synonymous with social and civic problems. St. Louis applies the term to the string of towns sprawled along the opposite bank of the great river, and it is appropriate in its civic as well as its geographical connection. But while New York's East Side has problems of encrusted congestion, St. Louis' East Side consists of comparatively new satellites, their growth so much in process that its shaping is both possible and worthwhile.

These Illinois towns are linked to the larger city by four big coupling pins—the bridges across the broad, brown Mississippi. Directly facing St. Louis, and as close to the river bank as a network of railway terminals will permit, is a scattered mass of business buildings, dwellings, and tall chimneyed industrial plants. This is East St. Louis, and it is linked to the city proper by two bridges. On its northern edge between a sluggish, dirty-looking stream and some railroad tracks is an extensive stockyards. Beyond lies a low swampy stretch, criss-crossed with railways and dotted with occasional factories and houses. Still farther north, where the third bridge leads over from St. Louis, the settled area peters out into a cluster of houses and hovels. This is Venice, unkempt, half amphibious. The trolley cars from across the bridge spend little time on their way through Venice to another and larger community set to the northeast a mile or two back from the river bank. Like a huge city wall, the big manufacturing plants are ranged along its western edge, while the stacks of a steel mill serve as sentinels to the east. The first section that the cars enter is made up of miscellaneous small houses with occasional ugly larger buildings. This is Madison. You go on into a better set-up section, Granite City, which is slow-creeping out into the prairie with skirmish lines of box-like dwellings. To one side is a forlorn neighborhood beyond the western bulwark of industries and railroads. This is "Hungary Hollow."

East St. Louis, Madison, and Granite City are not an overflow of St. Louis industry—for few factories have actually shifted their location from one side of the river to the other. But the modern tendency to utilize industrially the outskirts of large centers of population has here been based not alone on the factors which commonly operate. Special economic advantages, some of them arbitrary and artificial, are shared by all three Illinois towns over St. Louis. St. Louis has been reluctant to admit that such advantages existed. Until recently her principal commercial body would rather have thrown a new industry to Kansas City, nearly three hundred miles away, but in the same state, than to any one of the Illinois towns just across the river.

But the last couple of years has seen the beginnings of a new spirit; the old jealousies are being laid aside, and the real unity of the metropolitan industrial district is becoming recognized on both sides of the river. In seeking to bring in new industries, the Business Men's League of St. Louis, which is increasingly representative of the Illinois as well as the Missouri side, now seeks to explain fairly the relative advantages of locating in St. Louis proper, on its western outskirts, or in the towns of the East Side. Many plants find that St. Louis sites, with better sewerage and the cheap power which will be furnished from the dam across the Mississippi at Keokuk, are preferable to those with the advantages of the East Side. . . .

Cheap land and cheap coal have thus been the greatest factors in attracting industries to which one or both are important. In the removal of the St. Louis stockyards to East St. Louis, for instance, cheap land was of course the main consideration. So it was in the development of the railway yards and terminals on the Illinois side. But in the heavy steel manufacturing which plays so important a part in the development of the whole East Side, cheap land in large tracts and a large supply of cheap coal are prime factors. The East Side has rapidly become, therefore, the section of the St. Louis industrial district into which heavy industrial processes, usually the dirtiest and dingiest, have been shunted.

In 1890 East St. Louis had but 15,169 population while Granite City and Madison did not show at all in the census returns. . . .

In 1912 East St. Louis was estimated to have about 70,000 people, and Granite City—the 1910 census of which omitted two wards—about 12,000. The growth of this group of towns from 1900 to 1910 was no less than 108 per cent. St. Louis in the same decade increased only from 575,238 to 687,029, a growth of but 19 per cent. . . .

"Hungary Hollow"

Perhaps the most important social problem in Granite City is that presented by the picturesque and isolated mass of immigrants in "Hungary Hollow." No group in the community is more neglected, unless it be the Negroes, of whom about 1,000 are employed in the plants. All the latter live, however, in nearby squalid towns since there is an unwritten law in Granite City that no one shall sell or rent real estate to Negroes. Counting Granite City and Madison as one community it includes one of the largest settlements of Bulgarians and Macedonians to be found in this country.

There is no point in which on their civic side American industrial communities fail more conspicuously than in their handling of the lowest paid immigrant labor. The very unwillingness of such towns to have their immigrant conditions described or considered as typical is evidence of this. Yet the fact that such labor is more essential in these towns than elsewhere warrants especial attention to the conditions under which immigrants live and work. "It is true," said a factory official, "that the district is an eye sore to Granite City, yet 'Hungary Hollow' is necessary to the success of the large plants and the conditions are no different than with foreign communities of a like class which may be found in other cities. The large plants require common labor and Americans will not accept these positions." And then, as if to defend his city's prestige, he said, "Granite City is practically isolated from its foreigners and Americans do not mingle with them either socially or in a business way." But he pointed out some of the difficulties which surround efforts at betterment, by adding, "the majority are here today and gone tomorrow, adopt the least expensive mode of living and do not come to the United States with the intention of becoming American citizens."

To a description of the work and life of the Granite City Bulgarians and Macedonians the Federal Immigration Commission devoted much space in its report, and this document has been drawn upon for much of the information here set forth. It is estimated that in 1907 the number of Bulgarians reached 8,000 though some of the best informed citizens think this figure too large. But the general industrial depression of that year sent many back to the fatherland and reduced the number to only a few hundred. The group has since increased, although temporarily diminishing in the summers owing to the exodus for railway construction work. In the fall of 1912 as many as 600 went back to fight in the Balkan war. Of the 1,000 who were left, a large proportion lived in "Hungary Hollow." A further cause for their diminishing numbers is that plant superintendents have declared the Macedonians unsatisfactory workmen. One man said he would rather have two Negroes than three Macedonians.

More than 90 per cent are men—some single, but many with families in the old country. More than 90 per cent have been in this country less than five years. About 61 per cent are employed in the steel plants, but less than 3 per cent are affiliated with trade unions. While their sobriety is said to be above the average American standard, they are not adaptable in their work, require much supervision and are generally the least effective industrially of the immigrant races. But increasingly the younger men who have some intention of staying in this country attend school. Their earnings are from fifteen to seventeen cents per hour for common labor, and some of them on piece work in other departments earn as much as thirty cents or more. At the time of the Immigration

Commission study, practically all earned less than $600 a year; nearly 92 per cent less than $400; and about 25 per cent less than $200; these figures would now probably be from ten to fifteen per cent higher with the present higher rate of wages. But in addition account must be taken of other earnings during the periods in the summer when the steel plants are sometimes not in operation. As has been said, many of the common laborers go out on railway construction jobs. Some of them, however, find work in other industries in Granite City, particularly the Corn Products Refining Company which operated even above the normal output during the period of depression—affording a significant example of what diversity of industries means in a community.

7 | Post–World War I Suburban Expansion

Satellite cities represent only one form of the kinds of communities that were developing outside the old, central city in the early twentieth century. Between 1920 and 1930, for example, the population of St. Louis City grew by only 13 percent, but the population of St. Louis County increased by 110 percent. Stimulated by the enormous increase in automobile ownership and the building of roads and highways, this period marks the beginnings of the modern automobile suburb. There are many types of suburbs and various ways of analyzing and classifying them. For example, suburbs can be categorized by function: political (county seat towns); recreational (towns near parks or beaches); educational (college or university towns); institutional (towns dependent on hospitals or prisons); or residential (towns whose citizens commute to work in the central city). Another method, the one employed in the following selection, accepts these functional categories but incorporates them in another framework: the degree to which the suburb is absorbed into the core city. Among its uses is that it draws on ways in which the historical relationships between communities have changed. This excerpt from a 1939 urban sociology text by two Washington University professors, is an example of what can be called the "St. Louis School of Sociology." Although the authors delineated seven degrees of absorption, only four types are considered here. Stuart A. Queen and Lewis F. Thomas, The City: A Study of Urbanism in the United States *(New York: McGraw-Hill, 1939), pp. 280–86.*

1 | AN ISOLATED COMMUNITY IN A METROPOLITAN AREA — In the northwest part of the St. Louis metropolitan area lies the little municipality of St. Ferdinand. This village of 1,000 inhabitants, seven miles from the St. Louis city limits, stands in interesting isolation from the rest of the metropolitan population. It was settled late in the eighteenth century by the French. After the Civil War many Germans came in, later a few Irish and a scattering of a few other nationalities. At first the French and the Germans were most hostile, as was indicated by their maintaining separate Catholic churches and carrying on Saturday night saloon brawls. In later years there has been much intermarriage, until the community is now very closely knit. Life is simple in St. Ferdinand. Houses are separate frame dwellings; there is no general water or sewage system. An ancient charter limits the municipality's borrowing to a maximum of $1,000. A voluntary fire department serves those homeowners who have paid an annual fee and display an appropriate symbol on their premises. A sample study showed over one-half of the population to have been born in Florissant and one-third in other places in Missouri. Two-thirds were Catholic. Less than one-third owned either cars or radios; only a little over one-third of the families subscribed for a newspaper. . . . St. Ferdinand thus offers an illustration of the most extreme degree of separateness and isolation that is likely to be found in a metropolitan area.

2 | A RELATIVELY INDEPENDENT COMMUNITY — An interesting contrast to St. Ferdinand is furnished by another outlying municipality, Ferguson, four miles nearer to central city and on a direct line between St. Ferdinand and St. Louis. Its fine old homes with wide lawns and friendly shade trees bespeak a different economic level. Its steam railroad, electric railway, and bus lines betoken a more intimate contact with the great city. Yet Ferguson too is a community apart, separated from the continuous, built-up area of Greater St. Louis by Maline Creek, and having its own local institutions. . . . Casual inquiry and observation make it plain that the life of Ferguson is much more closely bound up with that

of St. Louis than is the case with St. Ferdinand, but Ferguson has a more marked individuality than some other suburbs which we are about to describe.

3 | SUBURBS COALESCING WITH THE CENTRAL CITY — . . . Clayton is another suburb of the same general type [as Webster Groves], but with some quite different characteristics. In 1875, by act of the Missouri legislature, St. Louis City and St. Louis County were legally separated. After some delay a committee of prominent citizens selected 104 acres, donated by Mr. Clayton and Mrs. Hanley, to be their county seat. Previous to this, no town existed where Clayton now is. Trees, brush, and stumps had to be removed to make room for the new county buildings. By 1883 it was reported that "Clayton now includes twenty dwellings, three hotels, one grocery, three printing offices, three attorneys, one singing hall, and the County buildings." Up to 1892, the trip between the new town and St. Louis was slow and inconvenient. One might take a hack from the courthouse to Wells Station and from there a narrow-gauge steam railroad to Grand Avenue. Otherwise he might spend a half day traveling on horseback or by carriage. Not until 1904 was there a paved road connecting the two places. However, in 1892 an electric car line was extended out to Clayton. Although agitation for telephone connections began in 1881, service was not established until 1900. As late as 1905 there were less than 50 telephones in Clayton, but by 1930 the number had grown to nearly 3,000.

Clayton possesses its own city government with the usual municipal institutions, one of the important retail subcenters of metropolitan St. Louis, 10 churches, 3 of them metropolitan rather than local, and a variety of social, civic, and professional organizations. Throughout its history it has maintained one or more newspapers, usually published weekly, dealing with local politics, promoting trade with local merchants, and thriving on official advertising. The survival of its banks has doubtless been aided by the deposits of county funds.

Today Clayton is to the eye merely a part of Greater St. Louis. Apart from a small business district surrounding a dingy courthouse, there is little tangible evidence of its separate existence. We have no count of the residents whose employment and business activities take them to other parts of the metropolitan area, but casual observation indicates that the percentage is very high. The population appears to be fairly stable; but this matter too awaits enumeration. The age distribution of the population is about like that of St. Louis, but the sex ratio is lower, only 80 males per 100 females. The people are predominantly native white of native parents. Out of 10,000, only 350 are Negroes and 700 foreigners. Thus, like Webster Groves, Clayton has the homogeneity, stability, local institutions, loyalty, and pride which make it a community. Yet it too has intimate relations with St. Louis and no longer exists apart from the central city. Starting as a "political suburb," it has come to be much like an "overflow suburb."

4 | OVERFLOW SUBURBS: RESIDENTIAL — We turn now from the suburb which grew up as an independent town and was gradually drawn into the orbit of the metropolis to the suburb created *de novo* to provide for the surplus population of the inner city or at least to attract people from the center to an outlying section. St. Louis has a number of such suburbs along its western borders. Representative of this type is University City, a municipality of nearly 30,000 inhabitants created through a series of real estate subdivisions which began in 1904. It is commonly described as middle-class, but like Webster Groves and Clayton is really well above a statistical median. Most of the homes are single dwellings whose characteristic value is about $15,000. They are of brick and often quite showy, suggesting the predominance of the *nouveaux riches*. In the eastern part of University City, close to the St. Louis line, are many apartment houses. Business is pretty well concentrated in the "Loop," which is one of the most important subcenters in the whole metropolitan area. It is the hub of transportation facilities east, west, north and south; streetcars, busses, and "service cars" carry passengers in all directions. In addition there are some business houses along Olive Street Road, a string street extending east and west through University City. All told, there are nearly 350 business houses in this suburb—garages, cleaning and dyeing establishments, restaurants, clothing stores, food stores, beauty shops, drugstores, and many others. In the northeast part of University City are a few small industries and large commercial yards, but most of the inhabitants of this suburb find their employment in other sections of the metropolitan district.

8 | Suburban Subdivisions: Lake Forest, 1929

By examining the constituent parts of the suburbs which Queen and Thomas treated as entities, it is possible to view more concretely the causes and process of growth. Clayton, although originally a political suburb, came to contain several discrete residential enclaves. These subdivisions tended to imitate the movement for elegant isolation that was manifest in the "place" movement of nineteenth-century St. Louis. One such exclusive area had its origins in the country estate of Edward Gay, a St. Louisan who made a fortune from a Louisiana sugar plantation before the Civil War and then built a summer retreat outside the city. The property remained unchanged, as suburban developments were built up around it. In the 1920s, a suburban development company purchased it from his heirs and laid it out as an exclusive and expensive subdivision, which has maintained its character through the 1970s. This document is an excerpt from the company's promotional brochure. Charles A. Shaw and Estill W. Francies, How to Buy a Home with Safety *(St. Louis: McMullen Company, 1929), pp. 35–40.*

As the years passed . . . the widening limits of St. Louis began to stretch out toward the estate. In Forest Park, a bare mile and a half to the east, the World's Fair was held. The old St. Louis Country Club was opened across the road.

After the perfection of the automobile, the encroachment of the city was rapid. Homes began to appear. Directly east of the tract of land on which stood the mansion, Hampton Park, an exclusive residential section, sprang up. A mile to the north the fine homes of Carswold, Brentmoor, West Brentmoor, Forest Ridge, were built.

While the city grew up all about it, the 57 acres on which the house stood lay idle, with summer sunshine drenching the leaves of the great trees, or winter blasts sending snow swirling across the ice of the little lake.

At last, however, Mrs. Crow consented to sell. Yet her love for it persisted to the end! When, shortly before her death, she deeded it to the Lake Forest Development Corporation—named from the lake upon the estate—she wrote into the bargain restrictions that, by setting a minimum cost of $25,000 for residences built upon it, guarantee its development into a region of high-type homes. . . .

Two of its boundaries are formed by Hanley road and Clayton road, the latter of which has been expanded recently into a 100-foot boulevard. Thirty minutes away, by motor, lies the business district, and the drive downtown is one of the most beautiful in the city, leading as it does through Forest Park and along Lindell-Olive boulevard.

There are more than 1200 trees upon the ground, and 900 of these have trunks a foot or more in diameter. Even after the property is divided into 124 lots, there will with but few exceptions be at least three or four trees on every lot, while some will have from 15 to 20. . . .

The land is located in the heart of the fashionable west end. Because of the reluctance of Mrs. Crow to part with it, it has been held back from development, until now it is the one remaining undeveloped section in that district situated so close to town. All about it are fashionable homes. . . .

Typical of the residences that will be built in Lake Forest is the English-type house planned by William G. Kaysing, president of the Kaysing Iron Works. The house has eight rooms, with three baths and a two-car garage. Whitewashed brick walls will give an antique note that will be carried out in the interior.

There have been homes that, to meet the servant problem, have had to send motors to bring maid or cook out from town. Those who sometimes find it difficult to keep servants will therefore note with interest that the Kirkwood-Ferguson car line runs near the west edge of Lake Forest, while the Clayton car is within walking distance to the north.

Given the choice of working in a home that can be readily reached by street car, or in one that can be gotten to only by a difficult and circuitous route, a servant undoubtedly will prefer the former. And from Kirkwood-Ferguson cars, transfers can be made direct to the University, Hodiamont, Delmar, and other main line cars.

Families in which there are children will mark, too, that the John Burroughs and the Country Day School are near—and that several good city schools are in the neighborhood. For girls, the new Mary Institute, Hosmer Hall and Fontbonne College are not far by motor car. Washington University, a short distance to the northeast, can be reached either by street car or highway.

Suburban shopping districts, with stores of all kinds, are in easy walking distance.

9 | Country Club Swingers: Suburban Society, 1929

As the preceding promotional brochure suggests, one of the attractions of the Clayton subdivision of Lake Forest was its proximity to the St. Louis Country Club. It was around such institutions —rigidly organized according to religious, class, ethnic, and racial distinctions—that social life for elegant suburbanites swirled and sparkled. Every city that had the visible wealth to afford such recherché institutions by the 1920s also had a new kind of journalism to match. The New Yorker, founded in the mid-1920s under the tasteful motto "Not for the old lady from Dubuque," was the best known and the longest running, but all cities, even midwestern ones, made spirited literary efforts to explore the amusements, brand preferences, and prejudices of upper-class suburban society. "At the Country Clubs," Whip and Spur, I (August 1929), p. 6; (September 1929), p. 6.

There seems to be little enough for the stay-at-homes during these uneventful late summer months, but summer activities at the country clubs are adventure enough for any man. All roads lead to the country clubs and with the hordes of cars that go ricocheting over the many roads, it would seem that the less fortunate St. Louisans are finding diversion enough at their clubs.

The swimming pools at the various clubs are proving to be a popular rendezvous, with morning, afternoon, and evening swimming parties. Golf is running a close second for popularity, with a number of local tournaments in the last rounds. Several local tennis tournaments are drawing goodly throngs of interested spectators, in lieu of some fascinating inter-city polo matches recently played off in St. Louis. While we might say ecstatically that this is the height of the summer season—it is most certainly not the height of the social season, hence the *divertissement à la mode* continues to be country clubs.

. . . Soon the sun-tanned army of vacationists will be welcomed in our midst again. Sun-tanned, and how, for now that an ebony hued skin has become not only fashionable, but the rage, none—not even our fairest and most beautiful of daughters—seems to care a hang how many coats they acquire of it, while the doctors applaud vigorously.

However, I do not think that we neglected stay-at-homes need grow gray hairs for fear our own complexions will suffer by comparisons, for surely the various activities offered by our numerous country clubs afford every opportunity to burn to any degree which the exacting Goddess of Fashion dictates—and, judging from the looks of the assembled multitudes, we certainly have made the most of it.

Shades of Aesop, are we in danger of losing our identity as Anglo-Saxons, and becoming one with the Ethiopians?—or is this a phase through which we will safely pass and perhaps next year be compelled to tint ourselves a pale green to harmonize with the scenery! We'll find out and let you know. Where and how you acquire your favorite shade of tan is a matter of little importance, but I notice an increasing number of the fair sisterhood on the fairways of the golf links lately—I am finding out every day forty-eleven new things that golf is good for, and in meandering over the green hills I hear some good stories, apropos of which is this one—believe it or not, as you choose:

"My dear, I am so thrilled, I simply must tell you about it. I have learned to play golf, Yes—absolutely. It is just the easiest thing, really. Especially if you can line up an up-to-date pro to teach you. I picked Jack Travis because I had seen his picture in a golf magazine, and he is just my ideal,—tall, dark, and romantic looking, sort of the Antonio Moreno type, you know—I wore my pink wool ensemble, and took along a copy of 'What Every Golfer Should Know'—I thought I might need it.

"Well, Jack (of course I didn't call him that to his face), handed me a club, the brassie or the mashie, I can't remember which, anyway it doesn't make any difference—and told me to hold it just the way he did. My dear, his hair waves in the most fascinating way over his left brow!

"Everything clicked until we reached the eighth hole. I was all fagged and anyway I thought the game was over, but Jack said there were ten more holes to play, and he looked as though he had lost a lot of pep, too. So I suggested we take time out for a smoke.

The caddy was a cheerful pup. He grinned as though he was thinking of something funny all the time. I told Jack I wanted to win a cup. They look so cute on the mantelpiece and make everybody ask questions about how you won them, and everything.

"When we had finished, Jack was the sweetest thing, and said he knew I would make a 'hole in one' player. I must look that up in the book. I wonder if he meant it!"

10 | The Separation of the City from the County

The metropolitanization of St. Louis led to a serious and enduring political problem—the fragmentation of the area into a host of independent political units that rarely cooperated with each other. Except in the South and Southwest, the political boundaries of American cities stopped expanding between the turn of the century and World War I. This trend reversed the nineteenth-century pattern in which the spatial growth and the political growth of cities were kept in conjunction through the annexation or consolidation of suburbs. In 1876, St. Louis City separated from St. Louis County, thereby becoming one of the first cities to freeze its boundaries. Prior to 1876, there were five expansions—in 1822, 1839, 1841, 1855, and 1870—which enlarged the city from the original three-quarters of a square mile to nearly eighteen square miles. The largest single enlargement occurred in 1876, when St. Louis' size more than tripled, to its present sixty-one square miles. Along with this new land mass, the city gained a home-rule charter from which it was hoped more efficient and responsible government would emerge. Although occasionally voices were raised in favor of renewing the outward movement of the city's boundaries, the issue was not put to the vote again until 1926. It failed then, as it has on several subsequent occasions. Consolidation became an issue in the 1920s because of the massive population growth in the county compared to the city. This movement resulted in a proliferation of political units, which, from a regional point of view, hindered the efficient management of area resources and a rational approach to common problems. The perspective of city leaders on the subject is presented in this document, which is a historical review of the annexation movement, an outline of the consequences of limited city boundaries, and, as the title indicates, "a plea" for renewed expansion. Office of the Mayor, A Plea to the Constitutional Convention of Missouri for Enlargement of Boundaries of the City of St. Louis *(St. Louis, 1944), pp. 5, 11–12, 26–27.*

The City of St. Louis is in the throes of a great calamity and an impending disaster. Circumscribed by artificial boundaries, the City suffers like one whose feet are hobbled, whose hands are manacled and whose body is enclosed with a steel corset, which prevents the normal operation of all his vital functions. It is manifest that the City of St. Louis cannot remove or escape from the chains by which it is bound, unless relief shall come from the sovereign State of Missouri of which it is an important part. . . .

The [present] Constitutional Convention has the power to strike off the fetters and remove the unholy shackles that prevent the City of St. Louis from developing in accordance with divine and natural law.

There has been presented to the convention a proposal . . . which enlarges the boundaries of The City of St. Louis. The boundaries established by said proposal consolidate portions of St. Louis County, which in truth and in fact are already physically, naturally and economically a part of the city and also a reasonable area in which the city may further grow and develop. . . .

[The present boundary] represents what the people of 1876 considered a convenient limit for the municipal jurisdiction of the City of St. Louis, but it is in fact but a mark made in the shifting sand by the fallible finger of man. Our forefathers never intended that the boundaries thus empirically established should be immutable and serve as a prison wall to confine the resolute will and dauntless spirit of an ever expanding community and arrest its natural growth.

Emancipated from the County, the City of St. Louis became an independent political entity, enjoying a charter of its own creation and embarked upon the novel enterprise of municipal home rule. . . .

In 1900 and 1910, St. Louis ranked fourth in population among American cities. Beginning in 1910, the restricted boundaries of the city began to militate greatly against its growth. During a century and a half St. Louis had constantly increased and developed; earnest and enthusiastic citizens envisioned a city of a million souls. They organized the Million Population Club to hasten the consummation of their ambition. But, alas, the unfriendly attitude of St. Louis County in refusing to relinquish to St. Louis politically, what it had economically and physically created, constituted an insuperable barrier to our natural expansion.

The people of St. Louis have always been devoted to the cause of individual family homes. Between the Missouri River on the north and the Meramec River on the south, the terrain westward presents a pleasing prospect and invites habitation. The natural lay of the land, and its availability for homes confirmed the sentiment of our citizens against being tenementized. Adequate public transportation and the lessening cost of the automobile encouraged the building of homes beyond the city boundaries. . . . The migration westward beyond the city limits was stupendous. Conscious of the debilitating effect of this loss of population and resources, St. Louis sought relief by promoting a constitution method of enlarging its boundaries. The people of the State realized the plight that had befallen their fair and honored metropolis and in 1924 adopted the constitutional amendment [allowing consolidation of City and County]. . . .

Proceeding in accordance with the . . . constitutional amendment, a Board of Freeholders met on June 15, 1925, to prepare a scheme of consolidation. The Board did not finish its labors until June 3, 1926. The scheme submitted to the voters proposed the absorption of the entire county and the government of the entire area by the City of St. Louis. The scheme was submitted to the electors of the City and County on October 26, 1926, and was approved in St. Louis City by a vote of seven to one, but was rejected by the County electors by a vote of approximately three to one.

In 1930 there was submitted to the people a constitutional amendment proposing a consolidation of certain services. . . . This amendment received a favorable vote in St. Louis but the St. Louis County vote and the vote of the entire State was adverse and the amendment was not approved or adopted.

During the decade from 1920 to 1930, the population of St. Louis increased from 772,897 to 821,960 or 12½ per centum.

During the same decade St. Louis County's population increased from 100,737 to 211,593 or 110 per centum. In the decade from 1930 to 1940 the population of St. Louis County increased by 62,637 whereas St. Louis had decreased in population to the extent of 5,912, the first loss in population during its entire history. The canker worm is in the flower and only sound and heroic husbandry can prevent progressive and disastrous decay. St. Louis is defenseless and so circumscribed in its powers that it cannot rescue itself and, if impending calamity is to be avoided, relief must come from the sovereign State of Missouri as the *parens patriae.*

We have stated that in 1910 St. Louis was the fourth city of the country. In 1920 it ranked sixth; in 1930 it ranked seventh; in 1940 it ranked eighth. The superficial area of the eight largest cities of the nation [is] as follows:

New York City	299. square miles
Chicago	206.7 square miles
Philadelphia	129.7 square miles
Detroit	137.9 square miles
Los Angeles	448.6 square miles
Cleveland	73.1 square miles
Baltimore	78.7 square miles
St. Louis	61. square miles

That municipal government may effectively operate areas far greater than those assigned to St. Louis is amply demonstrated by the foregoing table.

11 | The Consolidation Plan of 1959

The 1950s witnessed the most recent efforts to effect a consolidation of the city with the county. Utilizing a provision of the 1943–1944 Missouri Constitutional Convention that authorized the establishment of metropolitan district agencies for the functional administration of specialized services in both areas, the St. Louis Sewer District was created in 1954. In the following year, a group of academics and interested citizens organized a study group that unsuccessfully proposed to the voters a metropolitan transit district. In 1958, another group put forward a far more ambitious plan, which caught national attention. They called for the Greater St. Louis City-County District, which would govern common services: traffic control, regulation of mass transportation, sewerage and drainage service, and coordination of police information and communication. Since observers believed that St. Louis had a better chance than most older cities to accomplish this plan, its failure in the 1959 election led to widespread disappointment. It also spurred newer cities in the South and Southwest to realize consolidation before outlying areas incorporated in order to forestall the difficulties that St. Louis encountered. Although, as the following analysis by local political scientists points out, there was considerable organizational support for the plan, it failed largely because of popular ignorance and disinterest. Despite the pleadings of academics and civic leaders, the citizens of Greater St. Louis lacked a sense of metropolitan imagination and community. Henry J. Schmandt, Paul G. Steinbicker, and George D. Wendel, Metropolitan Reform in St. Louis: A Case Study *(New York: Holt, Rinehart and Winston, 1961), pp. 38–42.*

The Line-up For

The business leadership of the community, with few exceptions, supported the district plan. Civic Progress, Incorporated early endorsed it as did both the city and county chambers of commerce and the heads of many leading St. Louis firms. The large business interests traditionally favored metropolitan reorganization, partly because they believe that the present fragmented system is not conducive to orderly and efficient administration, partly because they feel that reform will result in a better business and industrial climate, and partly because the development of their civic image requires them to promote such causes. The last motive appeared to be most prevalent among the businessmen supporting the district proposal. Many of the business leaders were only mildly interested in the proposed charter, viewing it neither as a desirable necessity nor as a threat. Yet, if for no other reason, their position in the community compelled them to voice approval of a civic proposal endowed with such respectable sponsorship.

A number of the religious groups also announced their support of the plan. Among those formally endorsing it were the Metropolitan Church Federation of Greater St. Louis and the Missionary Baptist Pastors and Ministers Union Conference, an organization of Negro clergymen. The Catholic hierarchy made no announcement, but the official Catholic weekly of the archdiocese editorially supported the proposal and expressed the wish that its readers would vote favorably on it. No Jewish association took an official stand, but a prominent rabbi gave personal endorsement. These expressions of support by religious groups were not surprising or particularly significant in the light of local tradition. It had long been common practice for the St. Louis churches to endorse movements for civic improvement, and the present campaign fell in that general category.

Although most of the trade and professional organizations remained neutral, a few such as the Realtors Association and the local chapters of the American Institute of Planners and the Institute of Architects publicly supported the proposal. Because of their concern with land use, each of these groups—realtors, planners, and architects—had something of a vocational or professional interest in the planning provisions of the charter.

The major civic organizations of the metropolitan area were also found in the ranks of the proponents. The ever-active League of Women Voters, including the suburban chapters, not only endorsed the charter but campaigned for its adoption. Other area-wide civic groups favoring the plan included the American Association of University Women, the Citizens Council on Housing and Community Planning, the General Council on Civic Needs, and the St. Louis Crime Commission. Local or sectional organizations such as improvement associations and neighborhood councils evidenced little public interest. Only three groups in this category took positions: two from the county in opposition and one from the city in favor.

The two metropolitan dailies, the *Post-Dispatch* and *Globe-Democrat,* gave full support to the district plan. . . . During the final week of the campaign both papers carried a huge banner headline in red ink across the top of the front page: VOTE YES ON METROPOLITAN DISTRICT PROPOSAL TUESDAY.

The Line-up Against

Organized labor was preponderantly against the district plan. It has always felt that its local political strength would be better enhanced through governmental consolidation than other types of reorganization. . . .

The central committees of the political parties in both city and county refrained from taking any stand on the grounds that the issue was not a partisan one. . . . All but a few of the ward leaders appeared indifferent to the election and those who announced their support made no great effort to deliver. In the county, despite official neutrality, the situation was quite different. Leaders of both parties were actively opposed to the plan. County Democrats wanted no part of any arrangement that would align them closer to their city counterparts in local governmental affairs. County Republicans, on the other hand, shuddered at the thought of an agency that might open the door to further Democratic encroachment on local offices. . . .

Opposition was also active among officials at the municipal level. While the mayors of several large suburban cities spoke in favor of the district plan, the overwhelming percentage of local office holders were against it. . . .

St. Louis County still has some agricultural land in its outer reaches although the total acreage is rapidly dwindling. Farmers in expanding metropolitan areas have always looked with suspicion upon attempts to change the local governmental structure, and those in the St. Louis environs have been no exception. It came as no surprise, therefore, when the St. Louis County Farm Bureau, with 200 members, voted unanimously to oppose the plan.

In contrast to the metropolitan dailies, the community or neighborhood weeklies took strong positions against the district proposal. Of the 29 such papers in the area (the majority of them in the suburbs), 22 expressed opposition and the others remained silent. . . .

. . . Protecting the virtues of the small community against the encroachment and evils of the big city provides them with a worthy, and at times dramatic, cause. And by fighting the "outsider," they are less likely to step on the toes of their local constituency. Metropolitan reorganization seems particularly worrisome to them probably because they feel that it may in some way pose a threat to their existence.

12 | The City Beautiful in St. Louis: Improvement of Kingshighway, 1903

The energies put forward in effecting a political plan for the region were matched by those spent in planning for its physical well-being. In large measure the objectives of physical and political planning were similar: establishing control over a community that was constantly expanding. The efforts in physical planning, however, brought more obvious results. Beginning in the 1890s, a succession of groups, dominated either by a few rich families or a single imposing professional, proposed a steady stream of creative and often innovative designs.

The catalytic event for much municipal redesign was Chicago's Columbian Exposition of 1893, which emphasized the erection of monumental buildings in large open spaces to provide an aesthetic and symbolic focus for community life. In preparation for the Louisiana Purchase Exposition of 1904, civic groups prodded the city government to create a commission that would search for a way of tying together St. Louis' open spaces. Reporting in 1903, with conscious reference to the City Beautiful Movement, the commission suggested a network of drives to join together the north and south sides of the city. City of St. Louis, Report of the Kingshighway Commission, March, 1903, *pp. 5–8.*

The direct purpose of the Kingshighway Commission is to show how the parks of St. Louis may be tied together and so become one system, susceptible of the greatest enjoyment and use by all classes of people. Parks, public playgrounds and parkways, which are the connecting links between parks, are recognized today as essential in a municipality, and in all cases they have been, and must be, constructed and maintained by the municipality itself. For the healthfulness of the great masses of our population who are unable, as a whole, to leave the city in times of summer heat, and as a proper recreation ground for them on holidays and the many half-holidays of the year, they fully justify their cost and maintenance.

St. Louis is showing its increasing love for out-of-door life in numerous ways. Compare the former light attendance in Forest Park with the crowds which now assemble there on a Sunday or a holiday. . . .

In laying out a park system with connecting parkways it is obviously necessary that the natural conditions of topography should be considered carefully. This has been done in Boston and Kansas City, and in the work contemplated here in St. Louis, we believe that the study of these natural conditions will show the ready adaptability of the park system and parkways as suggested by this commission. The hills and valleys west of the city present rolling country easily susceptible of increased park development. We have on the river at the northern and southern extremities of the city highlands or bluffs overlooking the Illinois shore, but the river itself cannot be utilized for pleasure purposes; therefore facilities for such other public recreation as driving, bicycling, a speedway, and the like, should be developed. . . .

This is eminently the time to plan the work of establishing such a parkway. Property is not yet so valuable in proximity to the suggested lines that it cannot be acquired, where necessary, at reasonable prices, and no doubt much property required for increased width of roadway or for parks could be obtained by donation, because of increased value to the adjacent property. In later years it will not be possible to treat the problem to such good advantage, or in such an unrestricted way. Then, too, we are about to commemorate the acquisition of the Louisiana Purchase by the Union, and what more fitting and lasting memorial for all time can there be than the improvement and beautifying of the old colonial Kingshighway? . . .

A city without pleasure and recreation grounds is like a home without adornment. If people are to remain in our city when their means enable them to reside elsewhere, if so disposed, how are we to retain them unless the city offers something in which they can feel a civic pride? The opportunity is here, if our citizens will but take hold and show the desire and enthusiasm necessary to carry out the plan suggested, and have the willingness and show the disposition to spend the comparatively small sum of money needed.

13 | The Model Street: A Contribution of the World's Fair of 1904

The Louisiana Purchase Exposition of 1904 is best remembered

*for its size: it was as large as the previous expositions in Phila-
delphia, Chicago, Omaha, and Buffalo together. The nascent city
planning profession also made its contribution to the fair. Leading
contemporary designers, including Frederick Olmsted, Daniel
Burnham, John Robinson, and Albert Kelsey, were invited to
prepare "improvement plans" for civic organizations and mu-
nicipalities preparing displays. The 1,271-acre fair site originally
was to include a complete model city, but this plan was scaled
down to a model city street. This exhibit demonstrated numerous
innovations that soon were introduced into American cities, as
planners moved from the "City Monumental" to the "City Efficient." Of particular value were examples of the various kinds
of surfaces that were needed for urban roads, "street furniture,"
and lighting standards. David R. Francis,* The Universal Exposition of 1904 *(St. Louis: Louisiana Purchase Exposition Company,
1913), pp. 340–42.*

Striking features of the Model Street were the various kinds of
paving used in the construction of the roadway. Beginning with
the Plaza of St. Louis, a Boston manufacturing company laid as
an exhibit 250 linear feet of the street with granite bituminous
paving. Continuing, a St. Louis company laid a strip of 200 linear
feet. Adjoining this the Exposition Company laid 150 feet of
macadam. The roadway across the square, 200 feet in length,
was laid by a prominent asphalt company. The rest of the square
was parked in lawns by the Exposition Company. Leading out
from the square at the right was 100 linear feet of typical New
Jersey roads made by the roads department of that state. The
same department, under the direction of R. A. Meeker, erected
a pavilion on the east side of the square and laid down a practical
exhibit of road-making showing its different stages of construction. Adjoining the New Jersey roads department, a paving company of St. Louis laid 100 feet of paving. The remaining 400 feet
of the street was laid down in macadam under the direction of
the National Good Roads Convention during the meeting in St.
Louis in May, 1904.

On both sides of the street were erected at intervals ornamental
street lamps, combination street lamps, letter boxes and sign posts,
tree guards and trolley poles, several styles of drinking fountains
and ornamental fountains, two advertising kiosks, one from Ber-

lin and one from Dresden, Germany, and many other features incident to modern street equipment. An exhibit of septic tanks, also of garbage disposal vaults illustrating auxiliaries of the well-kept city, were installed.

To the east of the public square was assigned a space fronting 250 feet on the Model Street and containing about 32,250 square feet or roughly three-quarters of an acre for a model playground, such as might be maintained by villages or towns at a comparatively small cost. . . .

The playground contained not only a complete outfit for a children's gymnasium and for children's outdoor sports, with shelters and rests, but also had special buildings for the care of smaller children and infants. It provided a convenient place where children of any age could be left by parents visiting the Exposition, with assurance of safety and careful supervision. . . . In addition to fully serving its purpose as a model of its kind, it cared for over 7,000 children during the exposition period, ranging in age from two weeks upward. Over 1,200 of these were given care free of charge.

14 | The Civic League's Plan for St. Louis, 1907

Within the movement for reform which swept across the country during the late nineteenth and early twentieth centuries, a group of St. Louisans in 1902 organized the Civic Improvement League as the local branch of the American League for Civic Improvement. By 1904 this group was sufficiently well established to host a convention of similar organizations from other cities. A 1903 article in a national magazine characterized the league in the following way: "It is a business organization, doing its work purely on a business basis, with a paid secretary and solicitor, and appealing successfully for support to the wealth and influence of the city. By the accomplishments of its comparatively short life it has taught the St. Louis business man that cleanliness and public beauty pay dividends." Renamed simply the Civic League in 1907, it published St. Louis' first comprehensive plan, one of the first for an American city in the modern period. Dealing with the problems of recreation, spatial expansion, and efficient transportation, the plan's greatest significance is that many of its recommendations were realized over the next half century. This

synopsis of the plan is excerpted from the Architectural Record.
C. M. R., "The City Plan Report of St. Louis," Charities and
Commons, *XIX (February 1, 1908), pp. 1542–45.*

Following a brief introduction, there is printed, as a "statement
of the general committee," a chapter of The Need of a City Plan
for St. Louis. In this the familiar arguments are rehearsed, the
examples of other cities are cited, it is stated that in the preparation of the report there has been "kept constantly in view the
practical and the attainable," and that as a result of the previous
lack of plan and insufficient regulation there has existed a "riot
of conflicting and selfish interests" before which the citizens were
helpless. The next chapter is an illustrated historical sketch of the
physical growth of St. Louis. In its considerable length this offers
an exceedingly interesting study of the undirected development
of a city from its village days.

Following that comes the first division of the report proper. It
considers the Public Building Group, and is a reprint, with "hearty
endorsement," of the report of the Public Buildings Commission
issued some three years ago.

The succeeding chapter, on Civic Centers or Small Building
Groups, is one of the most interesting and distinctive features of
the St. Louis report. The idea is the grouping around a common
center, especially around a small park or playground, of the various public, semi-public and private institutions which have for
their object the mental, moral or physical improvement of the
neighborhood. This is urged with the greatest earnestness, both in
general terms and specifically. The committee selects the sites
for such centers, reviewing the needs of each neighborhood and
the local advantages of the selected site. It develops a complete
system of civic centers, and in doing so confines itself to what
would seem to be the immediately possible; for it limits its recommendations of park reservations for this purpose to the $670,000
included in the bond issue. If the plan is carried out St. Louis
will have for its congested district a series of civic centers with
which only Chicago, in its South Park district, could compete. The
bulk of the argument is . . . social and philanthropic; though it is
pointed out that the [civic centers] . . . would foster civic pride
in the neighborhood. . . .

The discussion of Inner and Outer Parks and Boulevards comes next. There is mapped a complete system to connect the park and forest reservations of the county. For one of the most important of the inner links, the Kingshighway, nineteen miles long and extending from river to river and tying together the principal parks, the money has already been appropriated and detail[ed] plans are completed. As to the parks themselves, St. Louis takes rank among the first cities in the country for the relative acreage of its reservations, but heretofore it has lacked such connecting drives to bind them into a system. The report, besides discussing the Kingshighway, plans a second boulevard to follow the Des Peres River and to extend to Jefferson Barracks. The two together, it is claimed, would give to the city a "parkway system unsurpassed in variety and beauty of scenery by any city in the Union, with the possible exception of Boston. The total length of the drives and parkways would be about thirty-five miles." And yet this is only the "inner system."

In the way of "outer," or country, parks, there is planned a belt system of drives and reservations suggestive of the Essex County system in New Jersey, of the Metropolitan system about Boston, and of those proposed for Providence, Chicago, Washington and other centers. The beauty of the natural scenery around St. Louis, the rapid growth of the city, the need of pleasanter connections with the suburbs, are pointed out in general advocacy of the plan, but the committee frankly says it has no hope or expectation of seeing so much accomplished within the next five or ten years. This part of the plan is "offered as a comprehensive scheme toward which the city can strive for the next quarter of a century, adding section after section, as the circumstances demand and the finances of the city and county will permit."

In the chapter on Street Improvements there is reached the last chapter that deals strictly with the city plan. This includes suggestions for the river front, the railway entrance, street car lines, etc. The committee, stating that it has considered the streets "from two points of view—utility and attractiveness," adds that here there are "suggested only those changes which seem possible of accomplishment within the next decade."

As to the river front, the report calls attention to the present deplorable condition—the familiar municipal story in America: a noble site, almost abandoned by business, the city turning its back upon it and it becoming a resort of the vicious and depraved. But new plans are timely. There is not only agitation for a deep waterway to the Gulf, but the citizens of St. Louis have voted in favor of a free bridge, which in itself gives great opportunity. Inserted maps and drawings show conditions as they are and "as they ought to be." It is proposed that the property lying between the Eads Bridge and the proposed bridge at Poplar street and extending back from the levee to Second street, be purchased by the city, the bluffs for the whole width excavated to a level with the levee and a broad esplanade constructed the entire distance on a level with Third street. Under this esplanade, at the levee level, would be the railroad tracks. Warehouses at Third street would have basement connection with the freight tracks, and at intervals on the river side of the esplanade there would be little passenger stations for suburban trains. Between the river level and the esplanade there would be connection by elevators and inclined roadways, as at Algiers. The suggested treatment is simple, dignified and commercially beneficial.

Of the proposed street changes the most radical are those designed to improve the approach to the Union station. It is recommended that the city widen Chestnut street to 150 feet from the station to the municipal buildings group and develop it like the Champs Elysees, and that there be purchased two blocks for a small park. The report also discusses at some length the improved development of the streets, the restriction of the width of roadways on residential streets, the systematic planting of trees, the removal of unsightly poles and wires, the establishment of a building line, the adoption of better designs for street utilities. The final chapters of the report are devoted to an appeal for a Municipal Art Commission and to a discussion of the legislation that would be needed to make effective the recommendations of the [several working] committees.

15 | The Introduction of Zoning, 1918

In 1912, St. Louis established its City Plan Commission, thereby becoming the second American city to do so. This movement to city-sponsored professional departments was derived from European precedents, particularly those of Germany and Great Britain.

*The much-hailed reform of zoning also was a European import.
It had spread through Germany and Great Britain at the turn of
the century. One of its great virtues was that it promised much
but cost nothing. Through regulation of the size of buildings and
the amount of the lot they covered, it was expected that the types
of structures and their uses could be predetermined and the real
estate market thereby would be made predictable. In addition,
zoning requirements were expected to control congestion, which
had long been a major objective of public health and social reformers. For a short time, zoning was the panacea both for reformers who sought to humanize the city and for businessmen
who wanted to rationalize the marketplace. In reality, only the
business interests were to be satisfied, since reformers traditionally
have had little power on the zoning boards that manage the ordinances and issue variances.*

*In 1916, New York led the way with the first zoning ordinance.
The St. Louis code of 1918 made a significant advance by more
clearly connecting zoning to land use. This article is one of the
first that was written by Harlan Bartholomew, then engineer for
the St. Louis City Plan Commission, later the principal owner in
the largest city planning firm in the United States. Harlan Bartholomew,* Zoning for St. Louis: A Fundamental Part of the City
Plan *(St. Louis: The City Plan Commission, 1918), pp. 10–17.*

Zoning for St. Louis

When a building intended for residential, commercial, or industrial purposes is to be erected, it is taken as a matter of course
that the plans be first prepared by architects and engineers in
such a way as to adapt the finished structure to meet the requirements which are to be subserved. It is clearly recognized that to
proceed without such a plan would be ruinous. But when it comes
to the application of this simple, common-sense idea to the planning of aggregates of such structures—to the physical arrangement of towns or cities as a whole—we have been strangely
remiss. Even the most casual observer must have noted the . . .
lack of definite grouping of structures with respect to their functions; the congestion here and vacant tracts there; and certainly
all owners of property must have deplored the widespread tendency toward instability of values. . . .

City planning has for its object the overcoming of such evils. It proceeds in two well-defined directions. First, the deliberate and conscious control of public property such as the streets, parks, playgrounds and public buildings, and incidentally of all means of transportation and of traffic movement; second, the control of private property to such an extent as is necessary to conserve the general welfare of the community.

The first function of city planning, the control of public property, is clearly within the legal right of any community, and involves no new feature save the fact that when its scope is made city-wide it takes official cognizance of the organic unity of the entire community.

The second function of city planning, the control of private property, is embraced under the meaning of the terms "zoning" or "districting." It . . . is clearly of the greatest importance if for no other reason than that private property constitutes the great bulk of the physical aspect of the community, and that the use or misuse of such property will either make or mar the aggregate. Obviously, there are limitations on the right of a community to impose restrictions or otherwise to control private property, and whatever form they may take they must still be within the scope of the police powers of the community, as defined, or in the future to be defined, by the courts.

Evils Due to Lack of Zoning

Overcrowding of Land

Up to a certain limit, the value of a piece of land will increase as the number and size of buildings upon it increase, and as the number of people living or working in those buildings becomes greater. But the significant fact is that *there is a limit to the intensive use of land beyond which values must decline.* As the density of population becomes greater, the space required for pedestrian and vehicular traffic must likewise increase, and as these space requirements are conflicting, there must be a point at which intensive development must cease if the highest efficiency is to be realized.

But over and above such economic considerations is the social consideration that a definite relation exists between the health and morals of the population and the degree to which it is congested. Dense population brings in its train such evils as high infant mortality, tuberculosis, adult crime and immorality, and juvenile crime, which has been defined as misdirected play, is the inevitable result.

The city has permitted such conditions to arise through its own negligence or short-sightedness. . . . [Suitable living conditions would] cure the evils and prevent their perpetuation. . . .

Inflation and Instability of Property Values

As stated above, the value of property is increased up to a certain limit by greater intensiveness of use. But if congestion exceeds this limit, a reaction inevitably sets in and values will decline. Familiar illustrations are found in many districts where skyscraper conditions prevail. The first few high buildings enjoy a certain popularity because of the advantages they offer in the way of light and air; but when other high buildings are erected in close proximity, these initial advantages disappear, and rentals decline. At the same time, street congestion increases markedly, and the usual outcome is the construction of another high building in a new location, thus carrying the evil to a new district and blighting the old one.

One's first impulse in thinking about high buildings is that the financial returns ought to increase with increasing height, because it appears at first sight that each added story means just so much more rentable space. But the case is by no means so simple. Added height necessarily involves more elevators . . . and more elevators very rapidly absorb floor area; moreover, columns must be larger and walls thicker, with the result that ground floor area falls off very rapidly. . . . Further, the administrative expenses increase rapidly with height. Because of these and other reasons, the very high building has not been found to be a good paying investment, and in the opinion of those best qualified to speak with authority, the limiting height consistent with good financial returns is in the neighborhood of twelve stories. There is thus an automatic tendency to check unlimited inflation of business property values.

Evils of a corresponding nature occur when too intensive development is permitted in residence districts. We think of them in connection with slum districts, where they appear in aggravated form. But we are slower to realize that the very thing which produces slums, namely, too great congestion, is being brought about under our eyes in many apartment house districts in what we fondly refer to as the better class neighborhoods.

A second cause of unstable land values, and one which is perhaps more serious, is the indiscriminate intermingling of structures having nothing in common with each other. Residence districts often have great potential value, which value lasts until the district is invaded by a store, factory or apartment house even, when unusual decline of value occurs. . . . Great economic advantage may accrue to the invader, but this is many times offset by the loss to scores of occupants of the district invaded.

Here also it is of first importance for the city to recognize and attempt to regulate haphazard growth with its consequent economic loss. Individuals are damaged, but the city is damaged most. The taxable earning power of the city is reduced, business is retarded and substantial expansion is limited.

What Is Zoning?

"Districting" or "zoning" is the power of a city to control, to a limited extent, the character of all building development within the city. It means the establishment by the city of restrictions on the *height, area* (bulk) and *use* of all buildings. Zoning is a justifiable use of the police power in the interests of health, safety and the general welfare. To enforce a proper districting plan is to so fix growth and the tendencies of growth that stability will replace chaos and the destructive element of uncertainty in city expansion will largely be removed. Appropriate character and intensity of the use of land cannot fail to insure permanence, preserve life, conserve resources and increase the amenities of life.

16 | The Planned City, 1916–1944

The American Planning and Civic Association convened in St. Louis in 1944, forty years after its parent organization, the American Civic Association, held its original meeting in the city. This convention of articulate and active citizens supportive of planning provided Harlan Bartholomew with an opportunity to document how St. Louis became one of the nation's most planned, if not always the best planned, city in the period between the wars. In addition to reviewing past accomplishments, he outlined new challenges and articulated the important role planning had assumed in the development of the modern city. Harlan Bartholomew, "The Saint Louis Plan in Action," American Planning and Civic Annual *(American Planning and Civic Association, 1944), pp. 112–15.*

It was on April 1, 1916 that a new City Plan Commission received its initial appropriation, adopted a program of work and employed a staff to carry it out. The initial work was the preparation of a report "Problems of Saint Louis" in which were discussed the general nature of the city plan needed for Saint Louis and the specific studies which should be undertaken. . . .

This was a pioneer undertaking. Only a few other American cities had attempted to prepare comprehensive city plans. There were no precedents to follow. There were no state laws authorizing the work. There was no well established procedure to follow. The only authority for the work was an ordinance passed by the Board of Aldermen in 1911. An earlier attempt to do this type of work for which a previous commission had been appointed had ended in failure.

The new city plan was accepted and followed by practically all administrative offices of the City Government. In 1923 an $87,000,000 bond issue was approved by the electorate which made available funds for carrying out much of the work shown in the proposed city plan. This bond issue also included funds for other public improvements such as additional hospitals, water supply, sewers, street lighting and the like.

The original program was supplemented by a special study of the riverfront undertaken in 1925. Two reports were issued from this study:

A Plan for the Central Riverfront	1928
Plans for the Northern and Southern Riverfront	1929

A report on Ten Years Progress on the city plan in Saint Louis was published in 1927. A special study of the integrated problems of population trends, land use, zoning and taxation was published in 1936 entitled "Urban Land Policy."

Thus for twenty-five years Saint Louis has followed consistently a comprehensive city plan. Something over fifty reports have been prepared, some of which have appeared only in mimeographed form. Over 8,500 maps, plans, drawings and studies have been prepared and are on file in the office of the Commission.

From the standpoint of comprehensive city planning, the City of St. Louis has been one of the most active of the large American cities. The City is now equipped with a full quota of public improvements of modern design. We have a water supply that is unexcelled. The entire City's area is provided with sewers and storm water drains. An unusually complete system of wide, well paved and fully lighted main thoroughfares serve[s] all parts of the City. . . .

Many neighborhood parks and playgrounds have been acquired and improved throughout the entire City's area. A large group of public buildings has been constructed around the Memorial Plaza. Seven blocks were acquired for the Memorial Plaza at a cost of approximately $4,600,000. Of these, six comprising 9.54 acres are now devoted to open space. The Soldier's Memorial Building has been constructed at an approximate cost of $1,000,000. The municipal Auditorium covers an area of almost six acres, and faces the Memorial Plaza. The Opera House seats 3,500 persons and the Convention Hall which cost approximately $5,000,000, seats 12,000. The Civil Court House, completed in 1930, is at the east end of the Plaza. Building and land cost about $5,600,000. Across the street from the Civil Court House is the new United States Court House and Custom House. Original buildings facing the plaza site consisted only of the City Hall, Municipal Courts Building and Public Library. Three blocks west of the Memorial Plaza is the Aloe Plaza comprising two blocks and having an area of 2.19 acres, which was acquired when Market Street was widened. The Fountain by Carl Milles, dedicated in 1940, depicts the Wedding of the Mississippi and Missouri Rivers. As a result of the Aloe Plaza the beautiful facade of the Union Station can now be fully appreciated.

The entire Central Riverfront comprising all of thirty-nine, and a portion of three additional city blocks, has been acquired for approximately $7,700,000 by the City of St. Louis and the United States Government for a National Monument to be known as the Jefferson National Expansion Memorial.

On the other side of the ledger are several new problems of great magnitude, such as decentralization of population and of business, declining property values, especially in centrally located slum areas and large surrounding areas of blighted districts. However, as a first step in meeting these problems, two low-cost housing projects have been constructed, and the site for a third project has been acquired. The projects completed are: The Clinton-Peabody Terrace, a USHA project for 657 white families, which consists of 53 two- and three-story fire-proof buildings with a total of 2,820 rooms in units of 3 to 6½ rooms, at a total cost of approximately $3,500,000.

The City Plan Commission was instrumental in having adopted a State Act providing for an Urban Redevelopment Corporation, to permit the assembling of land for housing projects to be financed with private capital. The Report "Saint Louis After World War II," published by the City Plan Commission in 1942 suggests a realistic land program that should be carried out after the present war to solve one of the greatest economic and social problems that confronts Saint Louis.

There are still unsolved problems of street congestion. The Major Street Plan adopted in 1917 was revised in 1942 making certain recommendations for opening and widening of streets. One of the Major Street undertakings, to be initiated after the war, will be an Interregional Highway from the southern city limits along the riverfront to the Jefferson Memorial Area, where it will then go on to the Third Street elevated roadway extending north of the Memorial Area, thence following the riverfront to the northern city limits. The projected Third Street elevated roadway was proposed by the City Plan Commission in its Central Riverfront Report published in 1928.

There is need for several additional neighborhood parks and playgrounds. In January 1944 the City Plan Commission completed its revision of the Master Recreation Plan and published a report entitled "Plan for Public Recreational Areas." The plan is an attempt to anticipate the City's needs in public recreational areas during the next two or three decades.

There is need for a new modern zoning ordinance which the Commission has drafted recently.

17 | Problem Areas of St. Louis, 1937

An important emphasis of the professional planning movement was the accumulation of factual information in order to assess more effectively social and physical problems. This data gathering became especially important during the 1930s, as local, state, and federal agencies attempted to cope with the terrible consequences of the depression. The research approach followed by the St. Louis Community Council, a local welfare agency, was one formulated by urban ecologists. The method was to delineate the dimensions of various pathologies and relate them to the city's neighborhoods. Although the roughly drawn maps that accompanied this report have not been included here, the tone and statistics are sufficient to convey the message: St. Louis' urban problems were concentrated heavily in the downtown and its surrounding inner-city areas. The focus on social problems marked a significant turning point in the direction of city planning in St. Louis. Previously, most proposals had dealt with the problems of growth. Beginning with the depression decade, arresting and eliminating decay became increasingly important concerns. St. Louis Community Council Research Department, "Problem Areas of St. Louis," Social Studies of St. Louis, XXVIII (March 1938), pp. 2–9.

To George Bernard Shaw "The old notion that people can keep to themselves and not be touched by what is happening to their neighbors, or even to the people who live a hundred miles off, is a most dangerous mistake." For, he adds, "The saying that we are members one of another is not a mere pious formula; . . . It is a literal truth; for though the rich end of the town can avoid living with the poor, it cannot avoid dying with it when the plague comes." Events have so conclusively established the truth of this assertion that most of us are inclined to take it for granted and cease to respond to its challenge. At any rate, social problems march on, despite our recognition of their hurtful effects upon us all.

For the past five years, this Research Department has studied annual changes in community conditions with which social work is concerned and discovered a persistent recurrence of certain serious social and health problems. Geographic analysis of these problems revealed their presence in almost every nook and cranny of the town, although the distribution was by no means uniform. Some neighborhoods, in point of fact, showed pretty high concentrations. What is more, they appeared to have the lion's share of, not one, but many problems—steadily, year after year. In view of the persistent prevalence of problems in these areas, we have termed them "the problem areas" of St. Louis. They represent not only the places where social problems are most numerous, but in a very literal sense, the "sore spots" of the community, the sources of our social infections.

These areas include seven districts: namely, Downtown, Beaumont, Garfield, Mill Creek, Soulard, Hyde Park and Lindell; extending over almost a fifth of the city's acreage. They are located in the heart of the city. We must go through some of them to reach the downtown offices, factories, stores, theatres and restaurants. Yet, not many of us are aware of them; of their physical deterioration, their dreadful housing, filthy alleys, lack of proper sanitation and of even minimum comforts of living; although a turn off the main traffic thoroughfares will land us in the midst of these conditions. Even fewer of us are aware of the conditions in these areas which do not as easily meet the eye: the widespread unemployment, low family incomes, dependency, family tensions, sickness, delinquency and vice.

The extent of these problems comes to light as we glance over the available statistics. Unfortunately, statistics are not kept on very many problems of neighborhoods. The few studies here were taken from the records of the City Bureau of Vital Statistics and the Social Service Exchange. They represent the situation in 1937 in respect to: births, illegitimacy, deaths, infant deaths, maternal deaths, child care, delinquency, diphtheria, insanitary conditions, tuberculosis, syphilis, family relief, and health care.

Analysis of the figures pertaining to these problems discloses that the seven neighborhoods which we have labeled "problem areas" account for a considerably larger proportion of the amount of each problem than is justified either by the number of people living in them or by the size of their territory.

Contrasted with the fact that these areas comprise only 34% of the city's estimated total population and only 19% of its total territory are these findings: That the problem areas are responsible for: 40% of all births; 75% of all illegitimacy; 41% of all deaths; 52% of all infant deaths; and 49% of all maternal deaths. That they are chargeable for: 60% of all child care cases; 66% of all delinquency cases; and 39% of all diphtheria cases. That they produce: 52% of all nuisances (insanitary conditions); 63% of all tuberculosis cases; 64% of all syphilitic deaths; 53% of all relief cases; and 47% of all health problem cases. . . .

. . . [There are] wide variations between districts in all but three problems: births, deaths and health cases. Of the seven districts labeled "problem areas" Beaumont stands out with excessively high rates in six problems, moderately high rates in five and a median rate in one. Mill Creek ranks as the second "problem area," with excessive rates in seven problems, a moderately high rate in one and median rates in four. Downtown places third, with excessive rates in six problems, moderately high rates in three and a median rate in one. Soulard comes fourth, topping in one problem, near topping in three, and averaging in seven. Garfield follows with moderately high rates in four problems and median rates in seven.

18 | Housing the Poor: Pruitt-Igoe

With the passage of federal legislation in 1937 and state legislation in 1939, St. Louis embarked on a program of building low-rent housing. The first two projects, Carr-Square and Clinton-Peabody Terrace, were completed in 1942. Despite the increase of substandard housing and low-income families, little else was done until 1949 because of a lack of money and the possibility that investment in such housing would not be tax-exempt. With new federal legislation in 1949 that provided funds and the classification of public housing as tax-exempt by the courts in the same year, there developed renewed interest in such projects. The most ambitious programs were the building of the Pruitt and Igoe apartments just north of the central business district. The Pruitt apartments, completed in 1955 at a cost of $21,689,000, were a complex of twenty eleven-story high-rises originally intended for *white tenants. The Igoe apartments, completed a year later for $14,438,000, were composed of thirteen eleven-story buildings for black tenants. After the Supreme Court decision of 1954 concerning nondiscrimination in housing, Pruitt-Igoe opened without racial quotas. In fact, from the beginning, almost all of the 11,500 residents of the 33 buildings were black. Initially, Pruitt-Igoe attracted attention because it was one of the largest and supposedly one of the best-designed public housing projects of the post-World War II period. Rather than remain a source of pride, the project quickly became a local and national scandal. By 1975, a contract had been let for its total demolition. Critics have debated what went wrong. There are basically two schools of thought: that which blames the architects and that which blames the tenants. The argument is actually about a century old, revolving around the question of whether behavior can be modified through environmental programs or whether people alone bear responsibility for the conditions under which they live. The two views are summarized by William Clay, a black representative from St. Louis who is critical of the architects, and Lenore Sullivan, a conservative, white representative from St. Louis, who finds the blacks unworthy by suggesting that others would have behaved differently.* Congressional Record, *92nd Congress, 1st Session, August 3, October 21, 1971, pp. 29209–10, 37303.*

KMOX Editorial:
The Shame of St. Louis—Pruitt-Igoe

MR. CLAY. Mr. Speaker, a recent editorial by KMOX-TV in St. Louis discusses the public housing shame of St. Louis—Pruitt-Igoe. The editorial expresses a sentiment that I have pointed up time and again—that no matter how much money is poured into this public housing structure, it would be a futile effort to try to reconstruct a disaster. . . .

An environment such as this induces acts of crime. In fact, crime and vandalism run rampant in Pruitt-Igoe. The only way to end these problems is by removing the source which creates them. In this case, the source is Pruitt-Igoe. . . .

I endorse the KMOX editorial and commend it to my colleagues' attention:

Pruitt-Igoe

More millions in federal money have been proposed to rehabilitate the public housing shame of St. Louis—Pruitt-Igoe. In KMOX-Television's opinion, this would be a futile repetition of other costly efforts to rectify a monumental error in the project's original concept.

Pruitt-Igoe was doomed the day it left the drawing boards. You can't concentrate almost 3,000 low-income families in 43 [*sic*] high-rise buildings and expect them to survive in an area that provided no shopping facilities, no health services, inadequate transportation, a minimum of job opportunities, and almost non-existent schooling, playground, and recreational facilities.

Discontent, crime, vandalism and subsequent low occupancy were automatically programmed into this ill-conceived project. Originally, 43 buildings were constructed 16 years ago at a cost of $36 million. Ten years later, another $5 million was spent in renovation. Today, only 17 of the buildings have occupants in about 600 apartments. The remaining 26 structures have been sealed shut to prevent further vandalism and opportunities for crime, at an additional cost of several hundred thousand dollars.

Mr. Elmer Smith, Area Director of Housing and Urban Development, has proposed this new attempt to salvage Pruitt-Igoe. He says if the city of St. Louis and representatives of all public housing projects, business, civic and labor leaders were to plan and work to change that area adjacent to downtown so that its residents become an integral part of the entire community, then Pruitt-Igoe can be saved.

Mr. Smith has an excellent idea—had it been proposed 16 or even 10 years ago. It might then have had some chance of success. But not now. It is much too late.

We agree that this area and its residents must be brought into and made a viable part of the community. And we urge more money should be spent on Pruitt-Igoe—but not for renovation. It should be leveled to the ground. Then new plans, new ideas and new public housing concepts can be devised without the 43 specters of failure casting their shadow over these blighted areas.

Lenore K. Sullivan:
A Tragedy of Social Bankruptcy

I think it is a tragedy of social bankruptcy that in my own city of St. Louis we are being urged to tear down a housing project built only 16 years ago to accommodate thousands of families, because no decent family wants to live in the units and few of the units are even habitable. They have been literally torn apart—destroyed—and turned into a jungle of crime, vandalism, and trespass, by drug addicts and others exercising squatters' rights.

Those who built the project with such high hopes only 16 years ago made many mistakes in planning and in format—they built wrong for the wrong size families, for one thing; for another, they made the by-now universally understood mistake of cramming thousands of children into huge high-rise buildings. Under the very best of environments, large numbers of young children usually are not compatible with high-rise buildings. Of course it can be accomplished without disaster if the children are under rigid discipline and control at all times. For instance, if you go into a high-rise apartment project in Singapore or in Hong Kong, full of people and especially full of young children, you hear a constant twittering of bird-like sounds composed of a multitude of quiet voices talking in Chinese sing-song, but there is order and control; the places are spotless; the people who live in them are buoyed in spirit and absolutely delighted with their step up the housing ladder to their very own private homes—even a single room for a family. These were families which previously lived in shacks or packing boxes, on boats, or out in the open.

American Patterns of Life Compared to
Those of Asian Refugees

Perhaps one day those huge Asian projects, too, will become uninhabitable slums, but I doubt it. They can be kept livable. But it requires a life style or life philosophy which is not generally characteristic of the way American families with children live—neither the rich, the moderate income, nor the poor. I mean, among other things, the absolute control over the children's activities, so that whether they are playing many floors below on an open playground or in the fields nearby or on the streets, they are respectful of the neighbors and the neighborhood. The children in the Asian projects I mentioned are multitudinous, but orderly —even when playing actively in groups, with or without constant adult supervision.

If 1,000 or more families from Singapore or Hong Kong were moved into one of our problem housing projects in a metropolitan area of the United States, I suspect they would carry this life style with them. Perhaps not. It would probably depend upon how many American families were also living there, and which group instructed, or "corrupted," the other.

Since American families as a rule exercise a certain degree of "social anarchy" in the mass, we cannot expect them to act like Chinese families living in Singapore or Hong Kong, or Japanese families in Tokyo. Yet our large high-rise housing projects were all built with the idea that the clean and sturdy surroundings would automatically instill in the tenants the same life-style characteristics of a refugee family in an Oriental metropolis, a family which had fled famine and regimentation in China and had come to another country where there was food and perhaps employment, too, but absolutely no place to live except what you created for yourself out of a few boards and a sheet of tin, until the authorities could move you into something better.

19 | The Comprehensive City Plan of 1947: Post–World War II Housing Problems

This document outlines the local context in which the Pruitt-Igoe tragedy occurred. Although St. Louis' population peaked in the early 1950s at 880,000, residential construction did not match this growth through the depression and World War II. Only outside the city, particularly in the postwar period, were homes built in substantial number. Recognizing that something had to be done, experts proposed not only putting up new public housing such as Pruitt-Igoe but a host of less expensive or no-cost measures to preserve or encourage the rehabilitation of existing housing. True to the traditions of the city in which discrete residential areas had existed for nearly a century, and in consonance with the teachings of modern planning that underscored the value of communities, the 1947 plan emphasized the need for neighborhood reconstruc-

*tion. But the brilliant initiatives taken under the City Plan Com-
mission three decades earlier could not be continued; it was easier
to build public facilities like roads, airports, and civic centers
than deal with the underlying social issues involved in rehabili-
tating older housing. City Plan Commission,* Comprehensive City
Plan, Saint Louis, Missouri *(1947), pp. 27–33.*

We cannot truthfully say that St. Louis is a good place in which
to live *when—*

We spend $4,000,000 general tax funds annually to maintain
our obsolete areas. (This sum represents the difference in cost of
governmental service and tax collections annually in these areas.)

We have 33,000 dwellings still dependent on outside privy
vaults. . . .

We have an additional 25,000 dwellings where toilets are
shared by several families.

We have 82,000 dwellings in structures built before 1900.

We have obsolete and blighted districts because our interest has
always been centered in the newest and latest houses and subdivisions in areas of new development. As home owners have
moved to successive outlying neighborhoods the earlier homes
have gradually been allowed to deteriorate. No matter how great
the extent of disintegration these old homes are seldom adequately
repaired and are rarely torn down. This is no way to build a
sound city. . . .

We have had no *Housing Policy* and no *Housing Program* other
than that of abandonment of old areas and of moving to new
fringe areas. This is a frightfully wasteful policy of which we
have not yet reckoned the full cost. It is a tragic policy because
of the poor housing conditions which must be endured by those
unable to move to the new outlying areas.

Our obsolete and blighted districts now embrace half the city's
residential area. . . . They will continue to expand until the whole
city is engulfed unless we remove the causes of this condition.
There is no reason why the older neighborhoods cannot be kept
wholesome and attractive. We can redirect our attention to creating
good living conditions in older central areas with much advantage
and profit. It is not difficult to visualize complete transformation of
the city by a new housing policy and a bold program. . . .

In order to study intimately the local conditions in all parts of the city, St. Louis has been divided into 82 residential neighborhoods and 17 industrial districts. . . . As a result of these studies, a definite constructive housing plan and policy is suggested herewith.

Obsolete Areas

Present obsolete areas must be cleared and reconstructed. This is a social necessity as well as an economic essential. The City of St. Louis cannot continue to thrive and prosper where there is nothing but progressive decadence in its housing supply, any more than it could with polluted water supply or smoke laden air.

The unit area for reconstruction must be the neighborhood. It is necessary to create a new environment. This can be accomplished only by large scale operations. Obsolete neighborhoods must be rebuilt, not merely with houses of good design and construction, but with more open space, more park and playground facilities, a good school and community center. . . .

Present high costs of building construction together with rent controls preclude immediate reconstruction of obsolete areas, either for public or for private housing. As construction costs become lower the city must be in a position to encourage wholesale reconstruction of these obsolete areas. This can be achieved by public acquisition of land so that it could be made available for housing and other needed purposes if private acquisition and construction fails to accomplish the needed results. The total cost of clearance would scarcely exceed public expenditure during the past 25 years for other types of public work such as streets, sewers, and airports. Unlike these, however, ownership of the land would be a sound investment. The land could be leased or sold, and much if not all of the expense involved could be recovered by (1) elimination of the present $4,000,000 annual deficit, (2) a long term increment in taxable revenues on private housing projects, and (3) participation in Federal subsidy programs. . . .

Blighted Districts

The blighted districts should be extensively rehabilitated before they degenerate into obsolete areas. This is both a social need and an economic essential because of high rates of juvenile delinquency, crime, and disease found in areas of poor housing.

Rehabilitation of blighted districts must be undertaken on a neighborhood basis also in order to protect environment and to create improved living standards. Because of the larger areas involved, special planning and experimentation is required. Obsolete buildings should be removed, some streets should be closed, new park, playground and recreation areas created, small concentrated shop areas established, and individual buildings should be repaired and brought up to a good minimum standard. The new Constitution of Missouri specifically provides for this type of rehabilitation. There is fully as much opportunity for private enterprise in this field as in the more spectacular large scale reconstruction housing projects.

The most important single requisite for the improvement of housing in St. Louis is the enactment of a Minimum Standards Housing Ordinance. The City Plan Commission, the Building Commissioner and the Health Department with the aid and assistance of the American Public Health Association, have collaborated in the preparation of such an ordinance which provides for:

1| Elimination of overcrowding by prescribing minimum standards of space per family and per person.
2| The number, area, and openability of windows permitting entrance of fresh air and natural light.
3| Screens on doors and windows to restrict flies and mosquitoes.
4| Elimination of basement rooms as dwelling units unless they comply with the provisions set forth in the ordinance.
5| Improvement of sanitary conditions by elimination of hopper water closets and privies in sewered areas within six years of effective date of ordinance.
6| The location of water closets and the number of persons using them.
7| Keeping dwelling units in a clean, sanitary, habitable condition and free from infestation.
8| Maintenance and repair of dwellings necessary to provide tightness to the weather and reasonable possibilities of heating.

9| Installation of flues which would permit the operation of heating equipment to maintain adequate temperature in each habitable room.

10| Adequate daylight or fixtures for artificial illumination in public halls, bath rooms and other habitable rooms.

Unless and until such an ordinance has been adopted and enforced, most housing areas in St. Louis will continue to deteriorate and blighted districts and obsolete areas will reach much greater proportions than at present.

The rehabilitation of blighted areas is the No Man's Land of housing. It is more important than reconstruction of obsolete areas. It is a field that has been completely neglected partly because it is less spectacular than large scale reconstruction and partly because the opportunities for profitable investment are presumably less than in a new development. Without a definite plan for the rehabilitation of the present blighted areas new obsolete areas will develop faster than present areas can be reconstructed. . . .

20 | Decline in Municipal Services: The School Bond Issue

As the middle classes left the city of St. Louis for the county, they were replaced by the poor, most of whom were black. This population transfer eroded the financial base on which good municipal services could be supported. The problem of providing quality public education has received the most attention because it touches more people on a daily basis than any other service and has therefore occasioned a large number of special elections for additional revenues. The following table of the forty-four tax and bond proposals between 1916 and 1969 indicates that the public schools could count on overwhelming support in the period from the First World War until 1959, as eighteen out of nineteen proposals passed. The one that failed received 62 percent of the vote, falling short by only 4 percent of a necessary two-thirds majority. In the 1959–1969 period, only nine out of twenty-five proposals passed. Moreover, the margin of failure from the necessary two-thirds majority expanded to 12 percent and 14 percent.

The failure to pass tax and bond issues in the recent period is a result of several factors. First, Catholics who have maintained a large number of separate parochial schools have always been hostile to increasing support for the public system. This hostility was aggravated when they failed to obtain state aid for the hard-pressed parochial system in the 1960s. Secondly, homeowners, who are largely white and pay much of the property tax that supports maintenance and expansion of educational services, have become increasingly unwilling to vote themselves higher taxes, particularly in a period of inflation. Third, black wards, which favor these proposals by as much as 93 percent, have extraordinarily low voter turnouts. What has in effect occurred is that white and Catholic areas, which have the heaviest turnouts, have been easily able to outvote black wards, which produce relatively little support. Fourth, the issue of education as well as that of other social services has been aggravated by racial animosities, with the white population believing that it would be white dollars paying for services to the city's blacks. Without the kind of popular support and consensus that existed through the first half of the twentieth century in St. Louis, it appears inevitable that the deterioration of municipal services will continue. For a more detailed analysis of this issue, consult Gary A. Tobin, The St. Louis School Crisis: Population Shifts and Voting Patterns *(St. Louis: Washington University, 1970), Table 6.*

TABLE 7
School Tax and Bond Elections, 1916–1969

Proposal No.	Date	Required for Passage	% For	Pass or Fail
1	Nov. 16, 1916	2/3	78.47	Pass
2	Nov. 11, 1919	Simple	58.44	Pass
3	April 8, 1921	Simple	74.18	Pass
4	March 28, 1922	Simple	74.27	Pass
5	March 23, 1926	Simple	90.68	Pass
6	March 25, 1930	Simple	88.11	Pass
7	Feb. 20, 1934	Simple	78.50	Pass
8	April 5, 1938	Simple	91.08	Pass
9	Feb. 17, 1942	Simple	81.36	Pass
10	March 7, 1947	Simple	62.15	Pass
11	"	2/3	62.45	Fail
12	"	Simple	61.47	Pass

Proposal No.	Date	Required for Passage	% For	Pass or Fail
13	May 1, 1951	Simple	66.05	Pass
14	"	2/3	66.39	Fail
15	June 5, 1951	2/3	73.77	Pass
16	April 7, 1953	Simple	68.06	Pass
17	March 11, 1955	Simple	81.38	Pass
18	April 12, 1956	Simple	68.00	Pass
19	March 18, 1958	Simple	63.04	Pass
20	April 22, 1959	Simple	44.36	Fail
21	March 22, 1960	Simple	64.14	Pass
22	"	2/3	63.50	Fail
23	"	2/3	65.92	Fail
24	May 17, 1960	2/3	62.55	Fail
25	Nov. 8, 1960	2/3	60.14	Fail
26	Jan. 23, 1960	Simple	67.16	Pass
27	"	2/3	66.60	Fail
28	March 6, 1962	2/3	73.60	Pass
29	March 5, 1963	Simple	50.15	Pass
30	April 2, 1963	Simple	29.15	Fail
31	May 4, 1965	Simple	46.30	Fail
32	May 26, 1965	2/3	83.20	Pass
33	June 2, 1965	Simple	68.33	Pass
34	Nov. 16, 1965	2/3	65.36	Fail
35	April 4, 1967	Simple	75.74	Pass
36	April 18, 1968	2/3	55.33	Fail
37	"	Simple	56.68	Pass
38	Aug. 6, 1968	2/3	57.45	Fail
39	Nov. 5, 1968	2/3	59.32	Fail
40	April 1, 1969	2/3	53.99	Fail
41	"	2/3	53.24	Fail
42	"	2/3	52.78	Fail
43	"	2/3	52.09	Fail
44	April 1, 1969	Simple	54.24	Pass

21 | Population Decline: The Nature of the Loss

The dimensions and character of population changes in the St. Louis region are outlined in a 1973 Rand Corporation report that was commissioned by the National Science Foundation. The report, entitled St. Louis: A City and Its Suburbs, *is an almost unrelieved jeremiad on the future of the city. While many local leaders reacted strongly to the pessimism of the report, no one denied the demographic data interpreted by Peter A. Morrison, a senior staff member of the Rand Corporation. Morrison's research, which appeared in several different forms, is a useful summary with interpretations of migration patterns in the metropolitan area. He devoted special attention to outmigration from the city of St. Louis because of its significance within the metropolitan fabric. This section of Morrison's study demonstrates the importance of demographic bases within the planning process. Peter A. Morrison, "Urban Growth and Decline: San Jose and St. Louis in the 1960's,"* Science, *CLXXXV (August 1974), pp. 758–61.*

The St. Louis SMSA encompasses the city of St. Louis and six counties lying on both sides of the Mississippi River: the counties of St. Louis, St. Charles, Franklin, and Jefferson in Missouri and the counties of St. Clair and Madison in Illinois. The city of St. Louis is entirely separate in area and jurisdiction from St. Louis County. (Hereafter, St. Louis will refer to the city, while St. Louis County will be so designated.) The closest metropolitan area of comparable size is the Kansas City SMSA, about 275 miles to the west.

In 1970, the population of metropolitan St. Louis stood at about 2.4 million. It had increased by 12 percent since 1960, a rate lower than the average national metropolitan increase of 17 percent. After 1970, population in metropolitan St. Louis, like that in 21 other formerly growing SMSA's, began to decline.

St. Louis attained a peak population of 880,000 in the early 1950's. But by 1972 it had dwindled to a city of less than 590,000. During the 1960s, St. Louis' population declined 17 percent while its metropolitan ring population increased 29 percent. The central-city decline was acute, compared with that of most cities. Examination of the demographic change components reveals why. . . .

The white population declined mostly because of massive outward migration, chiefly to the suburbs. Between 1960 and 1970, a net 34 percent of the white city dwellers moved away. But whites also declined because their death rate steadily approached their birth rate, and since 1965 has exceeded it. Those who remained in the city added only 2 percent to their numbers (nationally, the increase in the white metropolitan population for that decade was 11 percent).

It was a different picture for blacks. There was no gain or loss through net migration during the 1960's, but the black population rose 19.5 percent through natural increase, very close to its national rate of 21.6 percent. Annual population estimates, however, show St. Louis' nonwhite population to have peaked in 1968 at around 269,000. By 1972, it is estimated to have dropped below 250,000. In view of the black population's positive natural increase, the only explanation is that blacks have been migrating out of the city since at least 1968 (and almost certainly before).

The number and composition of households in the city also changed during the decade. The number of households declined somewhat more slowly than the population (13 versus 17 percent), and the average size of a household went down slightly. Households with only one person increased from 21 percent in 1960 to 28 percent in 1970, a reflection primarily of the growing frequency of widowed elderly persons.

Demographic trends were somewhat more uniform outside the city. Natural increase and net migration contributed equally to the white population's 26.6 percent increase during the 1960's. The black population's 53.8 percent suburban growth was attributable more to net migration than to natural increase. St. Louis' suburbs attracted migrants largely from the city but also from outside the metropolitan area. Increasingly, migrants of both races entering the St. Louis SMSA bypassed the city and settled in the suburbs (mainly in St. Louis County). It can be seen that the total stream of new arrivals to St. Louis between 1965 and 1970 was smaller (both absolutely and relatively) than it had been a decade earlier. For blacks, the inbound stream was numerically about the same; but in relative terms, newly arriving blacks increasingly favored the suburbs.

Persistent and severe migration away from St. Louis has altered the structure of its population. These changes bear heavily on the city's capacity to meet the needs of the increasingly disadvantaged population that remains and on this population's very capacity to regenerate itself.

Diminished replacement capacity. The white population's capacity to replace itself diminished during the 1960's. Heavy and prolonged out-migration among whites drew away potential parents and left behind an elderly population that no longer replaces itself. . . . By 1972, the services of the undertaker exceeded those of the obstetrician by a margin of 3 to 2. Since it is now undergoing natural decrease, St. Louis' white population will continue to shrink whether or not net out-migration continues. Only a dramatic rise in fertility or a massive influx of childbearing families can alter this situation. . . .

The city's black population has not undergone severe migratory change and retains its strong replacement capacity: in 1972 its crude birth rate was 24.9 per thousand, but its crude death rate was only 11.2. In 1969, however, the black population began to decline, indicating a net migratory loss severe enough to offset its natural increase. This recent shift could signify an increase in departing migrants, a reduction in entering migrants, or a combination of both. Indications favor the first of these explanations. . . .

Accumulation of disadvantaged citizens. As migration has changed the metropolitan-wide distribution of population, St. Louis has come to be composed disproportionately of those citizens who are disadvantaged or have special needs, as the following comparisons show:

1| Between 1960 and 1970, the black percentage of the city's population rose from 29 to 41 percent; it increased only from 6 to 7 percent in the rest of the metropolitan area.

2| The city's residents aged 65 years and older increased from 12 percent to constitute 15 percent of the population; they stayed at 8 percent in the rest of the metropolitan area.

3| For families and unrelated individuals, median income in the city was 79 percent of that for the St. Louis SMSA in 1959; by 1969 city income was only 68 percent of the SMSA income.

4| The proportion of relatively high income families declined sharply. In 1959, 11 percent of families in the city had incomes at least double the city's median family income; 10 years later, only 4 percent had incomes double the 1969 median.

5| The proportion of relatively low income families rose slightly. In 1959, 16 percent of families in the city had incomes less than half the city's median family income; 10 years later, 21 percent had incomes less than half the 1969 median.

Through selective out-migration, then, problems of dependency and poverty—not exclusively problems *of* St. Louis—have come increasingly to be located *in* St. Louis.

The Dilemma of Policy: Coping with Decline

The degree of population decline in St. Louis may be exceptional, but St. Louis is no exception to the rule. The phenomenon of local population decline is widespread now—a characteristic of entire metropolitan areas, not just their central cities. The policy dilemma in coping with decline and its local consequences is likely to intensify during the 1970's.

The dilemma is this. The local official responsible for what happens in a place like St. Louis is understandably alarmed by severe population loss and the bleak future in store for the city if it continues. The city's boundaries, which have not changed since 1876, separate the problems within St. Louis from resources in its suburbs. But from the standpoint of individual welfare, it can be argued that the people who left St. Louis now enjoy living conditions they prefer, and those who remain have benefited from a thinning out of people from formerly overcrowded areas. . . . Even the widespread abandoned housing in St. Louis can be viewed as a positive sign that many people have upgraded their living conditions, leaving behind a residue of housing no longer competitive within the market. Both views have validity, the choice depending on whether one's perspective is that of a local policy-maker or of a freely mobile citizen.

But that line of argument may amount to no more than a confusing piece of sophistry for the policy-maker, or even the objective student of urban affairs, who looks at careful statistics from respectable sources telling him unequivocally that St. Louis is much worse off than it used to be. Part of the confusion is due to the paradox that statistics can be deceptive even when they

are accurate. They can mislead us here, for example, if they
beguile us into confining our attention to the plight of *places,*
whereas our central concern is with the well-being of *people.* It
is hard to escape that situation, however. A major difficulty in
our way is that standard social and economic statistics are compiled and organized mostly by areas rather than by groups of
people. Consequently, we can observe the experience of places,
but not of people. These experiences can differ sharply. For instance, black in-migrants from impoverished rural areas in states
like Mississippi may be less affluent or employable, on the average, than the mostly white population they join in St. Louis. If
this is true in St. Louis as it is in other cities . . . , then area
indicators (for example, unemployment or poverty in St. Louis)
may register a worsening of local conditions. But measures of individuals' experiences (for example, their unemployment or poverty now, compared with what it was before they came to St.
Louis) may show marked improvement. In short, the place we
call St. Louis may be worse off because of in-migration while
the in-migrant people are better off than they were.

22 | The Gateway Arch: Symbol for the St. Louis Metropolis

*For nearly a century, St. Louis' chief urban symbol was the Eads
Bridge. When the arch was topped out in October 1965, it already had achieved the instant recognition comparable to the
Washington Monument or the Eiffel Tower. Seven years were
required to erect Eero Saarinen's 632-foot monument to westward expansion, and the construction was only the last phase
of a much longer effort. The City Plan of 1907 called for a
formal riverfront park, and a project to memorialize westward-
bound pioneers was discussed for many years before the first
funding came in 1935. As important as the completion of the
arch was the development associated with it. Nascently in the
late 1950s, more rapidly through the 1960s, a combination of
private and public effort brought forth a downtown renaissance.
These two articles—the first an editorial, "Topping-Out Day,"
the second examining the monument's significance a decade later
—together point out the real and symbolic importance of the
structure. "Topping-Out Day," St. Louis Post-Dispatch (Octo-*

ber 28, 1965); John McGuire, "Gateway Arch Now Spanning 10 Years," St. Louis Post-Dispatch *(October 27, 1975).*

Topping-Out Day

From zenith to horizon, a radiant blue sky formed the backdrop for placing the last silver gray section of the Gateway Arch. The day, crisply bright as fall days in St. Louis so often are, was as brisk as the ceremonial band music and the traditional topping-out flag. Entranced by the shine and sparkle, thoughts wandered, not disrespectfully, from what was being said.

Memories drifted back inevitably to that evening—Feb. 18, 1948, it was—when the drawings of the five finalists, chosen from 172 entries in the Jefferson National Expansion Memorial design competition, were projected on a screen in the Statler's banqueting hall. Each had been awarded $10,000 to detail his work, and the time had come to announce the winner of the $40,000 grand prize. . . .

All the designs were earnest efforts of competent men, but Saarinen's arch was uniquely symbolic of the great westward surge of trappers and missioners, soldiers and settlers through St. Louis into the Western wilderness. It fully deserved the praise accorded it by Aline B. Loucheim, then the architectural critic of *The New York Times,* as "symbolizing the 'Gateway to the West' —a modern monument, fitting, beautiful and impressive." She went on to say:

"Its symbolism is direct and convincing. Large in scale, the arch does not dwarf the other structures and its form is sympathetic with the courthouse dome which it frames. It has a simplicity which should guarantee timelessness: yet the audacious engineering, the material, and the implications of science in the choice of this curve make it wholly contemporary."

As Mrs. Eero Saarinen, widow of the arch's chief designer, she attended Thursday morning's ceremonies. With a very special interest, she must have felt that the selection of the design was not really the beginning, nor the topping-out the completion of the magnificent national undertaking on the riverfront. She knew, of course, that its realization began with the allocation of

$9,000,000 in WPA funds by President Roosevelt and the approval of a local bond issue in 1935. That made possible the clearing of the 40-block site, but the demands of war pushed aside all thoughts of further work. And by the war's end, what had seemed assured had become an uncertainty.

Congress, which never had made an appropriation for the monument, was bent on balancing the budget and slow to recognize the agreement of the late President and the City of St. Louis that the riverfront park should be a joint federal-local enterprise. Opportunists had their eyes on the site for a dozen different projects ranging from housing to a stadium. The reluctance of the railroads to move their tracks became a new obstacle—removed finally by an engineer-mayor in City Hall whose name unfortunately was not mentioned at Thursday's ceremonies, Raymond R. Tucker.

There were many such St. Louisans who would not let the vision fade. The strenuous efforts of a few had launched the competition for a design. Once that design was unveiled, they grew in numbers, in enthusiasm and in determination. In a very real sense, its realization and a new flowering of an old city became intertwined. Those who witnessed the placing of the last section of the arch had but to look about them for evidence of this.

Their celebration actually was premature. Much remains to be done to complete the arch and the park. Much also remains to be done to complete a thorough rehabilitation of St. Louis. The building of the arch, however, has engendered a fresh confidence. St. Louisans have learned how much they can really do. They have made the arch not merely the symbol of two hundred years gone, but also of a future, bright as the sky on topping-out day.

Gateway Arch Now Spanning 10 Years

At the base of either leg, the Gateway Arch is beginning to show its age, the telltale signs that 16,254,500 humans have passed by. It will be 10 years old tomorrow.

"Maurice loves Annette." "Johnny + Gwen." "Donald." "Connecticut." These are just a few of the graffiti scratched into the stainless steel skin. Handprints. Heart shapes. Angry, formless scrawls. On one section near the base of the north leg it looks as though someone took a hammer and chisel to the steel surface.

But from a few steps away, the graffiti disappear in the shimmering metal surface.

The Arch is like a magnet, attracting the adventuresome and oddities. An airplane flew through it—an illegal act. There have been weddings at its base and one held in an airplane flying overhead.

A peace symbol was stamped into the snow under it. And millions of persons have rubbed it, put their arms around its corners, spread out against it and behaved in strange, ritualistic ways. Once, a seer predicted that the Arch would fall into the river on a specific day. It didn't.

But perhaps the most impressive thing about the Arch's first decade has been its almost "Kilroy-was-here" influence on the surrounding territory.

The proliferation of Arch insignia, corporate symbols, company and organizational names is in a way the best example of the pervasive effect on the area that the 630-foot monument to westward expansion has had.

It is somewhat surprising that a local sports team has not come up with the name, Fighting Arches. (Maybe not so surprising, though, since as losers, they certainly would be known as the Fallen Arches.)

This strong identity with the Arch even surprises the National Park Service's new superintendent here, Robert S. Chandler.

"Look at the truck going by the window," he said. "The sign on the side reads Big Arch Trucking."

Despite the strong identity here, there are those non Archophiles about the land who are a bit confused about the nature of the Jefferson National Expansion Memorial, Chandler says.

"Some people have called and wanted to know if the Arch has one leg in Missouri and the other in Illinois," he said. Not such an absurd question when it is recalled that the designer of the Arch, the late Eero Saarinen, once considered such a plan.

"Others think the trains (which run up the legs to the top) make a complete loop underground," he said.

"There are a lot of people who think there's a restaurant at the top, and they call to inquire about the menu. . . ."

For millions who have come to the Arch since it was opened to visitors in 1967, the reaction is usually the same—the seemingly irresistible urge to caress (touch, at least) and to look skyward. And, of course, there have been the photographic records of family and friends—some standing stiffly against one of the stainless steel legs and others in comic moods, posing as though they were holding up the structure.

"All right, Eloise, look in this little square and press this little button here."

Eloise's companions were standing on either side of the north leg, each leaning against it with one arm, much in the manner of the Marx brothers.

Chandler thinks the Arch will become an even more meaningful attraction when the Museum of Westward Expansion is completed next summer. It is under construction off the lobby of the underground section of the Arch and will have 42,000 square feet of exhibit space, making it the largest museum in the National Park system.

The museum will focus on the people who settled the West: the fur traders, the railroad builders, the miners, the mountain men and explorers. There will be 600 exhibits and 1600 graphic displays, photo murals and slides, Chandler said.

There are other projects not completed. A grand staircase is under construction.

Two ponds that were to have gone on either side of the Arch, much of the landscaping and two pedestrian overpasses to Memorial Drive and Interstate 70, have not been financed by Congress.

"We're going to continue to ask for them in our budget requests, but I'm not optimistic," Chandler said. . . .

There is no doubt the Arch has had a profound impact on downtown St. Louis that has led to much revitalization. By some estimates, the Arch has stimulated almost $503,000,000 in construction since the 1960s.

Some statistics indicate that the Arch is the fourth largest visitor attraction in the world, behind Lenin's Tomb and the two Disney-theme parks.

Appendix

TABLE 8

Selected Characteristics of Population Growth

	Total City Population	National Rank of City	% of Population in City Non-White	Total Population in St.Louis County other than City	Total Population in SMSA	National Rank of SMSA
1790	1,318					
1800	1,039					
1810	1,400		28.6%	5,667		
1820	4,598			10,020		
1830	5,852		24.6%	14,125		
1840	16,469		12.5%	35,979		
1850	77,860		5.2%	27,118+		
1860	160,773		2.0%	29,751		
1870	310,864			40,325		
1880	350,518	6		31,888+		
1890	451,770	5	6.0%	36,307		
1900	575,238	4	6.2%	50,040	649,711#	6
1910	687,029	4	6.4%	82,417	828,733#	6
1920	772,897	6	9.0%	100,737	952,012#	7
1930	821,960	7	11.4%	211,593	1,293,516#	8
1940	816,048	8	13.3%	274,230	1,367,977#	9
1950	856,796	8	18.0%	406,349	1,400,058*	9
1960	750,026	10	28.8%	703,532	2,104,669	9
1970	622,236	18	41.0%	951,353	2,363,017	11

Notes: + Major Annexations to St. Louis City took place in 1841 and 1876
Metropolitan District as defined by U.S. Census Bureau
* Urban Area as defined by U.S. Census Bureau

Index

Agriculture: hinterland, 47–49, 67–68, 72; resource for area manufacturing, xxiii, 139; St. Louis, 6–7; St. Louis County, 174

Air pollution. *See* Smoke Problem

Allen, Thomas, 54–55

Alton (Ill.): abolitionists, 77; connected by ferry, 53

Amelung, Richard C., 17

American Bottoms (Ill.), xxvii, 142

Annexations, St. Louis: dates, 168; of 1876, xvi, xxiv, xxvii, 205

Arkansas, xxvii, 137–38, 145

Atlanta (Ga.), 83

Atwater, Caleb, quoted, 45–49

Automobiles: aid suburbanization, xxviii, 141, 160, 170; assembled in St. Louis, xxv; for upper class, 166

Baltimore (Md.), xxii, 79, 83, 171

Barrett, William, quoted, 95–97

Bartholomew, Harlan: identified, xxix, 182; planning history, 186–89; zoning, 182–85

Barton, David, 42

Barton, Joshua, 42

Bates, Edward, 42

Beer gardens, 71, 73

Bek, William G., 67

Benton, Thomas Hart, 76

Billisame, Alexandre, 40

Billon, Frederic L., quoted, 5, 15–16, 25–26

Bi-State Development Agency, xxxii

Blacks. *See* Negroes

Bond issue, of 1923, 186; of 1935, 208; schools, 199–201

Boston (Mass.): character of population, xxii; industry, 63; parks, 176, 180; subdivisions, 125; suburbs, 48

Boulevards, xxiv, 128, 131, 175–76, 180
Brackenridge, Henry M., quoted, 26, 28–31
Brockmeyer, Henry C., 74
Brooklyn (N.Y.), 62
Brotherton, James, 78
Buel, James, quoted, 93–95
Buffalo (N.Y.), 177
Burnham, Daniel, 177
Burroughs, John, School, 165
Business Men's League of St. Louis, quoted, 65–66; represents region, 157

Carr, William C., 42
Catholics, xvii, xx, xxi, xxxii, 7, 8, 37, 43–44, 106, 161, 173, 199–200
Central Business District: declines, xxxi; functions, xxiv, 144; problem area, 190; reshaped, 63–64; revitalized, 210
Chandler, Robert S., quoted, 209
Charity, 95, 104, 106–109
Charleston (S.C.), 79
Chicago (Ill.): area, 171; character of population, xxi; exposition, 177; industrializes, xxiv, 155; parks, 179, 180; rival to St. Louis, xxiii, 62, 64, 65, 138
Children, 10–15, 47, 79, 89–95, 147–52, 165–66
Cholera, epidemic of 1849, 103
Chouteau, Auguste, 22, 26, 29, 33; quoted, 3–5
Chouteau, Pierre, 21–22, 33
Cincinnati, Ohio: building costs, 47; industrializes, xxiv; site, 28; trade rival, 49, 53, 138; trade with St. Louis, 46, 53
City Beautiful Movement, 130, 175–76

City planning, xvi, xxiv–xxv, xxix, 173, 180–81, 185; organizations, 130, 133, 173, 178, 185; Plan of 1907, 206; Plan of 1947, 195–99
City services: fire companies, 35–36; garbage, 131; sewers, 103, 111, 157, 171. *See also* Schools
Civic League, 129–30; plan for St. Louis, 178–81; smoke problem, 113–17; tenements, 117–21
Civic Progress, Inc., 172
Civil War, xxii, xxvii, 59, 72, 84, 100, 103, 124, 150, 161
Clay, William, quoted, 192
Cleveland (Ohio), 125, 155, 171
Coal, impact of use, 46, 117, 140, 157–58
Columbian Exposition, 63, 175
Committee of One Hundred (anti-vice), quoted, 97–100
Consolidation, xxvii, 168–74
Conventions, xxvi–xxvii; hall built, 187
Country Day School, 165
Cruzat, Don Francisco (Gov.), quoted, 16–21

Dacus, Joseph, quoted, 93–95
Dallas (Texas), 139
Denis, Jacques, 15–16
Denver (Colo.), 138
Depression, of 1893, 65; of 1930s, xxv, 189, 208
Detroit (Mich.), 155, 171
Didier, Pierre, 35
Dueling, 42, 76

Eads, James Buchanan, 60, 62
Eads Bridge. *See* St. Louis-Illinois Bridge
East St. Louis (Ill.): manufacturing and railroad center, xxvii,

144, 155, 156; race riot, 150–55; in St. Louis metropolis, 53, 64, 142

East Side (Ill.), industry, xxvii–xxviii, 144; problems, 155–60

East-West Gateway Coordination Council, xxxii

Engineers' Club, 113, 115

England, policy affects St. Louis, xvii-xviii, 4, 23

Ethnic groups, xxxi, xxxii, 146, 154–55, 159–60, 173. *See also* France, Germans, Immigrants, Irish

Fairs, annual, 66

Famous-Barr Department Stores, xxvi

Finance, 65, 139

Fontbonne College, 165

Forest Park, 127–29, 133, 164

Forts: Bellefontaine, 25, 30; Chartres, 4; Jefferson Barracks, 180; Mandan, 28–29

Fort Worth (Texas), 139

France: policy influences St. Louis' development, xv, xvii–xix, 4; source of immigrants, 30, 80, 161; trade compared to St. Louis, 48

Francies, Estill W., quoted, 164–66

Francis, David R., quoted, 177–78

Franklin (Mo.), 45

Franklin County (Mo.), 202

Fur trade, regulations, 20, 23; St. Louis, xvi, xviii, xix, 48

Galveston (Texas), 138

Gambling, 95, 102

Germans: celebration, xxxi; influence in St. Louis, xxi, 66–74, 92; location, xxxi, 161; as workers, 144, 146

Government, local, xix, xx; corruption, xxiv–xxv, 130

Graebner, Thomas, quoted, 69–70

Granite City (Ill.), 157, 158

Greville, John Chester, quoted, 75–76

Hammond, George, 77

Hannibal (Mo.), 138

Harbor improvement, 54

Harris, William T., 71, 73; quoted, 85–91

Harris Teachers College, xxvi

Hempstead, Edward, 33

Herculaneum (Mo.), 46

Holt, Glen E., quoted, 7–15

Hosmer Hall (school), 165

Hospitals, xxvi, 37–40, 103, 104–105, 108

Housing: character, xxiv, 5–6, 25, 170; condition, xxix, 112, 195, 196–99; construction, 30; policy, xxx, 196; projects, 188, 191–95; rental rates, 41; tenements, 117–21; value, 163

Housing and Urban Development, Department of, 193

Houston (Texas), 138

Howard, Ebenezer, 156

Illinois: xxiii, xxxii; portions in St. Louis trade area, xxvii, 48, 137–38; source of immigrants, xix, 145

Immigrants: employment, 68, 158–60; origins, xix, xx, xxi, xxiii, 26–27, 37, 67–68, 92, 144–45; vote, 84–85

Indiana, 145

Indianapolis (Ind.), 138

Indians, xviii, 17, 18, 20–21, 23, 45; mounds, 29

Industrial Club of St. Louis, quoted, 145–47
Industrialization: xxiii, xxvii, xxviii, 57, 62–66, 140–41; educational response, 85–91; wages from, 159–60. *See also* Manufacturing
Industrial parks, xxviii
Industrial sections, 143
Initiative and referendum, 83–85
Iowa, xxiii
Irish: celebration, 74–76; immigrants, xxi, 92; location in St. Louis, xxxi, 71, 73–74, 82, 93, 161; as workers, 144, 146

Jefferson County (Mo.), 202
Jefferson National Expansion Memorial, 188, 206–10

Kalamazoo (Mich.), 65
Kansas, xxiii
Kansas City (Mo.): parks, 176; SMSA, 202; steamboat connects, 53; trade rival, 138
Kaysing, William G., 165
Kelsey, Albert, 177
Kentucky, xxvii, 137–38, 145
Keokuck (Iowa), 53
Kiel, Henry, 84
King, Edward, quoted, 71–74
Kingshighway Commission, 175–76
KMOX-TV, editorial quoted, 192–94

Labor: character, 144–46; origin, 145; strikes, 76, 154; unions, 152, 154–55, 174; wages, 146–47, 154, 158–60
Laclède, Pierre, xvii-xviii, 3–5, 7, 121
Lane, William Carr, 37, 76
Lead mining, 30, 46

Leffingwell, Hiram W., 127
Lewis and Clark Expedition, 22–24
Limestone, building material, 46
Littering, fines, 131
Little Rock (Ark.), 138
Localism, xxxii
Logan, Charles T., quoted, 62–66
Los Angeles, Calif., 171
Loucheim, Aline B., 207
Louis XV, xvii, 5
Louisiana, 46
Louisiana Purchase, xix, 26
Louisiana Purchase Exposition of 1904, xvi, xxiv–xxv, xxix, 129–34, 164, 175, 176–78
Louisville (Ky.), 46, 47, 53, 138
Lovejoy, Elijah, quoted, 76–80
Lucas, James H., 122
Lucas, John B. C., 26
Luedeking, Robert, quoted, 110–13
Lumber, 47, 139

McCall, Louis M., quoted, 130–33
McGuire, John, quoted, 208–10
McIntosh, Francis J., 76–80
McKinley, Andrew, 128
McNair, Alexander, 33
Madison (Ill.), 157
Madison County (Ill.): manufacturing center, xxvii, xxviii; in St. Louis metropolis, 141, 202
Manufacturing, 7, 73; companies, xxvii–xxviii, 130–33, 150–55, 160
Mary Institute, 165
Meachum, J. B., 44
Meeker, R. A., 177
Memphis (Tenn.), 138, 139
Metropolitan Chamber of Commerce, xxxii
Mill Creek Valley, xxiv, 29; industrialization, 143

Milles, Carl, 187
Million Population Club, 170
Minerals, St. Louis area, xxiii, 139, 145. *See also* Coal, Lead
Minimum Standards Housing Ordinance, 198–99
Minnesota, xxiii
Mission Sunday Schools, 95
Mississippi, 46, 145
Mississippi River, xx, xxiii, 28–30, 46, 47, 49, 57, 59, 139, 142; bridges, 156; explored, 23–24; flooding, 53, 142; trade, 55
Mississippi Valley, St. Louis trade, 54, 55, 61, 62, 137–40
Missouri: constitution of 1865, xxiii; Germans, 66–74; lead manufacturing, 46; population grows, xxiii; railroads, building of, 56; St. Louis trade, xxvii, 137–38; St. Louis workers, 145; statehood, xx
Missouri Botanical Gardens, 115, 125
Missouri Republican, cited, 56–57
Missouri River, xxiii, 24, 28, 31, 45, 49, 53, 140
Mitchell, Samuel, 42
Mobile (Ala.), 138
Morrison, Peter A., quoted, 202–206
Mulattoes, xviii, 10–15, 76–80. *See also* Negroes
Mull, William, 77
Mullanphy, John, 37
Municipal Art Commission, 181

Nashville (Tenn.), trade rival, 139; trade with St. Louis, 53, 138
National Good Roads Convention, 177
National Stockyards, xxvii

Negroes: colonial St. Louis, xviii; housing problems, xxix, xxxi, 192; location, xxix, xxxi, 82–83, 158, 203–204; organizations, xxxi, 80, 173; population, xxii, 10–15, 30; religion, 44–45; segregation, xxii, 82–85; violence against, 76–80, 150–55; as workers, 73, 145, 158–60. *See also* Slaves
Neighborhoods, xxxi, 74, 93, 158, 190; centers, 179; problems, 190; reconstruction, 195
Newark (N.J.), 63
New Orleans (La.), 55, 83; trade rival, 30, 138; trade with St. Louis, 45–46, 53, 69
New York (N.Y.):133; area, 171; character of population, xxi, 62; subdivisions, 125; tenements, 117–18; trade rival of St. Louis, 65; trade with St. Louis, 62; zoning, 182
New York Times, The, quoted, 207
Noonan, Edward A., 115
Northwest Ordinance of 1787, 8
Noyes, John, quoted, 125–27

Observer, The, quoted, 77–80
Ohio River, 30, 55, 140
Olmsted, Frederick, 177
Omaha (Neb.), 138, 177
Opera, 72–73, 187

Parks: xxiv, 127–29, 180; neighborhood, 187, 188; relation to boulevards, 175–76; riverfront, 187–88, 206–10
Peck, John Mason, quoted, 40–44
Peoria (Ill.), 53
Perry County (Mo.), 69
Philadelphia (Pa.): 5; area, 171;

exposition, 177; Negroes, xxii; population, 62–63; suburbs, 48

Pittsburgh (Pa.), trade with St. Louis, 46, 47, 53, 68, 77

Pitzman, Julius, 125

Playgrounds, xxiv, 178, 187, 188

Police: crime commission, 173; early history, 33–34; investigated, 100–103; and slaves, 34, 35; stations modernized, 131

Population: East Side towns, 1900–1910, 158; Florissant, 161; Midwest projected, 49; St. Louis city, xviii, xix, xx, xxi, xxv, xxviii, 5, 25, 26, 30, 64, 72, 110–11, 160, 169, 170–71, 188, 191, 202–206, 211; St. Louis city tables, 1764–1800, 6–15; 1790–1970, 211; St. Louis County, xxviii, 160, 170–71; St. Louis County table, 1810–1970, 211; St. Louis SMSA table, 1900–1970, 211

Pratte, Bernard, 33, 35

Private places, xxiv, xxxi, 124–27

Prohibition, xxii

Prostitution: brothels torn down, 80; licensing repealed, 97–100; red-light district, 98; regulation, xvi, xxii, 95–97

Providence (R.I.), 180

Public buildings, 114, 187; commission, 179

Public health, 100, 110–13, 132, 191

Pullman (Ill.), 155

Queen, Stuart A., quoted, 161–63

Railroads: 61, 133; as employer, 160; enter from east, 143; introduced, 55–57; number, 140–41; rate discrimination, 65; trade impact, xxiii, xxv, 59, 138–41; tunnel, 181

Real estate market, 64, 132, 157–58, 183–84; organizations, 64, 173

Reavis, L. U., quoted, 60–62, 127–29

Recreation, 7, 32–33, 131, 166–68, 188

Reform, in St. Louis, xvi, xxii, xxiv. *See also specific topics*

Regional Commerce and Growth Association, xxxii

Religion: Baptists, 40–43; Greek Orthodox, xxxii; Lutherans, 68–70; organizations, 173; Presbyterians, 47; protestants, xx, xxxii, 106. *See also* Catholics

Riis, Jacob A., quoted, 118–21

Riots. *See* Negroes

River Des Peres, 122–23, 128, 180

Riverfront plan, 180–81, 186

Rivers, xxiii, 23, 48–49, 53, 161. *See also* Mississippi, Missouri, River Des Peres

Rivers and Harbors Convention, 54

Robinson, John, 177

Roosevelt, Franklin, 208

Saarinen, Eero, 206–207, 209

St. Charles County (Mo.), 202

St. Clair County (Ill.), xxviii, 141, 202

St. Joseph (Mo.), 53

St. Louis (Mo.): area, 171; future, 45–49; incorporated, 31; seal of, explained, 49–50; separated from county, 162; site, 4, 28–30, 46–47, 141–44

St. Louis Board of Health, 95–97, 108–10, 112, 131

St. Louis City Plan Commission,

xxix, 181, 182, 186–89, 196, 198–99. *See also* City Planning

St. Louis Commons, 29–30

St. Louis Community Council, 189–91

St. Louis Country Club, 164, 166

St. Louis County (Mo.): finances railroads, 56; governments, xxxii, population, 211; separated from city, 162

St. Louis County Farm Bureau, 174

St. Louis Globe-Democrat, quoted, 81–82

St. Louis-Illinois Bridge, 60–62, 181, 206

St. Louis Labor, quoted, 82–85

St. Louis Land Reutilization Authority, xxix

St. Louis Post-Dispatch, 173, 207–10; quoted, 84, 151–55

St. Louis SMSA, xxvii, 202, 211

Saint Louis West-End Improvement Company, 122

Ste. Geneviève (Mo.), 4

Saloons, 102

San Francisco (Calif.), 62

Santa Fe Trail, trade, xix

Satellite cities, 62, 155–60

Scharf, John Thomas, quoted, 31–33, 35–36, 57–59

Schools: administration, 81; employer, as large, xxvi; finance, 199–201; for industrial and urban citizens, 145, 147–50; kindergartens, 89–91; Negroes, 80–82; parochial, 68–70, 190; suburban, 124, 165–66. *See also private schools by name*

Sedalia (Mo.), 138

Servant problem, 165

Shaw, Charles A., quoted, 164–66

Shaw, George Bernard, quoted, 189

Slaves: codes, 19–20, 31–32, 34–35, 71–76; in St. Louis' early growth, 8

Smith, Elmer, 193

Smoke problem, xxiv, 113–17, 158

Social class: xxi, xviii, xxix, 41–45, 166–68; in ethnic and racial groups, 72, 74, 150; in fire companies, 35; in housing, 124, 163, 164–66, 193

Socialist Party, 84

Spain, policy affects St. Louis, xv, xvii–xix, 8, 21–24

Springfield (Ill.), 138

Springfield (Mo.), 138

Steamboat: as Mississippi River ferry, 77; replaced by railroads, xxiii; on Seal of St. Louis, 49–50; trade, xxix, 53–55, 58, 59

Stiff, Edward, quoted, 37–40

Streets, cleaning, 131; congestion, 188; model, 177–78

Subdivisions, xix, 121–24, 164

Suburbs: xxxi–xxxii, 161–64; advertisement, 121–24; geography, 142; governments oppose consolidation, 174; method for study, 160–63; movement to, xxvii–xxviii, 64, 155, 156, 160–61, 170, 203; shopping centers, xxx; wealthy, xxiv

Sullivan, Lenore, quoted, 192–94

"Sunday Law," 102

Taussig, William, 121

Taylor, Graham, quoted, 156–60

Tennessee, 46, 145

Thomas, Lewis, quoted, 138–41, 142–44, 161–63

Tobin, Gary A., quoted, 200–201

Tourism, xxvi

Trade: area defined, xxvii, 137–44; character, 45–49, 59, 65;

future bright, 30–31; river-based, xxiii, xxv, 139–41
Transportation, local: buses, 161, hacks, 162; railroad, 123, 162; service cars (jitneys), 163; street railroads, 66, 141, 161, 162, 165; trucks, xxviii, 141
Troen, Selwyn K., quoted, 92
Tucker, Raymond R., 208
Turner, Frederick Jackson, 40

Unemployment, 206
United States, policy affects St. Louis, xxvi, xxx, 22, 23–25, 45, 54
Urban renewal, xxix, 188
Utilities: electricity, xxvi, 157; telephone, xxvi; water, 103, 111, 132

Venice (Ill.), 157
Vicksburg (Miss.), 79

Walsh, Patrick, 77
War of 1812, 25–26
Washington, D.C., 180
Washington University, 166; Medical Center, xxvi
Wells, Rolla, 129, 131
Western Sanitary Commission, xvi, 103; quoted, 104–105
Whalen, Michael, 152
Wherry, Mackey, 34
Wisconsin, xxiii
Women, 10–15, 105, 147, 149–50, 173
World War I, 113, 127, 137, 168, 190
World War II, xxviii, xxx, 192, 195
World's Fair of 1904. *See* Louisiana Purchase Exposition

Yeatman, James E., 103

Zoning, 181–85

About the Editors

Selwyn K. Troen teaches history at the Ben Gurion University of the Negev, Beersheva, Israel. He was educated at Brandeis University (B.A.) and the University of Chicago (M.A. and Ph.D.).

Glen E. Holt is chairman of the department of urban studies at Washington University, St. Louis. He was educated at Baker University, Baldwin, Kansas (B.A.) and the University of Chicago (M.A. and Ph.D.).